Fundamentalism, Fundraising,
and the Transformation
of the Southern Baptist Convention,
1919–1925

Fundamentalism, Fundraising, and the Transformation of the Southern Baptist Convention, 1919–1925

Andrew Christopher Smith

America's Baptists
Keith Harper, Series Editor

Knoxville • The University of Tennessee Press

The America's Baptists series will bring broader understanding of the places Baptists have occupied in American life. Many of these works will be historical monographs, but the series will embrace different types of primary and secondary works, including but not limited to annotated collections of diaries, letters, and personal reflections as well as biographies and essay collections.

Library of Congress Cataloging-in-Publication Data

Names: Smith, Andrew Christopher, 1979-
Title: Fundamentalism, fundraising, and the transformation of the Southern Baptist Convention, 1919-1925 / Andrew Christopher Smith.

Description: First [edition]. | Knoxville : University of Tennessee Press, 2016. | Series: America's Baptists | Includes bibliographical references and index.

Identifiers: LCCN 2015030173 | ISBN 9781621902270 (hardcover : alk. paper)

Subjects: LCSH: Southern Baptist Convention—History—20th century. | Fundamentalism—United States. | Church controversies—Baptists. | Southern Baptist Convention. Cooperative Program—History. | Church fund raising—United States. | United States—Church history—20th century.

Classification: LCC BX6462.3 .S64 2016 | DDC 286/.13209042—dc23
LC record available at http://lccn.loc.gov/2015030173

For Pam, Elizabeth, and Charlotte

Contents

Illustrations

Foreword

Most Americans are familiar with the "wall of separation" between church and state. Few, however, know that this phrase is not found in the Constitution or in the Declaration of Independence. Rather, Thomas Jefferson first articulated this particular conception of church-state relations in response to a letter from a group of Connecticut Baptists. Indeed, America's Baptists have been key players throughout the nation's history. Sometimes Baptists have been at the forefront of significant social and cultural change, as with the call for the separation of church and state. At other time they have commanded center stage either because of internal conflict or external enmity. In recent years, the centralization of power and dramatic changes in Baptist life associated with the rise of the Southern Baptist Convention have dominated news about the denomination and colored our understanding of Baptists' history and their future.

Books in the America's Baptists series will seek to bring broader understanding to the place Baptists have occupied in American life since the Colonial Era. Their ranks have produced Presidents and paupers, pulpiteers and pundits. Their story began as a people marginalized by cultural and political elites. Gradually, they moved to the mainstream, but, in the twenty-first century, they once again face marginalization. Baptist history is both integral to the main currents of the nation's religious history and a unique story, or series of stories, in its own right. As such, Baptist history reflects ecumenical, political, social, and certainly theological characteristics that, in many ways, are deeply American at their core, but also so unique that the Baptist trajectory in American culture is almost always controversial and complicated.

Such a rich, diverse, and complicated history merits close attention. The America's Baptists series will explore this history in all of its complexity. Many of these works will be historical monographs, but insights from sociological works like Clifford A. Grammich Jr.'s *Local Baptist, Local Politics: Churches and Communities in the Middle and Upland South* will also be included. Likewise, the series will embrace different types of primary and secondary works, including but not limited to annotated collections of diaries, letters, and personal reflections as well as biographies and essay collections in the vein of Nancy Tatom Ammerman's *Southern Baptists Observed: Multiple Perspectives on a Changing Denomination*.

In some ways it is only natural that the University of Tennessee Press would launch a scholarly series dedicated to Baptists in America. The press enjoys a reputation for publishing cutting-edge books on Baptists. In addition to the Grammich and Ammerman titles the press has published John Lee Eighmy's *Churches in Cultural Captivity: A History of the Social Attitudes of Southern Baptists* (1987), Ellen Rosenberg's *The Southern Baptists: A Subculture in Transition* (1989), and Howard Dorgan's *The Old Regular Baptists of Central Appalachia* and *In the Hands of a Happy God: The "No Hellers" of Central Appalachia*, to mention a few. Simply stated, there has never been a better time to delve into Baptist history. This series will build on these works and offer an independent, nonsectarian opportunity to publish the best scholarship related to Baptist history and Baptist life.

We proudly launch America's Baptists with Andrew Smith's *Fundamentalism, Fundraising, and the Transformation of the Southern Baptist Convention, 1919–1925*. Smith argues that, contrary to the perception that Baptists are non-hierarchical, Southern Baptist fundraising ventures between 1920 and 1925 reflected Progressive Era tendencies toward organization, structure, and bureaucratization. Moreover, Smith claims that the failure of the so-called Seventy-Five Million Campaign, coupled with the Progressive Era tendency toward organization and Northern-style Fundamentalism, actually paved the way for the modern Southern Baptist Convention. It is a fascinating story that Smith tells well, and it serves as an excellent beginning for the series.

The University of Tennessee Press seeks to be the leader in scholarly inquiry into Baptist life and thought in its American context. We hope scholars of all stripes will accept this as both a challenge and an invitation to explore the Baptist experience in its rich diversity. We welcome your inquiries.

Keith Harper
Southeastern Baptist Theological Seminary

Acknowledgments

To complete this project, I have relied upon the efforts of a group of people scattered across four states. I am grateful to Laura Botts and the staff of the Georgia Baptist Historical Depository; Jason Fowler, Director of Library Services at Southeastern Baptist Theological Seminary; the staff of the Archives and Special Collections at The Southern Baptist Theological Seminary; Al Lang at the Carson-Newman University Baptist Archives; and McGarvey Ice and the staff at the Disciples of Christ Historical Society. I am particularly grateful for Bill Sumners and Taffey Hall at the Southern Baptist Historical Library and Archives, where I worked five days a week for more than a year. A grant from the Vanderbilt University Graduate School helped to underwrite out-of-town research and particularly improved the quality of the study's fifth chapter.

I am thankful for the close readings of this document that several senior scholars have offered. I am particularly indebted to Dr. James Byrd of Vanderbilt University, who led me away from several blind alleys during this project's initial stages. Dr. Keith Harper of Southeastern Baptist Theological Seminary served as an unofficial "fifth reader" of the original dissertation and was one of my biggest cheerleaders. His enthusiasm about this project helped me to stay excited about it, too. I also owe a debt to Scot Danforth, Kathryn Peck, and the staff at the University of Tennessee Press for working to make this the best book that it could be.

Through it all, I have relied on the support of my family. My parents, Randy and Diane Smith, and my sister, Kara Diane Smith, never failed to listen to me. Above all, my wife, Pamela Hoppes Smith, worked to feed and house us while defending the time I needed to work, while my children, Elizabeth Diane and Charlotte Anne, often waited patiently for me to emerge from sessions of editing and revision. To them this book is gratefully dedicated.

Introduction

Beginning in the late 1970s, a group of conservative Southern Baptists began to assert that their denomination no longer served their best interests. Leaders among this group alleged that denominational employees were to the left of their constituency both theologically and socially. Further, conservatives claimed that these heterodox bureaucrats operated the denomination's colleges, seminaries, publishing houses, and missionary organizations in ways not reflective of the dominant theological position among rank-and-file Southern Baptists. Under the banner of biblical "inerrancy," conservatives successfully moved to oust their moderate opponents from power. By electing their own candidates to the Southern Baptist Convention's presidency every year after 1979, conservatives placed sympathetic individuals on the denomination's boards of trustees. These trustees, in turn, were able to dismiss professors, missionaries, and denominational employees not congenial to the Convention's new, rightward turn. Over the course of two decades, conservatives were able to successfully remold the denomination in their own image.[1]

For outside observers, the new shape of the Southern Baptist Convention simply confirmed the South's identity as the "Bible Belt." Meanwhile, insiders bickered over the meaning of the conservative program. Although the new conservative leaders of the SBC claimed merely to be implementing a "course correction" that would put the denomination back on its originally intended track, now-disenfranchised moderates asserted that the conservative program amounted to a "fundamentalist takeover" that imposed a foreign, Northern method of theological thinking onto the boards and agencies of the denomination. Behind both of these readings of the events of the 1980s and 1990s, though, lies the assumption that Southern Baptist identity had not been significantly influenced by Northern controversies during the 1920s. Strangely, although scholars and journalists have paid significant attention to the contemporary "Fundamentalist" tendencies of Southern Protestantism, they have paid much less attention to how the Northern Fundamentalist controversies affected Southern Protestants during the formative period of the former.

The subject of this book is the scope and character of the interaction between Southern Baptists and early Fundamentalism during the late 1910s and early 1920s. Despite their conservative theology, leaders of the SBC did not align themselves with the Fundamentalist movement during its formative phase, and Convention leaders suspiciously eyed those few Southern Baptists who did embrace Fundamentalist attitudes and practices.[2] Southern Baptist leaders recognized and avoided the divisive tendencies of the Fundamentalist movement but adopted many Fundamentalist theological emphases and strategies. Specifically, these leaders used Modernism as a foil against which Southern Baptists were urged to unite for the sake of more effective educational and missionary work. The Fundamentalist movement thus served as a catalyst that expedited the bureaucratization of the Southern Baptist Convention. Without the perceived threat of Modernism, Southern Baptist leaders might never have succeeded in overcoming the centrifugal forces of the denomination's tradition of congregational polity, transforming the Southern Baptist Convention into the centralized denomination that it is today.

The Historiographical Problem of
Fundamentalism in the South

The question of the interaction between Fundamentalism and Southern Protestantism during Fundamentalism's formative period (1919–1925) remains an open one, with literature on their interaction providing either impressionistic or inadequate answers.[3] In particular, much literature discussing the relationship between Fundamentalism and Southern Protestantism suffers from a tendency to conflate the antievolution crusade with Fundamentalism proper.[4]

Fortunately, scholars have begun to recognize the distinction between Fundamentalism and antievolutionism. The most recent treatment of Fundamentalism in the South, William R. Glass' *Strangers in Zion: Fundamentalists in the South, 1900–1950*, clearly brackets concerns about evolution out of its analysis. Quoting Ferenc Szasz, Glass suggests that "fundamentalists turned to antievolutionism while their campaign to oust liberals from the denominations was failing, and evolution came to symbolize for fundamentalists the cultural crisis that America faced in the 1920s."[5] By taking evolution off the table, Glass clears the way for a dis-

2

cussion of Fundamentalism proper as it surfaced in the South during the early twentieth century, defining it as a movement that "sought to affirm the supernatural character of Christianity, to defend the authority and inerrancy of the Bible, to promote holy living by imposing an individualistic code of ethics, and to encourage evangelism in America and overseas as a solution to vexing social issues."[6] Glass' definition of Fundamentalism works well in the context of the present study.

At the same time, Glass' study retains certain weaknesses. First, Glass suggests that the more established Southern denominations (the Baptists, Methodists, and Presbyterians) were almost uniformly opposed to Fundamentalism because they rejected the growing network of Fundamentalist educational and evangelistic institutions. Additionally, Glass notes that Southern Protestant wariness of premillennialism contributed to their distaste for Fundamentalism. While this analysis is true as far as it goes, it fails to distinguish between separatist, premillennial Fundamentalists such as W. B. Riley and J. Frank Norris[7] and more benign, denominationally loyal Fundamentalists such as Curtis Lee Laws. Glass shows conclusively that Southern Baptists, Methodists, and Presbyterians were not interested in participating in the support of Fundamentalist institutions, but this fact alone does not prove that Southerners had no interest in Fundamentalism as it was taking shape in the North. In fact, Southern Baptists who were commenting on Northern events openly supported the more moderate wing of the Fundamentalist movement that sought to oppose Modernists in the denominations without threatening to rupture those same institutions.

Students of Fundamentalism in the South, then, have come to agree that Fundamentalism was not native to the South and that antievolutionism and Fundamentalism are distinct phenomena that historians must study separately. At the same time, however, historians have yet to produce a study regarding the effects of the Fundamentalist movement in the South that acknowledges that disagreements over the importance of denominational loyalty divided early Fundamentalism. In addition, and more importantly, no study of Fundamentalism in the South has sought to investigate the influence of Fundamentalist thought on Southern Protestant denominational organizations, independent of Southern rejection of Fundamentalist-sponsored interdenominational evangelistic and educational institutions. This study explores the interaction between the Fundamentalist movement and Southern religion while taking these crucial insights into account.

3

Fundamentalism and the Southern Baptist Convention, 1919–1925

This monograph will explore the interaction between the Fundamentalist movement and Southern religion from 1919 until 1925 by focusing more closely on the Southern Baptist Convention, understood here as a group of congregations bound together by a network of associations, state and national conventions, and a number of educational institutions, mission boards, and other denominational organizations. As such, the SBC provides an excellent locus for the study of the interaction between Fundamentalism and Southern religion for two reasons. First, even before World War I, the Southern Baptist faith had emerged as the dominant form of Christianity in the Southern United States, representing forty percent of the South's white churchgoing population by 1910.[8] In addition to being numerically dominant, Southern Baptist churches and institutions identified more closely with Southern culture than did other denominations active in the region.[9] During the early twentieth century, by which time the Southern branches of Methodism and Presbyterianism had already begun to debate whether to reconcile with their Northern counterparts, Southern Baptists were distancing themselves from their Northern brethren. By identifying their region as a special place of pristine religiosity and unspotted virtue and in turn identifying themselves with that region, Southern Baptists living after the Civil War created what was, in essence, a new religious tradition.[10] One historian has gone so far as to suggest that, at times, "southern values and Southern Baptist values were the same."[11] To study Southern Baptists during the period between the Civil War and the Civil Rights Movement is to study the nerve center of distinctively Southern white Protestantism.

Second, the six years immediately following World War I, Northern Fundamentalism's formative period, also constituted a period of intense ferment for Southern Baptists. During this very short period of time, the denomination found itself fending off unwanted ecumenical overtures, organizing and executing a fundraising campaign of unprecedented size, dealing with ill-understood Fundamentalist dissent in Texas, and eventually drafting its first confession of faith in 1925 in response to the evolution controversy. The Southern Baptist Convention emerged from these events as a different organization than the one that had celebrated the end of World War I. White-hot from the fires of conflict burning both within and without, the Southern Baptist Convention of the early 1920s was especially susceptible to being molded by ideas that its members had no

4

hand in creating. Fundamentalist ideas, lingering in the atmosphere of the South after wafting there through hearsay, national religious periodicals, or the secular press, likely influenced Southern Baptist self-understanding during this critical period.

Available documentary evidence supports this hypothesis. Faced with pressure from the burgeoning ecumenical movement on the left and Fundamentalism on the right, leaders among Southern Baptists chose neither route but instead constructed a third way that reflected the influence of both. On the one hand, after spurning the Interchurch World Movement in 1919, Southern Baptist leaders borrowed the movement's tendency toward centralization, its methods of advertising and fundraising, and its vision of a world converted to Christ and American democracy in the wake of the Great War. On the other hand, SBC leaders recognized as legitimate the basic theological claims of Northern Fundamentalists and eventually adopted those ideas as a theological rationale for the Convention's policy of denominational isolation and missionary expansion. Unable to join institutional hands with either the Interchurch World Movement or many Fundamentalists because of what they perceived to be irresponsible practices on the part of both, Southern Baptist leaders joined elements of both groups' ideologies underneath their own increasingly-centralized organizational tent. Southern Baptists would take the gospel to the whole world, but theirs would be a gospel tempered by the doctrinal cautions of the Fundamentalist movement. Southern Baptist leaders, having come to associate "Fundamentalism" with reckless critiques of denominational institutions and with J. Frank Norris, resisted that label with fair consistency. At the same time, they affirmed the more moderate wing of the movement and allowed it to influence their own self-understanding.

The "Seventy-Five Million Campaign," a fundraising and organization-building drive that the gathered SBC approved in 1919, was the denominational movement through which the selective appropriation of Fundamentalist ideas occurred. The Campaign represented the largest push for funds and institutional expansion and centralization in the denomination's history to that date. It was in the course of gathering pledges and, even more importantly, of persuading Southern Baptists to make good on those pledges that Southern Baptist leaders reached for Fundamentalist ideas in order to better convince poor, independent-minded Southern Baptists to generously support their denomination and its increasingly centralized structure.

Susceptible to the pervasive influence of Progressivism, Southern Baptists had begun to centralize their denominational institutions under a single bureaucratic roof in 1916, and the creation of an Executive Board that year transformed the SBC into "a continuing, permanent organization with a central authority capable of overseeing the many institutions it comprised."[12] The Seventy-Five Million Campaign, however, placed flesh on the bones that the 1916 action had created. In the days leading up to the 1919 meeting of the Southern Baptist Convention, a number of Southern Baptist editors floated the idea of a massive fundraising campaign among Southern Baptists, intending to apply the funds to the denomination's missionary and educational efforts in the wake of the Great War.[13] By the time messengers reached Atlanta for the annual meeting, the discussion of a five-year program had become so feverish that the messengers voted unanimously to approve a plan to raise seventy-five million dollars over the course of five years.

Reflecting the Convention's increasing tendency to trust its business to small groups of leaders, the Convention voted to authorize the president of the Convention to form a commission of fifteen Southern Baptists who would determine both how to execute the Campaign and how the money received would be distributed. After dividing the expected funds between the various Southern Baptist missionary and educational institutions, members of this commission decided to collect five years worth of cash and pledges during the week spanning November 30 and December 7 of 1919, a week the group dubbed "Victory Week." Leaders associated each of the months of late summer and fall of 1919 with some aspect of the program; July was dedicated to "preparation," August was dedicated to expanding the circulation of the denominational newspapers, September was a month of coordinated prayer, October was designated as "Enlistment-for-Service" month, and November was dedicated to "Christian Stewardship."[14] Throughout these months, Southern Baptist print media were saturated with promotional material publicizing the Campaign.

Finally, during Victory Week, Southern Baptists offered pledges to their denomination in the context of the two Sunday morning worship services with Victory Week sandwiched in between. Campaign General Director L. R. Scarborough, already ensconced in the denomination's "Campaign Headquarters" located in the offices of the Baptist Sunday School Board in Nashville, received news of the pledges via telegraph. By the end of the first day of Victory Week, Scarborough had received word confirming that Southern Baptists had pledged at least fifty-four million dollars to the Campaign.[15] By the time news had been received from all participants early in 1920, that number had ballooned to more than ninety-two million, well

6

over the Campaign's original goal.[16] With characteristic optimism, some leaders proclaimed that the 1920 Southern Baptist Convention would be a "victory convention," although future SBC president George W. McDaniel ominously suggested that he was "afraid of people who spend very much time celebrating on promises."[17]

Experience vindicated McDaniel's doubts. Before the end of 1920, leaders realized that Campaign subscribers were not redeeming their pledges fast enough to cover the debts of the several organizations.[18] Southern Baptists had been hit hard by the economic depression that followed the wartime boom, and many Baptists found themselves unwilling or unable to fulfill pledges that they had made while caught up in the excitement of Victory Week. As a result, leaders turned to a variety of methods to jumpstart interest in the Campaign among rank-and-file Southern Baptists, including emphases on stewardship, tithing, and evangelism.[19] Despite these efforts, the Campaign ended in 1924 having gathered less than fifty-nine million of the ninety-two million dollars originally pledged, a result that led historian Barry Hankins to label the Campaign an "inglorious flop."[20] Southern Baptist institutions spent years retiring the debt that they accumulated by spending money that never appeared.

Because the institutional life of the Southern Baptist Convention during the years of the Northern Fundamentalist controversy was so entwined with its leaders' obsession with successfully completing the Seventy-Five Million Campaign, Southern Baptist responses to Fundamentalist claims were necessarily refracted through this overwhelming aspect of Southern Baptist institutional life. Southern Baptist leaders rejected those aspects of Fundamentalism that they felt threatened the Campaign while they appropriated those aspects of the movement that they believed could help prop it up, embedding them within the rhetoric of the Campaign and ultimately within the warp and woof of the denominational identity that they sought to promote. In other words, to paraphrase Paul Tillich, Fundamentalism contributed to the substance of the Seventy-Five Million Campaign, while the Campaign became a way for Southern Baptists to appropriate Fundamentalist ideas.

Discussion of Methods and Sources

German sociologist Max Weber provides the definitions of "bureaucratization" and "centralization" upon which this book depends. According to Weber, societies develop as they "rationalize," meaning that "magical elements of thought are displaced" while "ideas gain in systematic coherence and naturalistic consistency." [21] In Weber's work, the most rationalized institutional form is the bureaucracy, an institution in which charismatic impulses have been routinized, traditional habits have been modified or rejected for the sake of efficiency, and in which means and ends are systematically adjusted to each other through the administration of rules and procedures. Weber notes that bureaucracies rise due to the need to grant equal treatment to masses of people too large to be dealt with on a person-to-person basis. Weber's observations about the rise of bureaucracy as a form of organization were written primarily with government organizations in mind, but his ideas are helpful for understanding the rationalization of religious organizations as well. These ideas can be found in the predictably titled essay "Bureaucracy" and in the first part of his massive magnum opus, *Economy and Society.*

For the purposes of this text, I have grouped the characteristics of Weber's ideal bureaucracy under four headings. First, bureaucracies depend upon administration by specially trained experts. Second, bureaucracies depend on a steady flow of funds, allowing the organization to provide a salary to its expert administrators. Third, bureaucracies elicit this flow of money and compliance to its other rules and regulations through a system of coercion and reward. Fourth, bureaucracy cannot help but create resistance among those strongly committed to democracy, as rank-and-file recipients of the bureaucracy's administration come to realize that the authority with which bureaucratic functionaries are invested tends to mitigate against democratic decision-making.

First, bureaucracies, by definition, depend upon the administrative abilities of experts who have received specialized, technical training for their particular field of service.[22] Because performing bureaucratic duties depends upon the incumbent having requisite training, true bureaucrats are always appointed, not elected, which ensures that the bureaucrat's loyalties remain with their employing institutions and not with the people regulated through that institution.[23] In order for the bureaucracy to recruit appropriately trained individuals to fill its posts, the educational system of a state (or, in this case, a religious institution) must be adapted to provide trained employees who can fill posts within the bureaucracy.[24]

Second, bureaucracies require a steady flow of money in order to function. Because true bureaucratic functionaries are full-time employees,[25] they must be supported with salaries connected to their positions. As a result, "a stable system of taxation is the precondition for the permanent existence of bureaucratic administration."[26] Even as governments require

8

stable systems of taxation, denominations require stable sources of funding to pay their employees.

Third, bureaucracies depend upon a system of coercion and reward in order to elicit desired responses from their employees and those on payroll. On one hand, bureaucracies tend not to coerce their employees, instead depending upon the provision of salaries, social prestige, and opportunities for advancement to elicit cooperation.[27] On the other hand, bureaucracies do employ coercion to convince those people being regulated to comply with the bureaucracy's rules. While Weber defines the state as the organization that successfully monopolizes the use of force, he notes that means of coercion may be "physical" or "sacerdotal," a tantalizing hint about the non-violent means that ecclesiastical organizations might use in order to encourage compliance with church policies.[28]

Fourth, Weber notes that while bureaucracies are created out of democratic society's need to devise a method whereby large populations can be treated equally, democratic impulses tend to struggle against the process of bureaucratization. "We must remember this fact—which we have encountered several times and which we shall have to discuss repeatedly: that 'democracy' as such is opposed to the 'rule' of bureaucracy, in spite and perhaps because of its unavoidable yet unintended promotion of bureaucratization. Under certain conditions, democracy creates obvious ruptures and blockages to bureaucratic organization."[29] Weber believes that advocates of democracy, faced with the paradox between bureaucracy's intended inclusion of all worthy applicants, regardless of class background, and its creation of an elite group of expert administrators, eventually reject bureaucracy as a legitimate means to the democratic end.[30] While this brief discussion of Weber's theory of bureaucratization does not exhaust his analysis, it provides an outline of his thought that illuminates the extent to which the theory helps to explain events within the Southern Baptist Convention in the early 1920s. As Southern Baptist leaders sought ways to induce rank-and-file Southern Baptists to pay their pledges, these leaders turned to intense forms of persuasion that could be described as sacerdotal coercion, telling Baptists that their failure to pay their pledges might well affect their income or even their standing with God. Leaders also sought to reform Baptist colleges and seminaries by placing new emphasis on their ability to provide competent, professional employees for congregations and denominational organizations. As these changes developed, however, they were not without critics, as some observers labeled the emergence of a new, bureaucratic tendency in the life of the SBC as a threat to the denomination's original democratic ethos. In other words,

9

the rise and results of the Seventy-Five Million Campaign illustrate how the process of bureaucratization, as described by Weber, proceeded in an American denomination.

Even as Weber's thought provides theoretical shape to this study, Southern Baptist newspapers published during the period of study serve as chief primary sources for this text. By 1919, every state convention or association connected with the Southern Baptist Convention either itself operated or closely cooperated with a weekly or monthly newspaper. During the early 1920s, many Southern Baptist pastors worked less than full time and might only meet face to face with denominational leaders at an annual associational meeting. Given these tenuous links between the denomination and its churches, state Baptist newspapers provided an indispensable source of denominational information for pastors and laypeople as well as a way for denominational leaders to share their thoughts on issues facing the denomination at the state and national level. The editors of these organs, sometimes their outright owners but increasingly employees of their respective state Conventions, seem to have had wide latitude in what they included in their newspapers. Each issue contains at least one leading editorial, the work of the editors themselves. Editors also reproduced copy on issues of national, regional, and state interest to Baptists written especially for this purpose by Baptist leaders. Finally, and sometimes most interestingly, editors included letters from their readers when they could, providing extremely rare and valuable glimpses into the thoughts and lives of their workaday Baptist readers. Although editors who had a stake in the success of the Southern Baptist Convention were unquestionably the ones controlling these newspapers, they were not afraid to run pieces occasionally, such as letters to the editor, with which they disagreed. Editors did not run material that cast the Southern Baptist Convention as an illegitimate institution, but they were more than willing to print criticisms that they considered within the range of loyal dissent. Additionally, different editors, writing in different states, often held divergent opinions about matters facing the Southern Baptist Convention. The regularity with which these newspapers appeared, along with the comparative diversity of Southern Baptist opinion that they recorded, make them the best available sources for information about Southern Baptist life during this period.

The broad range of opinion published in Southern Baptist newspapers during the early 1920s helps to foreground in some cases the disagreements between Southern Baptists that elite leaders such as seminary presidents E. Y. Mullins and L. R. Scarborough wanted so badly to sweep under

10

the rug. While Southern Baptist newspaper editors R. H. Pitt or Virginia and L. L. Gwaltney of Alabama tended to approach Fundamentalism with suspicion, their fellow editors V. I. Masters of Kentucky and P. I. Lipsey of Mississippi offered fairly enthusiastic endorsements of the movement as soon as it became known to them. Each of these editors were united in their belief in a "supernatural" bible, but the tone in which they dealt with the problem of Modernism differed greatly. Similarly, editors differed in their attitude toward the denominational centralization about which they wrote on a regular basis. For example, J. S. Compere, editor of the Arkansas *Baptist Advance*, was uncompromisingly enthusiastic about centralization because his newspaper advocated Southern Baptist causes as opposed to resurgent Arkansas Landmark criticism. Meanwhile, Livingston Johnson of the North Carolina *Biblical Recorder* was willing to wonder in his newspaper whether the Campaign had caused an illegitimate growth in unnecessary denominational "machinery." Both men supported the Campaign in their respective newspapers and urged the prompt payment of pledges, but one was more cautious about denominational centralization than the other. Use of Southern Baptist newspapers as historical sources, then, foregrounds the contested nature of the changes they document.

Although scattered use of other sources such as personal papers and Convention records can be found in the endnotes of this study, the Southern Baptist press forms the bedrock of this analysis. Because each of the Southern Baptist newspapers published during this time period was identified with a particular state, however, such extensive use of the Southern Baptist press acutely raises the question of Southern regional identity. Three states considered part of Southern Baptist "territory," Maryland, Kentucky, and Missouri, had been non-seceding "border states" during the Civil War, raising the question of whether their Baptists should be considered in a study involving "Southern Protestantism." The identity of Missouri Baptists is particularly difficult to determine because Missouri aligned itself with both the Northern and Southern Conventions until 1919. Oklahoma and New Mexico pose a separate problem, as neither state existed during the Civil War, but by 1919 each boasted a Southern Baptist state convention that participated fully in the Seventy-Five Million Campaign. Even more unusual is the identity of the Illinois State Baptist Association (ISBA), an organization formed in 1907 in reaction to Modernism among Illinois Baptists. Having aligned itself with the Southern Baptist Convention by sending its mission funds to that organization in order to avoid associating with the Northern Baptist Convention, the ISBA began sending messengers to the SBC in 1910. Although churches aligned with

11

the ISBA were accepted as full members of the SBC from that year forward, they did not possess a hint of the Southern identity upon which the wider Convention depended for its identity. Each of these state conventions published or was associated with newspapers that served Southern Baptists but that were arguably not "Southern." Stated succinctly, the obscurity of Southern boundaries in 1919 leads one to question which Southern Baptist state newspapers can serve as sources for a study of that region's religion

Fortunately, historian Dewey Grantham's *Southern Progressivism: The Reconciliation of Progress and Tradition* offers a delineation of the early twentieth-century South that answers these questions. Grantham's analysis primarily examines states that seceded from the Union in 1861, but the historian adds two states to his analysis that seem to have adopted a Southern identity without actually having participated in the war. First, Grantham states that Kentucky, while officially neutral during the Civil War, began acting as a Southern state almost as soon as the war ended. Democrats won easy victories in the state's 1866 elections, and the state was undisputed Bourbon territory until the populist uprisings of the 1890s.[31] Second, Grantham includes Oklahoma in his list of turn-of-the-century Southern states, noting that its government was dominated by Southerners and that Oklahoma residents exhibited Southern racial attitudes and participated in the South's "cotton culture."[32]

This study, then, draws most heavily on the state Baptist newspapers associated with the state Baptist conventions of the eleven former states of the Confederacy plus Kentucky and Oklahoma, the "South" to which this book refers. The newspapers of some other Southern Baptist state conventions (Southern Illinois, Maryland, and Missouri) will appear from time to time, but only in order to support points not related to regional identity or to refer to copy written by top-tier Southern Baptist leaders.

The region that Southern Baptist leaders addressed during the early twentieth century was a South in transition. While Southerners clung tenaciously to the sense that their region was one set apart from the rest of the United States by a unique set of historical circumstances, the South was also subject to the influence of a number of political and social movements that affected the nation at large. Chief among these was Progressivism, the conviction that democracy was best served not through laissez-faire policies, but through bureaucratic regulation.[33] Large corporations would be checked in their greed by government restrictions, and local governments would be administered not by politicians, but by professionals dedicated to the science of urban management. Southern Baptists felt the effects of Progressivism, and some sought to harness it in order to bring the same order to the Southern Baptist Convention that the movement promised to bring to American government and economic life. The first chapter of this book describes the transformation that Progressivism brought to Southern Baptist ideas about democracy by focusing on the Southern Baptist Convention's most influential Progressivist, Edgar Young Mullins.

1

The Transformation of Baptist Identity: E. Y. Mullins and the New Baptist Democracy

The opening years of the twentieth century saw a move toward greater centralization among Baptists throughout the English-speaking world. Northern Baptists reorganized their societies into the Northern Baptist Convention in 1908, and British Baptists continued to expand the influence of the newly-formed Baptist Union of Great Britain and Ireland under J. H. Shakespeare, one of their most influential secretaries.[1] The most profound shifts in polity, however, occurred among Southern Baptists, as the leaders of a denomination traditionally opposed to ecclesiastical centralization came to embrace a reading of Baptist polity that severely circumscribed the roles of rank-and-file Baptists. Although many Southern Baptist leaders helped to move their denomination in this direction during the first quarter of the twentieth century, Edgar Young Mullins (1860–1928) stands as the most important.

Remembered primarily as a theologian, Mullins, the fourth president of the Southern Baptist Theological Seminary (1899–1928), also served as the president of the Southern Baptist Convention (1921–1924) and of the Baptist World Alliance (1923–1928).[2] As a constructive theologian, Mullins was a pioneer among Southern Baptists; the way he used the work of non-Baptist thinkers like Friedrich Schleiermacher, William James, and Borden Parker Bowne placed him in a class all his own. Mullins used these ideas in order to create a theology located at the crossroads of liberalism and evangelicalism, emphasizing the freedom and responsibility of individual believers before God, an idea that Mullins distilled into the now-familiar concept of "soul competency." The resulting corpus of theological work has continued to attract the attention of Baptists and others in the decades since his death.

One group of Mullins's readers, counting both insiders and outsiders among its members, finds in Mullins's thought a "magna carta" of Christian freedom and the true meaning of Baptist democracy. In a 2008 article, for instance, Russell Dilday, the former president of Southwestern Baptist Theological Seminary, responds to critics who have accused Mullins of baptizing American "rugged individualism" by pointing out that Mullins claimed "the American government" was, in fact, a "shadow" of the polity of the New Testament church.[3] Strikingly, Dilday seems to accept Mullins's assertion that the freedoms of speech and worship claimed by Americans are rooted entirely in the witness of the Baptist people. For Dilday and many other Baptist readers, Mullins's work continues to be cherished for his clear articulation of a vision that places spiritual freedom at the very center of the Christian life.[4] At the same time, Mullins's theology won him at least one extra-ecclesial admirer. Although not a Baptist himself, Harold Bloom's reading of Mullins's theology also pinpoints his emphasis on individual religious experience. Bloom probably took individualist interpretations of Mullins's theology to their logical conclusion when he asserted that Mullins, "the Calvin or Luther or Wesley of the Southern Baptists," reframed Southern Baptist theology in terms that were subjective, apophatic, and ultimately Gnostic.[5]

A second group of readers, while finding the same emphasis on religious experience and individuality in Mullins's work, criticizes this emphasis as being both damaging to legitimate forms of religious authority and a misrepresentation of the historic Baptist position. In a 1959 volume discussing changes in American Baptist ecclesiology over the course of its history, Winthrop Hudson declared that Mullins's doctrine of soul competency weakened Baptist ecclesiological thought by "mak[ing] every man's hat his own church."[6] R. Albert Mohler, the current president of the Southern Baptist Theological Seminary, builds upon these criticisms in his introduction to a 1997 edition of Mullins's 1908 monograph *The Axioms of Religion*. Expanding his critique of Mullins beyond the ecclesiological, Mohler charges that Mullins's emphasis on the subjective experience of the individual undermined the doctrinal bases of the Southern Baptist Convention and "threatened to dissolve into doctrinal ambiguity."[7] For Mohler, Mullins's embrace of the religious experience of the "autonomous individual" as an organizing center for Christian theology represents a methodological shift away from emphasis on biblical authority, theology's legitimate center.

It would be difficult to overestimate the amount of animosity that has developed between these two parties as they continue to discuss Mullins's

16

legacy, yet the two groups do have at least two things in common. First, members of both groups rightly tend to gravitate toward *The Axioms of Religion* as the focus for their interpretations of Mullins. Widely recognized today as the most important segment of the Mullins corpus, *The Axioms of Religion: A New Interpretation of the Baptist Faith* was popular immediately upon its release by the American Baptist Publication Society and was embraced by Baptists throughout the Anglophone world.[8]

Second, contemporary discussion of E. Y. Mullins's legacy revolves so completely around his emphasis on "soul competency" and its effects on Southern Baptist life that other aspects of Mullins's thought and leadership often recede into the background of the discussion, sometimes disappearing altogether. In his introduction to the *Axioms*, for instance, Mohler hints that Mullins was a "Southern Progressive" who sought "the rise of a new Southern Baptist Convention in a New South," but Mohler's discussion of Mullins's leadership quickly veers into a discussion about Mullins' authorship of various confessional statements.[9] Mohler correctly identifies Mullins as a man of his time, but along with most of his conversation partners, he fails to read Mullins's work through the lens of his Southern, Progressive identity.[10]

This is the identity through which Mullins's *The Axioms of Religion* must be read. Although the *Axioms* represent a strain of Southern democratic thinking common first to elite, antebellum ministers and then to postbellum ministers influenced by the "New South Creed" and later by Progressivism, Mullins and others were aware that adherents of a second strand of Southern democratic thinking viewed them with suspicion. These heirs of the rhetoric of Jacksonian democracy believed that democracy was rooted in the virtue of common people; they resented Progressivism's tacit suggestion that only elites like Mullins could be trusted to govern the institutions of church and state, sometimes going so far as to condemn denominational institutions as "Romanism in a Baptist cloak."[11] Among Southern Baptists, these Jacksonian ideas of democracy came to be identified with the "Landmark" movement, a nineteenth-century web of ecclesiological and theological claims that insisted that Baptists, by virtue of an unbroken line of churches reaching back to the first century, were the only true churches in existence.[12] By the early twentieth century, Landmark ideas had so permeated the Southern Baptist Convention that the Progressive leaders controlling it did so only by constant vigilance against the ubiquitous possibility of Landmark revolt.

Evidence suggests that Mullins should be read as an adherent of the first strain of Baptist thinking about democracy. Heavily influenced by

17

Progressivism and professionalism, Mullins was an upwardly mobile minister who believed in the professionalization of the clerical office and who was heavily influenced by Progressive ideas about leadership and social organization. In fact, Mullins was the finest possible example of an elite, Progressive Southern Baptist minister.[13]

Although Mullins was a pastor formed in the tradition of the first strain of thinking about the meaning of Baptist democracy, his thinking and writing were always tempered by the political reality of Landmarkism, the second strain. Like other Progressive Era leaders, Mullins would learn to cast his reservations about democracy as a plea for its defense and extension. When the *Axioms* are read closely through the lens of Mullins's professional, Progressive identity, the book becomes an apology for Progressive-style professional governance of the Southern Baptist Convention. Although Mullins takes visible care not to offend superficial Landmark sensibilities, the book's larger theological argument is necessarily paired with a subtle yet sophisticated plea for professional control of convention activities.

The final section of this chapter includes analysis of several editorials written by Baptist leaders in 1919 and 1920, showing that Mullins's new interpretation of Baptist democracy was not idiosyncratic, but was similar to those held by leaders seeking to elicit participation in the Seventy-Five Million Campaign. By the beginning of the Seventy-Five Million Campaign, the Progressive-influenced reading of Baptist polity that *The Axioms of Religion* so clearly articulates had saturated the thinking of most Convention leaders.

Two Strains of Democratic Thought: Southern Baptists before Mullins

The Baptist tradition in the United States has always been one whose members have been concerned with preserving a democratic church polity. Isaac Backus (1724–1806), a leading pastor among New England's Separate Baptists, was originally fearful of the associational tradition common among English Baptists, fearing that it could lead to an informal episcopacy that would exert illicit control over Baptist churches.[14] Backus could only be enticed to lead his own congregation to join the newly constituted Warren Association upon seeing its constitution amended to emphasize "that such an association is consistent with the independency and power of particular churches because it pretends to no other than an advisory council, utterly disclaiming superiority, jurisdiction, coercive right

18

and infallibility."[15] Somewhat later, Backus's fellow New Englander John Leland (1754–1841) included both Jeffersonian and Madisonian notions of democracy in his account of both legitimate government and authentic Christian faith as he worked to secure religious liberty for the Baptists of Virginia.[16] As the Baptist tradition in the South took shape, Leland helped to infuse it with a concern for democracy that closely aligned Baptist church polity and Jeffersonian politics: "Liberty and equality, the boast of democracy, is [sic] realized in the church . . . as far as church government on earth is the government of Christ, it is of democratical genius."[17] The preachers that spread the Baptist faith throughout the South, often preaching on Sunday after a week of agricultural labor, frequently received these ideas with their mothers' milk.

Not every pastor of the antebellum South was a backwoods exhorter, however. Many of the clergymen that served the South's rising urban congregations were well-to-do and well educated. These pastors, preaching as they did to up-and-coming congregations full of physicians, lawyers, and teachers, tended to see themselves in the same professional light. Placing themselves in a category far from that of the frontier preachers who still labored in rural areas of the South, these professional ministers offered themselves as learned specialists in their field, mediating meticulously gathered theological knowledge to their congregations.[18]

People formed by the culture in which they lived, these Southern ministers expressed their developing elitism not only by distinguishing themselves from part-time and uneducated pastors, but, more tellingly, by their explicit approval of the developing Southern social hierarchy. The sermons of these town pastors consistently "exhibited a . . . description of society as a gradation of aristocrats, middling classes, masses, and slaves." While these preachers did not encourage abuse or exploitation of society's lower classes, they did believe that these distinctions were God-ordained and should be respected.[19] Heirs of the classical republican tradition, these pastors also harbored a distrust of unregulated democracy. One Presbyterian pastor read de Tocqueville's *Democracy in America* and concluded that he had always been right to distrust the unwashed masses. "The people" were unable to make good political decisions, and calls for betterment of society through a redistribution of wealth were simply out of accord with the will of God. Because God had decreed poverty and misery for the better part of mankind as punishment for the fall, any attempt to ameliorate the situation of the masses could only be described as a utopian pipe dream. This pastor's attitudes were typical of the town pastors of the South.[20]

19

Over time, the elite status of the South's aristocratic town pastors was tacitly woven into the structure of various denominations' polity. Educated, town-dwelling clergymen were consistently overrepresented in the leadership of their various denominational bodies. Those preachers who knew that they would never be able to aspire to such visibility or influence within their denominations often felt ambivalent (to say the least) about their ambitious de facto leaders, but they continued to elect them to positions of responsibility anyway.[21] By virtue of education and position, then, these town preachers became their denominations' Southern spokespeople as well, and it was from the ranks of pastors such as these that the Southern branches of the denominations drew their theologians.[22] As the debate over slavery intensified after 1830, these theologians became some of slavery's most ardent defenders, assuming intellectual responsibility to defend the "peculiar institution" and later developing theodicies that made sense of Southern defeat and humiliation.[23] These events solidified the mutual dependence between elite Southern clergy and the region's governing class.

After 1848, however, a form of protest against the growing power of this Baptist ministerial elite began to take root among Baptists in the Old Southwest. Much of the scholarly literature on Landmarkism has focused on its idiosyncratic interpretation of Baptist history and extreme anti-ecumenical tendencies, but many of the Baptist leaders criticized by J. R. Graves (1820–1893) and his associates held the same successionist viewpoint regarding Baptist origins as did their antagonists.[24] While on the surface Landmarkism was concerned with the aggressive promotion of Baptist isolation, the movement was actually motivated by an animus against eastern ministerial elitism.[25]

Graves was not the first Baptist leader to reject the "meddling" of eastern leaders in western affairs. During the 1820s, John Taylor and Daniel Parker led frontier revolts against the perceived eastern elitism of the Baptist clergy. These leaders saw behind the formation of the Triennial Convention an attempt to separate simple western Baptists from their money and place them under the yoke of an eastern-controlled national organization.[26] Taylor and Parker resorted to a rigid Calvinism in order to refute the claims of foreign-missions advocates, but by the time Graves rose to prominence the American political winds had so changed that the rising demagogue had access to a new language of political resistance.

Andrew Jackson's election to the United States presidency in 1828 energized the people of the "Old Southwest" and underscored a growing

The Transformation of Baptist Identity

feeling of resentment among southwesterners toward the Southern ruling elite in Virginia and South Carolina. As the population of the southwestern states grew, their residents began to demand greater influence over the new nation's destiny. While the classical republicanism that had influenced the founders affirmed the theoretical equality of all white men while accepting as natural the de facto social stratification of society, the rise of Jackson marked the beginning of an era in which common people began to reject this social stratification in favor of the idea that everyday people were capable of living the virtuous lives required by democratic government without elite supervision.[27]

It was this rhetoric championing the political rights of everyday people that J. R. Graves participated in as he resisted the perceived pretensions of elitist ministers and ecclesiastical organizations. In Graves's hands, the rhetoric of Jacksonian democracy and its message of political emancipation for the common people merged with traditional Baptist emphases on voluntary church membership, the separation of church and state, and adult believers' baptism. As a result, Graves was able to cast himself in the role of the people's defender against every conceivable form of ecclesiastical "tyranny."

Graves believed tyranny pervaded American Protestantism. He wrote one book criticizing the "great iron wheel" that was the Methodist itinerant system and wrote another against the baptismal theology of Presbyterianism, but he might have fought most viciously when he was at close quarters with other Southern Baptist leaders.[28] The demagogue never hesitated to accuse eastern Southern Baptist leaders of manipulating Convention structures to aggregate power in their own hands at the expense of everyday Baptists.[29] For instance, during his contest with R. B. C. Howell, pastor of Nashville's First Baptist Church, Graves made it clear that Howell was among those eastern elites who sought to control the publication of Southern Baptist Sunday school literature to their own advantage.[30] The conflict between the two men escalated until Graves was expelled from First Baptist Church. Graves formed a new church that was recognized as legitimate by the Landmarkist Concord Association after that group expelled Howell's congregation, but this turn of events did not prevent Graves from fuming about his exclusion. "Baptists of Tennessee and the South are told by Doctors of Divinity that the act of one church, whether according to the law of Christ or not, is binding upon every other Baptist church in *Christendom* itself! Concede this authority to the disorderly First Church in this city, and would not Nashville become a Rome

21

in one day, and the pastor of the Church universal and sovereign pontiff of Baptists!"[31] Graves's method of associating a distrusted Baptist leader with the Pope, a rhetorical turn not to be taken lightly in nineteenth-century Nashville, clearly illustrates his frame of mind. For true democracy to flourish among Baptists, the denomination would have to be steered not by "Doctors of Divinity" but by common people set free from peonage.

Howell resigned the presidency of the Southern Baptist Convention in 1859, defusing the Graves-Howell controversy. The Civil War violently disrupted the lives of Southern Baptists, and in the dark years immediately following the conflict, Graves achieved detente with his former opponents. Landmarkism, however, had come to the South to stay. Landmark teachings about the church and, more importantly, about the nature of democracy had thoroughly permeated much of the territory of the Southern Baptist Convention. Postbellum Southern Baptist leaders soon realized that any attempt to organize their people for missions, education, and benevolence would have to take the aftermath of the Landmark movement into account.

The social hierarchy that elite Southern ministers had defended so doggedly sustained a near-fatal blow when slavery collapsed in 1865. Almost immediately after the cessation of hostilities, a number of new Southern spokespeople began searching for a means by which the South might be delivered from its economic and social problems. The proposed solution, articulated in subtly different ways by its various proponents, was to abandon the feudal values of the "Old South," to diversify the Southern economy to include manufacturing as well as a wider variety of crops, and to cooperate with Northerners willing either to migrate South or to provide capital.[32] At the same time, thinkers advocating these changes harbored a familiar social conservatism; their rhetoric masked an attempt to maintain the South's old social hierarchy within a new constitutional framework.[33] This "New South Creed" gave the North an excuse to end Reconstruction even as it motivated the Southern "Redeemers" who took the reins of various state governments in 1877.[34] Business-oriented and socially conservative, these "Redeemers" were the political embodiment of the New South.[35]

Northern interest in Reconstruction may have waned in part because of the overwhelming social problems that vexed that region during the last third of the nineteenth century. During this period of remarkable population growth and industrial development, Americans began to search for ways to ameliorate the social disruptions caused by the rise of large corporations and uncontrolled urban expansion.[36] The solution around which America's best minds eventually gathered was that of bureaucracy. Americans had long been fascinated with the idea of professionalism, the idea that a person could gain entrance to the middle class by mastering a body of knowledge that they would then mediate to needful clients.[37] Progressivism, as a social and political movement, was born when Americans applied the professional ideal to the problems of governing a "distended society."[38] A bureaucrat was simply a professional whose expertise was in the art of government. Historian Robert H. Wiebe notes the incredible power that early twentieth-century political thinkers were willing to entrust to well-trained bureaucrats. Some of them envisioned a society led by

> a public man, a unique and indispensable leader. Although learned enough to comprehend the details of a modern, specialized government, he was much more than an expert among experts. His vision encompassed the entire nation, his impartiality freed him from all prejudices, and his detached wisdom enabled him to devise an equitable and progressive policy for the whole society. Corps of servants received his general directives and translated them into their particular areas. At the same time, they channeled basic information back to the public man, so that all government activity was ultimately coordinated in his mind.[39]

Although the government of the United States was never modified to accommodate such a vision, it serves to illustrate the profound trust that many educated Americans placed in the idea of professional government during the Progressive Era.

Southern political leaders, primed by their acceptance of the forward-looking "New South Creed," eagerly grasped Progressivism as a means by which the problems of the South, no less than those of the North and Midwest, could be addressed. Progressivism provided methods that the South could use to address the growing problem of urban administration and to reform Southern farming habits.[40] At the same time, however, Progressivism provided a new, scientific justification for elite government through its reliance on the ideals of professionalism. More than equal to this task, Progressivism provided the rhetoric necessary to disfranchise Southern blacks along with a significant number of poor or landless whites.[41] Through Progressivism and the scientific language of

23

professionalism, Redeemers were able to justify a hierarchical social order that could no longer be propped up by appeals to tradition. Progressivism, therefore, provided an alternative to Jacksonian notions of democracy.

Widowed by the death of the old plantation culture, leaders of the Southern Baptist Convention and of the South's other major denominations came to identify themselves with the conservative, pro-business Democrats that now governed the South.[42] Southern Baptist leaders of the early twentieth century, then, had been steeped in Southern aristocratic tendencies, were heirs of a tradition of alignment with the South's most powerful interests, and were continuing defenders of a conservative regime. In pastors and theologians with such a pedigree, the paternalistic and bureaucratic tendencies of Progressivism could only find good soil.

At the same time, however, Landmarkism and its Jacksonian definition of Baptist democracy had not disappeared. Having been reconciled to the dream of a "New South," many Landmarkers settled into cooperation with the Southern Baptist Convention and Southern state conventions, but pockets of Jacksonian resistance to this pattern of accommodation still remained.[43] A series of conflicts in turn-of-the-century Texas and Arkansas illustrates the continuing explosive potential of Landmarkism.

In 1886, Texas Baptists moved to consolidate a number of redundant denominational organizations into a single Baptist General Convention of Texas, a classically Progressive gesture of "efficiency." Samuel A. Hayden, editor of *The Texas Baptist and Herald,* had himself been instrumental in the merger, but immediately used his position to censure the administration of the new organization on the grounds that it was controlled by a small clique of insiders.[44] Hayden accused the leaders of the new state convention of building an illegitimate hierarchy, paying its employees exorbitant salaries and otherwise mismanaging funds.[45] Mutual recrimination continued on both sides until Hayden was denied a seat in the BGCT in 1897, an act that Hayden condemned as a usurping of the prerogatives of the local church since, by his interpretation, denominational bodies should be obliged to seat whomever churches, acting autonomously, choose to send. Hayden sued the BGCT and a number of its representatives in retaliation, and while these lawsuits were settled out of court, Hayden's followers had left the BGCT by 1900 to form the Baptist Missionary Association of Texas.[46] Hard feelings remained following the split; J. B. Cranfill, one of Hayden's adversaries, fired a pistol at him in a train station washroom five years later.[47]

24

A similar controversy broke out in Arkansas immediately upon the settlement of the Hayden lawsuits and the withdrawal of the Baptist Missionary Association. In 1899 Ben Bogard, the newly arrived pastor of the Baptist church in Searcy, Arkansas, launched a movement aimed at gaining control of the newly formed Arkansas Baptist State Convention. The attempt failed, and Bogard led his followers out of the state convention and into a merger with Hayden's group in 1905. The resulting organization, renamed the American Baptist Association in 1924, endured a split in 1950 but has continued operating to the present day.[48]

These two conflicts are best discussed as a unit. Both conflicts were fought in terms of Landmarkist ecclesiology, but while many scholars have tried to explain them as theological scuffles, in actuality the defenders of the BGCT and the ABSC were as committed to Landmarkism as were their critics. In fact, adherents of post-war Landmarkism who carried the movement into the New South fell into two groups.[49] The first group of Landmarkers identified with the "Lost Cause" and the promise of the New South so completely that their Landmarkism lost its Jacksonian edge. For these Baptists, Landmarkism was a set of ecclesiological commitments compatible with professionalization and denominational centralization.[50] More radical Landmarkers, however, retained the stubborn commitment to the Jacksonian fear of centralization and elitism that had motivated J. R. Graves.[51] In the Arkansas and Texas conflicts, Landmarkism had become the common vocabulary that these Baptists used to debate the merits of two conflicting forms of democracy: Jacksonian democracy, characterized by a distrust for elite authority and jealous defense of the autonomy of common people, and Progressive democracy, which took for granted the idea that the greatest good was best pursued by placing a few competent, trusted individuals in positions of power and influence. To put the matter somewhat differently, Paul Harvey notes that "centralizing efforts of denominational leaders . . . clashed with the pervasive localist ethic of rural congregations. . . . The theology of antimissionism and Landmarkism served as the rallying cry for Baptist localism."[52] Many Southern Baptists had a hard time seeing proposals that sought to modify Baptist democracy as anything but an attempt to destroy it altogether.

The conflict between J. B. Gambrell and Samuel Hayden illustrates the tension between these conflicting notions of democracy. Gambrell, a Mississippi pastor who came to Texas after serving as the president of Mercer University, became the BGCT Superintendent of Missions in December 1896. Like other BGCT partisans, Gambrell took it upon himself

25

to defend the organization and to respond to Hayden's criticisms. In the process of defending the BCGT from Hayden, Gambrell accused the editor of being both an advocate of T. P. Crawford's "Gospel Mission" movement, a late nineteenth-century Landmark challenge to the Foreign Mission Board, and even of being a follower of Daniel Parker, one of the early nineteenth-century founders of the Primitive Baptist movement.[53] In actuality, neither of the charges was true; while Crawford rejected the legitimacy of mission boards and Parker rejected the legitimacy of missions altogether, Hayden did neither of these things. The new organization that Hayden founded in 1899 barely differed from the BGCT in its structure.[54] Hayden's complaint was merely that a handful of leaders dominated the organization and mismanaged its funds, but Gambrell's accusations emphasize the fact that Hayden had become the latest bearer of the Jacksonian banner that so many nineteenth-century Baptists had carried. Gambrell and Hayden shared a commitment to Landmark ecclesiology, but while Gambrell represented a Landmarkism that had abandoned Jacksonianism in order to accommodate itself to the organizational realities of the Progressive Era, Hayden retained the older understanding of democracy and saw Gambrell as a "pontiff" whose burgeoning organization threatened the rights of ordinary Baptists.[55]

As in the Texas controversy, Landmarkism provided the language in which Ben Bogard scolded Arkansas convention leaders. Upon close inspection, however, his opponents were as likely to identify themselves with Landmarkism as were his followers. Rather than a conflict over ecclesiology, the Bogard conflict was a religious manifestation of rural resentment towards the New South leadership of both the state government of Arkansas and the ABSC.[56] In fact, the ABSC president who drew so much ire from Bogard, James P. Eagle, was also a former governor of Arkansas and a committed promoter of a New South agenda in both church and state.[57] As president of the state Convention, Eagle promoted a state missions strategy that emphasized the founding and strengthening of county seat churches, ministerial education, and the emulation of American business methods in church administration.[58] Eagle hoped that this quintessentially Progressive strategy would reinforce the financial base of the ABSC, but it also provoked a reaction among those Baptists who felt that it disproportionately favored townsfolk over yeoman farmers. The most reliable predictors of a church's alignment during the Bogard controversy was not its self-definition as "Landmark Baptist" or connection with J. R. Graves, but its distance from a railhead.[59] As indicated by the fact that he was able to entice a number of primitive Baptists to participate in his

26

new organization, Ben Bogard represented the latest defender of Jacksonian democracy in a New South increasingly inhospitable to it.[60]

Edgar Young Mullins: Professional and Progressive

If Samuel Hayden and Ben Bogard carried the Jacksonian banner into the twentieth-century South, E. Y. Mullins most fully exemplified the sort of urban, professionalistic, Progressive leadership against which they crusaded. Although the influence of professional and Progressive ideals over Mullins is just as important as the ideas he absorbed from Schleiermacher, James, and others, readers tend to neglect this aspect of Mullins's thought.

Mississippi natives, Mullins and his family relocated to Texas after the Civil War. Mullins eventually received his undergraduate degree from Texas A&M and planned a career in law, but after being converted during a revival at the First Baptist Church of Dallas, Mullins found himself planning for a career in the Baptist ministry. In 1881, Mullins left Texas for Louisville to enroll in the Southern Baptist Theological Seminary.[61] As one of the student graduation speakers at the seminary's 1885 commencement, Mullins chose to speak on "Manliness in the Ministry." The recent graduate placed Christian ministry among the professions, and stated that he expected ministers to be compensated appropriately.[62] Later, as a pastor, Mullins revealed his Progressive leanings as he managed his congregation in much the same way as the "public man" was to manage the United States: "He knew that he must know his church as nobody else knew it, from its topmost man to the humblest; that he must X-ray its official organization and understand its every department as no one else did; that he must vision possibilities of growth and spiritual culture of which none of them had dreamed; that he must keep a league ahead of them in everything if the heavens fell, and that he must do all these things without letting anyone know he was doing them."[63] Mullins seems to have managed his denomination's oldest seminary in the same fashion. The professor managed the seminary's fundraising efforts personally, "directing the movements of many workers over the South" and often working himself into exhaustion and illness.[64]

Like other elite Southern ministers, the young Mullins was drawn to and served in middle- to upper-class urban congregations. While Mullins was frustrated with the need to "popularize" his sermons in his first, small-town pulpit, the middle-class congregation was a far cry from the rural chapels where most Baptist preachers labored. Later, when Mullins left that first congregation for Lee Street Church, he entered an environment

27

where he found an opportunity to demonstrate his affinity for Progressivism through his involvement in the social problems of Baltimore. Mullins challenged the idea that alcohol abuse causes all poverty, supported striking miners, and applauded the electoral defeat of corrupt politicians. He also revealed a paternalistic streak in his support of the Baltimore Charity Organization Society and in his fears that some African Americans were worsening race relations through their insistence on social equality.[65] Mullins became more conservative in his approach to social issues as he aged, but he never completely turned his back on the Social Gospel or the Progressivism that it mediated to American Protestantism.[66]

In short, E. Y. Mullins was everything that elite, urban Southern Baptists ministers had always been. He was a professional, he advocated ministerial professionalization, and he employed professional models in his roles as pastor and administrator. His affinities with Progressivism were also apparent in his sensitivity to human suffering and in his paternalistic approach to remedying it. Heralded by so many as a prophet of freedom, Mullins actually exhibited the marks of Progressivism that would seem to indicate a lack of faith in unfettered democracy.

The Axioms of Religion as a Progressive Document

When *The Axioms of Religion* is read through the lens of Mullins's identity as a professional and a Progressive, the document takes on new meaning. Rather than a spirited defense of Christian freedom, the text contains a vision of Baptist life that legitimizes the professionalization of Baptist denominations' leadership. Drawing on the work of James, Schleiermacher, and Bowne, Mullins was able to reinterpret Baptist egalitarianism in psychological terms. Believers were equal to each other because they enjoyed equal access to God. As a result of this shift, Baptist democracy became a matter of discernment instead of debate, as Christians were expected to fall in line behind beliefs and courses of action thought to be the will of Christ in any given situation. Dissent was no longer a democratic right but a sign of a faulty sense of God's will. Further, by removing decision-making from the center of his definition of democracy, Mullins created an "administrative" role for the denominational expert. Ultimately, Mullins authorized these experts to collect the spiritual energy of autonomous believers for the purpose of channeling it as those experts saw fit.

Despite criticisms of Mullins's theology and how it may have affected Baptist thought about the church, Mullins explicitly wrote at least in part out of the same concern for the institutional church that later motivated his critics. Mullins knew that the American denominations had been forged in the fires of interdenominational debate and controversy. The theologian believed that such debate was no longer productive, but that the decline of denominational spirit was raising the specter of institutional dissolution. "There is indeed a marked movement toward an anti-institutional Christianity," Mullins noted. "If the mass of individual Christians is to become simply a vortex ring of dancing atoms, each moving aimlessly around its own center, Christianity will soon spend itself."[67] The idea that a man's hat could be his own church bothered Mullins no less than it did his late twentieth-century critics. Mullins wrote *The Axioms* to shore up the idea that churches and denominational structures are integral parts of true Christianity, and throughout the book he attempted to show how those structures could exist without occluding the equal access of their members to God. Mullins achieved this goal by contracting the sphere of the individual Christian's competency, expanding the role of the religious professional by defining denominational work as "administrative," and finally by stigmatizing non-cooperation with these professionals.

First, Mullins radically redefines the meaning of Baptist egalitarianism, positing "soul competency" as the "historical significance" of the Baptist denomination.[68] Interestingly, when Mullins introduces this concept, he is careful to explain what soul competency is not: "There is no reference here to the question of sin and human ability in the moral and theological sense, nor in the sense of independence of the Scriptures. I am not here stating the Baptist creed."[69] Elsewhere in the book, Mullins spends more time explaining the areas to which soul competency does not extend. Before even introducing the concept of soul competency, Mullins explains that "freedom by itself does not imply capacity for self-government."[70] Later, Mullins notes that "equality of privilege in the church of course has no reference to the mental and spiritual capacities of men. . . . Nor does the [ecclesiastical] axiom assume that one man is as well fitted as another for official position in the church."[71] Whatever Mullins means by "soul competency," he does not mean that all people are necessarily competent to govern themselves, nor does he mean that all people are individually competent to adjudicate knotty theological and ethical problems.

When Mullins does try to positively explain the nature of the connection between individuals and the divine, he reaches not for strict definitions but for a series of metaphors. The connection between Christians

29

and God is free, abundant sunshine,[72] electricity in a wire,[73] the geological pressure that turns carbon into diamonds,[74] and the wind that creates waves on the surface of the sea.[75] Like Schleiermacher, Mullins avoids finding an ethical impulse or the revelation of particular information at the center of true "religion."[76] Instead, these four metaphors indicate that Mullins believes soul competency, properly exercised, makes it possible for God to infuse Christians with spiritual energy. This spiritual energy, Mullins suggests, is the key to maintaining denominational vitality in an age weary of theological disputes. "All church problems are at bottom problems of spiritual temperature. God's Spirit supplies the flame. Earthly conditions furnish the fuel. Well-directed effort raises the temperature to the desired point."[77] This metaphor of heat appears repeatedly in the Southern Baptist literature of the period and helps to illustrate the fact that, for Mullins, the energy that competent Christians receive from God, like fire, brings with it no epistemological content.[78]

Second, even while drawing such a tight circle around the meaning of soul competency, Mullins tacitly lays out an expansive role for church and denominational leaders. While these leaders are forbidden from exercising spiritual authority, Mullins understands this only as one person's usurpation of the spiritual prerogatives belonging to the individual believer. Because these prerogatives are so narrowly and negatively defined in terms of infusion of spiritual energy, Mullins actually posits a broad space in which leaders can act with considerable latitude.

Mullins explicitly states the need for the church to designate leaders who are charged with doing "administrative" work within churches and denominations. The author assures his readers that the idea that the "right of every soul to deal with God for itself . . . does not forbid the setting apart of ministers or officials to perform certain specified duties for the sake of convenience or expediency in the church."[79] Later, Mullins reminds his readers that "no one regards all men as possessing equal natural ability or learning. . . . Diversities of gifts and offices and administrations are clearly recognized in the New Testament churches and as clearly set forth for our guidance."[80] While Mullins strongly criticized John Henry Newman's theology of church development, he did admit that "New Testament Christianity is susceptible of infinite development" in the area of administration.[81]

The range of activities that Mullins understands as being within the category of "administration" is easily extrapolated when he offers examples of those ecclesial systems that are unacceptable by Baptist standards. For example, Mullins defends the idea that human agents mediate the love of God and implies that any Christian can mediate God's grace, rejecting the "priestly and exclusive manipulator of sacraments."[82] Mullins was thinking along the same lines when he claimed that the Donatists were "suppressed in the early centuries because they insisted upon prophesying. This meant that they asserted their direct relation to Christ through the Spirit as against the indirect relation through the priesthood."[83] Later, when Mullins compares civil government to the government of the Church, he says:

> It might be a logical procedure for a given community owning
> a large body of real estate in common to delegate the control
> of its mines and the distribution of its coal to a commission.
> The nature of the case would require some such administra
> tion perhaps. But it would be absurd to appoint a commission
> to control and distribute the sunlight. In this respect the in
> habitants would only need to keep out of each other's light.
> Every man would simply have to avoid building his house or
> ordering his life so as to obscure the sun from his brother. As
> the Baptist sees it, papacies and episcopacies are commissions
> to control the sunshine.[84]

The anti-Catholicism in Mullins's remarks must have appealed to many in his audience, but Mullins's heavy reliance on anti-sacerdotalism to explain to his readers what Baptist leaders cannot do indicates that for Mullins, the category "administrative" could actually stretch to cover any non-priestly task. Mullins translates this broad definition of administration into Southern Baptist terms when he echoes the founding documents of his denomination and explains that "general organizations . . . have no ends to serve save those of eliciting, combining, and directing the missionary, educational, or other forms of energy among the churches and smaller societies, for the advancement of the kingdom of God on earth. In short, they are simply means of co-operation on an entirely voluntary basis."[85] Mullins intends to show that Baptist denominations are strictly limited in their actions, but Mullins, consciously or not, is actually making it theoretically possible for Baptist denominations to function in the same way as their more hierarchical counterparts. Baptist leaders harvest the spiritual energy of competent Christians and apply it to professionally planned denominational projects.

Mullins grants that Baptist denominational officials do the same work as their counterparts in other denominations: "Our superintendents and secretaries of missions perform the work of bishops without any of the authority of bishops." The author quickly qualifies this, however, by noting that these officials "have no semblance of authority over any congregation however small." Instead of dispensing ecclesiastical commands, Baptist leaders only work by "means of suggestion."[86] Mullins, like other Baptists, cherished the tradition of voluntarism that formed the heart of Baptist polity, but the theologian gives the tradition a Progressive spin. A close reading of *The Axioms* shows that while Mullins believed that churches were free to walk separately from the denomination, he also believed that such use of Christian freedom was a clear sign of spiritual indolence.

First, Mullins consistently equated cooperation with congregational health and associated non-cooperation with disease. For example, he noted, "If a local church becomes worldly and dies spiritually it may also pass out of existence as a visible organization. It cannot remain as a burden to its sister churches. It is simply isolated from the rest by its own worldliness. The spiritual churches, however, may unite in their Associations and Conventions for mutual helpfulness."[87] When Mullins refers to the temptation to worldliness in this context, he explicitly frames it as "over-emphasis of individualism" and as "unwholesome controversy" among churches. The theologian reminds his readers that Baptists occasionally choose to follow "demagogues" rather than "wise leaders over limited areas and for a brief period."[88] This oblique reference to the Hayden and Bogard controversies reveals that the worldliness to which Mullins refers is not theological or ethical, but organizational.[89] Later, Mullins admits that while "Baptist polity has its shortcomings," it also boasts "unmatched advantages. It localizes disease in the particular church and generalizes health through larger organization."[90] Sick churches, Mullins seems to be saying, isolate themselves, protecting their denomination. Healthy churches reach out, making their spiritual energy available to other churches and to denominational organizations. Mullins affirms that churches are free from denominational control but assumes that a church's decision not to cooperate with other churches and larger organizations is de facto evidence of its spiritual lassitude. Intentionally or not, Mullins laid the groundwork for the construction of a system in which dissent against denominational programs would be taken as evidence of spiritual failure.

Mullins's concept of congregational democracy as the creation of "consensus" acts to reinforce this identification of dissent with spiritual weakness.[91] Mullins affirms the Baptist tradition of democratic governance of the local church and of larger denominational bodies, framing decisions made by congregations as the "consensus of the competent."[92]

The Transformation of Baptist Identity

Mullins hints at what he means by "consensus" when he writes, "Man's capacity for self-government in religion is nothing more than the authority of Christ exerted in and through the inner life of believers . . . in accordance with his revealed word."[93] Elsewhere, Mullins expanded on this idea:

> Because the individual deals directly with his Lord and is immediately responsible to him, the spiritual society must needs be a democracy. That is, the church is a community of autonomous individuals under the immediate lordship of Christ held together by a social bond of common interest, due to a common faith and inspired by common tasks and ends, all of which are assigned to him by the common Lord. The church, therefore, is the expression of the paradoxical conception of the union of absolute monarchy and pure democracy. This we might say is the formula of the church.[94]

In other words, Baptists do not make decisions, but work together to reach consensus as to what Christ wants them to do. If Christ's commands are clear, the mere presence of dissent within a Baptist church or denominational body can only mean that at least one party to the discussion is being disobedient to Christ. Baptist leaders like Mullins would soon learn how to control the content of the Southern Baptist consensus and to claim for themselves the high road of following Christ as opposed to their very real denominational opponents.

The continuing presence of Landmarkism among Southern Baptists during the first decade of the twentieth century guaranteed an abundance of opponents for professional denominationalists like Mullins. *The Axioms of Religion* was published on the heels of the Hayden and Bogard controversies, and the threat of further defection from organized Southern Baptist ranks was still an active possibility. Mullins was aware that the denominational structures whose existence he defended rested on an uneasy alliance between the Baptists of the Atlantic slope and the reconciled Landmarkers of the western part of the Convention's territory.

As a result of this political fact, Mullins was careful to build the argument of *The Axioms of Religion* on an ecclesiological foundation that Landmarkers would find acceptable.[95] In fact, the rhetorical methods by which he contrasts "New Testament Christianity" with Roman Catholicism and Protestantism bear the direct stamp of Landmark thought. First, despite his positive attitude towards monasticism, Mullins is not above using Roman Catholicism as the counterexample against which he articulates the idea of soul competency.[96] When Mullins claims that "the Roman Catholic system is the direct antithesis to the doctrine of the soul's competency," he is adopting a familiar Landmark theme, dressing it up in more respectful language.[97] Second, Mullins tacitly draws a line between Baptist "New Testament Christianity" and Protestantism, a system that "attempts to harmonize two principles which are essentially contradictory to each other."[98] This characterization of Protestantism as a hybrid of biblical Christianity and the errors of Rome is, again, a familiar Landmark theme.[99] While Mullins never explicitly states that Baptists are not Protestants, he provides a significant amount of space for those who choose to interpret the theologian's words in those terms.

In summary, Mullins transformed the meaning of Baptist democracy by locating it at the intersection of a Schleiermacherian understanding of religion as feeling and a Progressive-era trust in administration by experts. When the Baptist tradition of egalitarianism is conceived as the prevalence of a "soul competency" defined in terms of a psychological connection to God through which spiritual energy flows, the administrative tasks of the church can be trusted to experts who channel the spiritual energy of laypeople toward chosen ends. When Baptist democracy is framed as a method of discerning the will of Christ, dissent from the resulting consensus appears as ugly evidence of disobedience within Baptist ranks. The Progressivism articulated in *The Axioms of Religion*, properly understood, sets the stage for the bureaucratization and centralization of the Southern Baptist Convention by giving leaders the theologically sanctioned responsibility to make decisions on behalf of the larger Southern Baptist family.

Putting the Axioms into Practice

Admittedly, the idea that Southern Baptist polity rests on consensus was not an idea that Mullins had spun out of whole cloth. In *Southern Baptist Politics: Authority and Power in the Restructuring of an American Denomination*, Sociologist Arthur Farnsley shows that the democracy that messengers to the Southern Baptist Convention practiced throughout the nineteenth century presupposed that participants would gather in order to articulate the consensus of the denomination rather than to hash out their differences through parliamentary procedure.[100] Southern Baptists never surrendered the idea of democracy as the discernment of consensus, but by 1913 Southern Baptists had created so many boards and agencies that convention attendees voted to approve a "Commission on Efficiency," which would be responsible for studying "the organization, plans and methods of this body, with a view to determine whether or not they are best adapted for eliciting, combining and directing the energies of Southern Baptists and for securing the highest efficiency of our forces and the fullest possible enlistment of our people for the work of the kingdom."[101]

The focus on "efficiency" was as Progressive as the 1916 Commission recommendation that the SBC create a strong executive board. While the board was, for the most part, limited to advising the boards and to planning the annual meeting of the Convention, it was also empowered to "act ad interim on such matters as may arise pertaining to the general business of the convention and not otherwise provided for in its plan of work."[102] Before 1917, the Southern Baptist Convention arguably had no legal existence when not in session. After that date, the Convention increasingly retained the services of professionals who were entrusted with the task of directing Southern Baptist efforts. The relationship that Mullins had articulated in *The Axioms of Religion* between lay-produced energy and the professionals that distribute it had been written into the structure of the SBC.

Not only was this relationship between leaders and laypeople codified in the SBC's emerging bureaucratic structure, it was also adopted by leaders responsible for encouraging laypeople and pastors to pledge money to the Seventy-Five Million Campaign. During the impassioned months of 1919 when Southern Baptists prepared for Victory Week, Southern Baptist editors and leaders wrote scores of articles and editorials pressing the case of the Campaign and reporting on progress made in "enlisting" churches, pastors and laypeople in the cause. After the close of Victory Week, the pace of publicity slowed, but leaders continued to press for the collection of pledges, ensuring a continued flow of written comments. The language that leaders use in these disposable news items is suggestive of the denominational framework implied in *The Axioms of Religion*. First, whether or not Mullins originally conceived of the energy provided by spiritually competent Christians in terms of fire and heat, L. R. Scarborough and other leaders clearly indicated that they had adopted this metaphor as their own. These leaders implied, like Mullins, that such spiritual energy should be channeled into programs expertly crafted by designated leaders. Second, campaign leaders, like Mullins, affirmed that while Baptists were free not to participate in denominational activities, this freedom could never be exercised without revealing spiritual failure on the part of non-participants.

L. L. Gwaltney, editor of the *The Alabama Baptist*, was among the most thoughtful and denominationally oriented of the editors that managed the various state Baptist papers in the territory of the Southern Baptist Convention. In an editorial published on August 7, 1919, Gwaltney describes the role that pastors would play in eliciting lay participation in the Campaign: "It is well for our pastors . . . to begin to give the people line upon line *now*. Some phase of the 75 million program ought to be worked into every sermon, every speech before every body of Christians, into every Sunday school lesson and felt and heard in every prayer that is offered up to a throne of grace. And the truth needs to go from passionate souls; it needs to fall like sparks of holy fire and kindle in the people a *will to win*."[103] Gwaltney wanted Alabama pastors to set their people on fire for the campaign, a fire that burned in the will, rather than in the mind. The fire that would consume laypeople would provide energy, not new ideas. F. M. McConnell, corresponding secretary of the Baptist General Convention of Oklahoma, expressed nearly the same sentiment when he said, "We will never stop the fires of hell from surging through the world until the Lord's fire is blazing in our hearts. Let us actually have faith in God–a faith that will dare to do exploits for Him. Let us tackle this $75,000,000 job and 'not come back 'till it's over.'"[104] That "the Lord's fire" might cause people to reject the campaign was not something McConnell was prepared to imagine.

When L. R. Scarborough, General Director of the Seventy-Five Million Campaign and president of the Southwestern Baptist Theological Seminary, used the same metaphor in an article syndicated to several Baptist newspapers in September 1919, he was even more expansive and explicit than either Gwaltney or McConnell. "The brotherhood throughout the South will be glad to know that the tides of Baptist enthusiasm are rising and that the spirit of our people is mounting high. The 'will to work and win' has gripped the whole denomination and Dr. Gambrell's Baptist pot is boiling from the bottom." Spiritual heat, provided by laypeople, was providing energy needed to propel the denomination to bigger and better things. "Good word comes from every section. The Baptist pot is boiling. Put fuel to the fire. Create the 'will to work and win.' Every church organized now, every church endued with heavenly power now, is the slogan from this office."[105] Scarborough, like Mullins, identified "heavenly power" with the "fire" that heated the denomination and made its activities possible.

When Victory Week had passed and the denomination moved on to the more tedious work of encouraging people to make good on pledges offered in a season of spiritual excitement, leaders continued to use the metaphor comparing spiritual energy to the heat that drives denominational work. Almost one year after the end of Victory Week, Scarborough noted in another syndicated article:

> Our programs will be better carried out by our people if our conventions have hours of transfiguration and vision when the mighty ties from the heavenly hills come in to sweep their souls up and out into heavenly places. Our people are a great deal easier enlisted when their souls are set on fire. Programs are good; organization, complete, systematic, worked out in detail—is very fine. But when the programs and the organization are led and backed and put over by people whose hearts are aflame and whose faces are aglow with the light and life supernal, when abounding and sustained enthusiasm nerve their hearts and propel their activities, the kingdom goes by leaps and bounds.[106]

The image could not be clearer.

Southern Baptist leaders sought positively to make the campaign a success by stoking the spiritual fire underneath the growing bureaucracy of the denomination, but they also occasionally sought to encourage participation by claiming that non-participation, while a Baptist right, is actually unjustified and evidence of spiritual laziness. J. B. Gambrell, a veteran of the Hayden controversy and president of the Southern Baptist Convention during the first half of the Seventy-Five Million Campaign, was never accused of failing to speak his mind. For years after his death, Baptist newspapers continued to fill odd bits of space by printing various *bon mots* attributed to the deceased leader. Though Baptist to the core and a fierce defender of democracy as a principle of church government, Gambrell made no secret about what he thought of those who opted out of the Seventy-Five Million Campaign on the grounds of church independence.

> Baptists are a free people. . . . But the best use of liberty will lead any Baptist to do those things he is not compelled to do. . . . Every intelligent Baptist knows that all the work of the

37

> Baptist people goes on the volunteer principle and fully recog-
> nizes the freedom of both individuals and churches, associ-
> ations and state conventions. For an intelligent Baptist now
> to insist that because he or his church is asked to co-operate
> in a great enterprise there is an attempt to boss him exhibits
> a serious element of insincerity; and one who proclaims this
> as his reason for not helping in a great enterprise, proclaims
> either his weakness or his perversity.[107]

Although the increasing bureaucratization of the SBC apparently had its critics, its leaders were becoming increasingly comfortable with identifying the programs of the Convention with Christ's will for all (white) Baptists residing in its "territory." Mullins's "consensus of the competent" was growing teeth.

Changes in Southern Baptist Democracy

Southern Baptist democracy was, by 1919, undergoing a series of changes related to the shifting political climate of the early twentieth century. Many Southern clergy, having embraced the assumptions that their nineteenth-century forebears had passed on to them, were well prepared to accept Progressivism as a program through which Southern denominations could be reformed. Many Southern Baptists participated fully in this trend, a fact illustrated vividly by the career of Edgar Young Mullins. Recognized by many as a pioneer in the defense of Baptist freedom, his best remembered work, *The Axioms of Religion*, actually helped pave the way for the bureaucratization of the Southern Baptist Convention. Mullins psychologized the freedom of the individual Baptist, opening the field of decision-making to experts who would direct the Convention's spiritual energies towards denominational programs. While this movement had its critics, it was bound to become the dominant organizational method behind the programs of the Southern Baptist Convention.

In early 1920, J. B. Gambrell published an article in which he averred that Southern Baptists were demonstrating the power of spiritual democracy to a world still impressed by the recent triumph of political democracy on the battlefields of Europe:

> The great campaign has given to the Baptists themselves and
> to the whole world a valuable lesson as to the working forces
> and the general efficiency of a great spiritual **democracy**. . . .
> Just as in the great war America gave all the world a demon-

38

stration of the power of a great democracy to mobilize quickly and to fight furiously and to win quickly, so the Baptists have given a demonstration of the efficiency of a spiritual democracy. The inside lesson of it all is that religion goes not by overhead authority, but by the stimulation, releasing, and directing of the spiritual forces in regenerated hearts. When people really want to do a thing, they soon find a way to do it. The way to pop corn is not to pick it open with machinery, but to heat the pan and give it a shake or two. [emphasis his][108]

After Victory Week, Southern Baptist writers would endlessly repeat the comparison between the Allied victory in Europe and the success of the Seventy-Five Million Campaign. Southern Baptists took advantage of the anxious, overheated atmosphere permeating the United States immediately following the World War, but they were not the only American Protestants to do so. When faced with the rise of the Interchurch World Movement (IWM), an organization that proposed in the wake of the Great War to unite American Protestantism for the sake of a more effective engagement with the needs of the world, Southern Baptists opposed it tooth and nail. Seeing in the IWM the advent of a Protestant superchurch replete with "machinery" but bereft of biblical doctrine or vital spirituality, Southern Baptists reacted by creating their own in-house alternative. The story of that creation forms the core of chapter two.

E. Y. Mullins and the New Baptist Democracy

The Clock of the World: Southern Baptists, the Interchurch World Movement, and the Seventy-Five Million Campaign

In the wake of World War I (1914–1918), Southern Baptists moved to launch the Seventy-Five Million Campaign as a means of strengthening Southern Baptist efforts to develop denominational institutions at home and spread the gospel abroad. Like other Protestants, Southern Baptists believed that the post-war world was ripe for new missionary expansion, and, like members of other denominations, they framed a fundraising campaign that would support a new wave of foreign mission activity. Southern Baptists repeatedly asserted that the Campaign was the result of divine intervention in the proceedings of the 1919 meeting of the denomination, but close attention to historical sources tells another story. Frightened by the advent of the Interchurch World Movement, a new ecumenical organization that many Baptists in the South believed was designed to usurp the prerogatives of America's denominations, Southern Baptists moved through the Seventy-Five Million Campaign to demonstrate the superiority of their own "democratic" polity to the "autocratic" methods allegedly practiced by the new organization.

Ironically, however, the Campaign framed at the 1919 SBC relied upon several methods for its administration that differed (when they differed at all) only slightly from those of the feared ecumenical organization. While Southern Baptists criticized the IWM for having been mapped out by its leaders and then submitted to the denominations, the masterminds of Southern Baptist life similarly conceived the Seventy-Five Million Campaign before the 1919 Convention. Submitted to the gathered messengers, the program received an enthusiastic rubber stamp. In addition, the program required Southern Baptists to set up an unprecedented bureaucracy that then required churches to process a similarly unprecedented amount of paperwork. Throughout the entire process, Southern Baptist leaders used methods of promotion reminiscent of those that the IWM had pioneered. In short, the Seventy-Five Million Campaign was created and executed as an in-house, denominational alternative to the Interchurch World Movement.

Denominational Fundraising Campaigns

While the Interchurch World Movement projected its activities and budget on a scale that American Protestants had never before imagined, it was not conceived in a vacuum. Several denominational campaigns, themselves ambitious in scope and fired by the pressures of war, preceded the IWM and heralded a new era in denominational fundraising. In 1913, for example, the Disciples of Christ launched a "Men and Millions Movement" that aimed to raise $6.3 million over the course of the decade. While the program began as an attempt to raise one million dollars for foreign missions, other Disciples agencies quickly adopted it, hoping to expand their own work by participation. The involvement of these new agencies made it necessary to increase the fundraising goals of the movement. When a millionaire offered one million dollars of his own money provided that the denomination's colleges and schools be included and that Disciples raise a further $5.3 million, the first major denominational fundraising campaign of the twentieth century was born.[1] The program included a number of features that would become commonplace in later campaigns, including the Baptist Seventy-Five Million Campaign: it sought to reach churches through the use of the "every member canvass,"[2] it emphasized recruiting young people for service,[3] it focused on the need for all denominational institutions to work together,[4] and its leaders tended to insist that it was an educational, rather than a fundraising, campaign.[5] In fact, Disciples of Christ leaders claimed that the Men and Millions Movement served as the direct model used both by the leaders of various other denominational fundraising drives and by the framers of the Interchurch World Movement as they drew up their own program.[6]

Other denominations did not begin their campaigns until fired by the enthusiasm created by the World War. The Northern Methodists launched their campaign for "$8,000,000 a year for five years" in September 1917 with the remark that Methodism needed to be reconsecrated as a church "adequately equipped, manned and munitioned for the conquest of the 150 millions whose evangelization is the accepted task of Methodism."[7] Not only had the excitement of war transformed the vocabulary of denominational leaders, it had also created an impulse of cooperation between the Northern and Southern branches of American Methodism. The two branches shared plans and personnel, promoting the same denominational objects with their respective constituencies.[8] In both cases, leaders of the Joint Centenary Movement used promotional methods that were borrowed from the government's domestic management of the war. In addition to placing paid advertising in a wide variety of periodicals, Methodists adopted the government practice of recruiting "minute men" to promote the Movement. During the war, the federal government had used a network of "Four Minute Men," volunteer public speakers, to promote the war effort among laborers, potential purchasers of Liberty Bonds, and others.[9] Methodists picked up this strategy and recruited their own band of "minute men" to scour Methodism for recruits to the goals of the Movement, often employing "the very men who did similar service for Uncle Sam in his war for democracy."[10] The Disciples folded this method into their own program, and the practice soon became a fixture of post-war denominational fundraising.

By the time the Presbyterians formally launched their own New Era Movement in October 1918, the thoughts of Americans, Presbyterian or otherwise, had turned to the conclusion of the war and the needs of both the returning soldiers and of the wider world. Rev. Dr. David G. Wylie, a Northern Presbyterian minister, asserted that "Responsibilities over 100 per cent more urgent and important than the Church has ever known before have been placed upon its membership in every city and hamlet in the country and the Church must be ready to do its share in the great work of rehabilitation at the close of the conflict." Presbyterians apportioned the money that they hoped to raise in their campaign with an eye toward peace in Europe. Of the projected seventy-five million dollar goal, they earmarked one million dollars for the rehabilitation of returning soldiers and another $1.5 million for the reconstruction of European churches.[11] What American Protestants did not anticipate before the Armistice, however, was the overheated and tense atmosphere that permeated the United States in the wake of the conflict.

"It's Over / Over There"

If Robert Wuthnow was able to characterize the years immediately following World War II as a period of "promise and peril" for America's religious institutions, the same could easily be said of the feverish months following the First World War.[12] While church leaders saw the post-war

43

period as an unparalleled opportunity for ecclesiastical expansion, they did so in an environment that offered more than a few hints that the war had left both international and domestic problems in its wake. While church leaders remained optimistic, these problems tempered the responses of ecclesiastical policy-makers to the post-war world and served as catalysts for action on the part of America's denominations.

The Russian Revolution of 1917 underlay many of the fears that attended the year or so following the War. Viewed as a new autocracy that was seeping into the power vacuum left by the defeat of the Central Powers, Americans feared Bolshevism both as an international force and as the ideological engine behind real or imagined acts of violence at home.[13] A series of mail bombings in the United States fired a Red Scare in which suspected Communists and other foreign radicals were commonly denied the rudiments of constitutional justice. Viewed from this angle, 1919 was a year of violence and distrust, culminating with the *U. S. S. Buford* departing for Russia. This ship, dubbed the "Soviet Ark," deported to Russia Emma Goldman and other outspoken radicals along with "200 people whose only offense was espousal of radical ideas."[14]

Closely related to the threat of Communism in the popular mind was the rash of labor disputes that marred American industrial life in the months immediately following the War. Seeking to make permanent the wartime gains of organized labor, workers walked off the jobs in the steel and coal industries.[15] Even police officers went on strike in Boston, provoking a stern rebuke from then-Massachusetts governor Calvin Coolidge. Whether or not the strikers in these industries had the better part of the argument between themselves and their employers, the fear of Bolshevism that permeated the American mind during 1919 made it impossible for organized labor not to lose ground. These conflicts ended almost as suddenly as they began, but the threat of violence that haunted them for as long as they lasted added further strain to already-tense national circumstances.

The presence of radical political ideas in the United States and in the wider world and their real or imagined rapid spread after the conclusion of the war only accentuated the belief that the world was entering a new phase of "plasticity." Even before the turn of the century, many Americans had been musing about the coming of a new era in which technological change would be coupled with increased contact between industrialized and developing nations. Americans felt that they were moving into a new day in which the people of the developing world would be increasingly open to new ideas of all stripes. As the war ended, the sense that autocracy had been defeated and that the world was moving into a new democratic phase was widespread. At the same time, however, the Russian Revolution was offering to the world an alternative to American-style democracy, and American ecclesiastical spokespersons felt that American churches would have to act quickly and decisively in order to mold the emerging world into an American shape. The conclusion of the war did not guarantee a bright, new era in world history; it only made the construction of a new world possible.[16]

In light of this sense of unparalleled danger and opportunity, Protestant leaders began to search for a means by which they could make their influence felt on the new, emerging post-war world. The ideas and organizational tendencies that would coalesce as the Interchurch World Movement were all present and familiar by the end of the war. All that remained was for some individual or group to call for the creation of the new organization.

A few days after the Armistice, Nashville, Tennessee hosted a meeting of the Presbyterian Church's Board of Foreign Missions Executive Committee in the United States.[17] The chair of the group, James Vance, was the pastor of Nashville's First Presbyterian Church and was already known nationwide as a leader among ecumenically-minded Protestants. After the group spent almost the entire meeting discussing the recent war and the opportunities that its conclusion presented to American Christians, they decided to call American Protestants into action on behalf of a malleable, war-torn world.[18] The committee resolved to call the denominations to a cooperative fundraising effort that would provide the money needed "for equipment and support of all their Foreign Missions work, and to recruit a sufficient force of evangelists, teachers, doctors and nurses to go to the front, that the non-Christian world may be immediately evangelized, and Christian education, medical and sanitary work, and social service may be adequately done in non-Christian lands."[19] When Vance forwarded this resolution to the American Protestant Foreign Mission Boards, he indicated that the interdenominational program of fundraising that his committee was suggesting was "the only hope of creating permanent peace conditions."[20]

The enthusiastic response to the committee's call exceeded their most optimistic expectations. At a December 1918 meeting that included one hundred thirty-five representatives of various American Protestant mission boards, a sense of expectancy filled the air—one that many participants compared to the energy that must have permeated the gatherings of the first apostles.[21] William Adams Brown later reminisced that

> No one who was present in the upper room on that momentous December day when the Interchurch World Movement was born can forget the thrill of expectation which stirred those who had gathered there. They were men of long experience—secretaries of church boards, professors in theological seminaries, veteran workers in the cause of home and foreign missions, and they knew the weaknesses and limitations of the bodies they served to the full. But they had seen a vision— the vision of a united church uniting a divided world, and under the spell of what they saw all things seemed possible. Difficulties were waved aside, doubters were silenced. In the face of an opportunity so unparalleled there seemed but one thing to do, and that was to go forward.[22]

The enthusiasm of that meeting was distilled into the creation of a Committee of Twenty, chaired by James Vance himself. Chosen to devise a plan of action, the Committee completed its work in less than a month.[23]

A thoughtful onlooker almost could have predicted the details of the plan as framed by the Committee of Twenty. It was this committee that first suggested calling the new undertaking the "Interchurch World Movement," recommending the movement include in its scope all activities "outside of the local church budget which are naturally related to the missionary enterprise."[24] The members suggested an organization springing from a General Committee of about one hundred members, a smaller Executive Committee, a national-level Cabinet and a number of lesser administrative bodies. The Committee also listed two immediate founding goals for the IWM. First, the organization would complete "a thorough united survey of the home and foreign fields of the world for the purpose of securing accurate and complete data as to what ought to be done by the combined churches to meet the needs of the hour, and of at least the next five years." Further, the Committee recommended "a thoroughgoing educational publicity campaign to carry the facts of the survey to the entire Protestant church constituency in America and to every mission station where the churches of North America are at work."[25] This publicity campaign would culminate in a collection during the spring of 1920. When this plan was presented to a meeting of interdenominational mission agencies the following January, it was overwhelmingly approved. The General Committee was formed by the end of the month and held its first meeting in February. In this rush toward ecumenical organization, many Protestants felt that American Protestantism was headed toward the most decisive moment of its existence. "[T]he church faces its biggest opportunity," one editor noted. "If it is to meet the hour, it must project its work on a larger scale than any it has yet attempted. . . . The clock has struck for the church of God."[26]

The IWM lost no time in employing the best available methods of advertising and promotion to secure its goals. Most of these methods had already been proven during the denominational fundraising drives earlier in the decade, and the new organization's leaders were anxious to put them to work. In fact, the leaders of the IWM were so impressed by the success of the Methodist Joint Centenary Movement in particular that they adopted it as a model, borrowing or purchasing many of their educational materials and tapping a number of their leaders to serve in the IWM.[27]

Tyler Dennett, who had served the Joint Centenary Movement as its head of publicity, was among the most important of these Methodist leaders. Selected to serve essentially the same role within the IWM as he had within the Methodist organization, Dennett oversaw a massive program of "scientific" advertising influenced by the government's efforts to sell war bonds and designed to assist the IWM in raising the massive amount of money that would be needed for it to accomplish its goals.[28] While denominations had been experimenting with advertising in the months following the war, it was Dennett's advertising campaign that first sought to promote a religious enterprise with the same tools and expense as might accompany the promotion of a business concern. Dennett's office cranked out advertising copy for every imaginable class of periodical, secular and religious, and also produced millions of posters and pamphlets. Underneath all this promotional activity lay the conviction that any organization, including the Protestant denominations, could raise any amount of money, provided that it was advertised "scientifically."[29]

While the IWM depended heavily on advertising in an exhaustive variety of magazines and newspapers, it also took steps to secure and publish its own monthly magazine, *World Outlook*. Originally, IWM leaders had hoped to buy and combine some well-recognized missionary magazines into a single publication, but many of these periodicals refused to sell. As a result, the IWM purchased the *World Outlook*, a Methodist missionary publication that was running at a thirty thousand dollar deficit. When the *Outlook* published its first issue under IWM auspices in November

1919, it still employed the same editorial staff that it had before the IWM had purchased it.[30] The *Outlook* itself, however, had changed drastically. Intending to compete with other popular magazines with a nationwide circulation, the new *World Outlook* boasted high quality photography, serial stories, and cutting-edge advertising. Such innovations proved a wise investment: by April 1920 the *World Outlook* had increased its circulation to over sixty-three thousand subscribers.[31]

Predictably, the IWM also employed a number of "minute men," volunteer public speakers, as had the denominational movements that foreshadowed the creation of the later ecumenical organization. The IWM supported an army of several thousand speakers through the provision of hundreds of thousands of prints and lantern slides, along with one thousand ready-made speeches that were coordinated with the various visual aids.

When the leaders of the IWM had gathered these instruments of publicity, they played them in a patriotic key. Having witnessed the power of militant nationalism during the war, Protestant leaders moved not to critique it but to harness it for their own purposes. The IWM song sheet contained wartime songs like "Onward Christian Soldiers" and the "Battle Hymn of the Republic."[32] Protestant spokespeople claimed that "Christian churches mobilize when armies demobilize" and suggested that war had always been a chief catalyst of missionary expansion.[33] Even after the rest of the nation had signaled their desire for a "return to normalcy," IWM leaders were still in a crusading mood. One Disciples editor pressed the point: "This is war! . . . The supreme issues of the military war were not settled; the way was merely cleared for their settlement. It is the Christian war that must permanently save the world from greed and lust and tyranny."[34]

Many IWM leaders failed to notice that such rhetoric had fallen out of style by early 1920—an oversight that contributed to the Movement's eventual failure. Planned in the heat of wartime excitement, the Movement was not equipped to deal with the quick return of what its leaders regarded as denominational selfishness. Although the IWM sought to represent all of Protestant America, denominational participation never rose to the level that its leaders had hoped for. Northern Baptists asked that only "evangelical churches" be allowed to participate in the movement, while other denominations, still managing their own campaigns, carefully guarded their own well-to-do members from solicitation for funds.[35] In the end, this unwillingness of Protestant leadership to channel funds into the IWM instead of into their own denominational coffers, along with the miserable failure of a fundraising drive aimed at denominationally unaffiliated Protestants, proved the undoing of the Movement.[36] Mortally wounded by the summer of 1920, the Interchurch World Movement was declared dead on April 8, 1921.[37]

Southern Baptists and the Interchurch World Movement

In 1919, however, the Movement's eventual (and probably predictable) demise still lay in the future. Early that year, the IWM had begun to recruit the various Protestant denominations of the United States to participate in the new organization. It fell to J. Campbell White to take the good news of the new movement to the 1919 meeting of the Southern Baptist Convention, but when he arrived he found himself in the middle of a beehive of anti-ecumenical sentiment.[38] "The union question was the livest [sic] thing in the Atlanta meeting," one editor noted. "Some reference to it was made in almost every speech."[39] Southern Baptists had not been insulated from rumors that the Interchurch World Movement was attempting to "unionize" America's Protestant denominations. Perhaps even more important at first, though, was the sense among Southern Baptists that the federal government itself had turned against them in their handling of religious work among soldiers during the World War, both in stateside camps and in Europe. Due to their perception of government unfairness, Southern Baptists perceived the post-war period more negatively than did many other Protestants. Southern Baptists agreed with other Protestants that the world was entering a moment in which missionary intervention would be decisively influential, but they also identified it as a moment of threat in which a world hungry for "Baptist" democracy could well be deprived of it because of runaway ecumenism.[40] Now that the exigency of wartime had passed, Southern Baptists were determined to speak their collective mind and to remind the world of the special mission that was entrusted just to them.

Southern Baptist disapproval of the government's handling of wartime religious work focused on the central role that the YMCA played in administering Protestant preaching and worship to soldiers. First, Southern Baptist leaders were appalled at the quality of the ministrations that the "Y" provided to soldiers who, facing imminent danger in battle, could have faced God's judgment at any minute. J. B. Gambrell, President of the Southern Baptist Convention, expressed what was probably a commonly held Southern Baptist criticism of the YMCA's war work when he

49

noted that the organization "undertook to syndicate religion with Sunday theatricals, 'stunts,' and sometimes Sunday dances, and in every such combination Christianity was cheapened and played out."[41] Not only did the Y cheapen the Christian faith; its representatives also seem to have developed a reputation for neglect of the soldiers with whom they were entrusted. George W. McDaniel, a Virginia pastor and future SBC president, went on record in the Richmond newspaper claiming that the YMCA overcharged soldiers for food and cigarettes and that it was unnecessarily rigid with its prices. He also accused YMCA workers of avoiding unpleasant trips to the front, where their services were most urgently needed.[42] Some criticisms were even more pointed. The *Western Recorder* reprinted a list of criticisms against YMCA representatives that was borrowed from the *News and Truths*, a conservative Baptist newspaper published in Western Kentucky:

1. They were slackers.
2. They were extortioners
3. They sold the boys things that were sent as gifts to the soldiers in their care.
4. They always served officers first.
5. Where their canteens were side by side with Government stores they sold things higher than the Government.[43]

Had the failings of the YMCA been the only target for Southern Baptist criticism, the Convention's leaders might simply have spoken their minds, made a mental note to avoid the organization in the future, and let it go at that. Southern Baptists were unable to let the issue rest, however, because they believed that the federal government had violated their religious rights when it decided that all Protestant work with the soldiers had to be filtered through the eventually despised organization. Insult thus added to injury as Southern Baptists saw in the government's decision a threat to their theology and polity that was impossible to ignore.

In a report offered to the 1919 Southern Baptist Convention, a committee consisting of J. B. Gambrell, a number of influential Baptist newspaper editors, and a number of other leaders explained their frustration with the War Department's policies. First, the committee explained that the government commission appointed to mediate between the nation's religious organizations and the War Department was made up of six religious leaders whom the denominations themselves had not selected.[44] Next, the committee (along with a number of other observers) was offended that Roman

Catholics and Jews were allowed to enter the camps through their own organizations while Protestants were expected to submit to the oversight of the YMCA. Baptists were doubly offended at being lumped in with Protestants with whom many Southern Baptists claimed to have no historical connection. Finally, and perhaps worst of all, the committee cited a public statement from the Third Assistant Secretary of War that "the whole trend and the whole desire of the Department is in the interest of breaking down, rather than emphasizing, denominational distinctions."[45] For Gambrell and others, this was a smoking gun. The government's actions had not grown out of ignorance or an oversight, but from an active desire to press an ecumenical agenda.

When Southern Baptists received news that the Interchurch World Movement had been created, they saw in it an attempt to extend the interdenominationalism of the YMCA into the peacetime life of the churches. J. W. Porter, the editor of the *Western Recorder* in 1919, received an invitation to an IWM gathering during that year and mused about the meaning of its leadership roster in an editorial. "It is significant that of the three names of the officers appearing on the letter-head two of them are John R. Mott and Fred B. Smith," Porter wrote. "It will be recalled that the former of these is the present head of the YMCA, and the latter formerly occupied the same position. Is it mere coincidence that these particular men should be the acknowledged leaders of this union enterprise?"[46] By the time V. I. Masters was able to ask Baptist readers all over the South "Who Steers . . . And Stokes the Union Boat?", it had become clear that Southern Baptist fears of "unionism" had blossomed into a full-blown "conspiracy theory."[47]

J. Campbell White stepped into this cauldron of distrust when he addressed the Convention on the subject of the Interchurch World Movement. In a speech not recorded in the convention annual, White "read the findings of Dr. Gambrell on the principle of union movements and declared that he accepted these principles in full. He urged that Christian people get together and confer on the needs of the world and talk over the best means of meeting these needs."[48] Not surprisingly, the Convention was not moved by White's appeal. When the committee spoke to the offer of cooperation with the IWM, they made it clear that they saw in it nothing but a "vague scheme" that could only hinder Southern Baptists' ability to offer their own "distinct witness" to the world.[49] The Convention's anger towards the YMCA had spilled over into its attitude toward the IWM.[50]

Southern Baptists, the Interchurch World Movement, and the Seventy-Five Million Campaign

The committee continued by offering what would eventually become a monotonously familiar refrain in Southern Baptist discussions of the ecumenical movement. Southern Baptists hold other Christians in "fraternal regard" and affirm the unity for which Christ prayed but define this unity as a "spiritual" phenomenon rather than as an "organic" union that would have to be created through "schemes of federation, cooperation, or other forms of common action by Christian denominations." In the meantime, Baptists have had entrusted to them a special message, peculiar to them, the integrity of which could only be lost through an alliance with other denominations. Because denominational differences are legitimately rooted in conscience, they must be respected.[51]

In the months following the 1919 Southern Baptist Convention, writers for the Baptist newspapers continued to develop their critique of the Interchurch World Movement, casting more light on the ideological motives that led to its rejection. First, Southern Baptists agreed with other Protestants that the Allied victory was ushering in a new age, but Southern Baptists tended to identify the emergence of this new era as a specifically Baptist phenomenon. In an article titled "The Times Reset to Baptist Doctrines," one Baptist leader observed, "The political autocrats of the world are falling fast before the march of human freedom, and all Ecclesiastical Autocracy is nervous over the spirit of liberty clamant for spiritual independence, the rights of conscience in creed and worship, the separation of church and state and the eradication complete and final of every phase and form of presumptuous interference with the dignity of individual choice and private judgment in matters of religion. All autocracy must speedily follow in downfall political autocracy to its doom."[52]

Another author in the very same issue of the Texas *Baptist Standard* noted that the events of the First World War ensured that "the whole world is ready to hear the Baptist message, the message of the democracy of believers, of regenerated church membership, of a spiritual religion, of the sufficiency of the Scriptures, the Lordship of Christ . . . the whole world is tired of forms and ceremony, and is seeking the true spiritual religion."[53] Amos Clary, a pastor writing in the South Carolina *Baptist Courier*, summed up the typical Southern Baptist attitude about the hoped-for results of Allied victory when he wrote, "This is pre-eminently a Baptist age. Had German imperialism won the war soul-liberty would have gone over board."[54] Southern Baptist leaders were sure that "the clock of the world had struck twelve for Baptists."[55]

52

At the same time, Southern Baptists did not believe that the advent of a new age of democracy was necessarily an unmixed blessing. Rufus Weaver, president of Mercer University, noted that "the spread of the unrestrained democratic spirit, the untrammeled assertion of human opinions, the breaking down of the accepted standards of authority, the virulent growth of Bolshevism, are creating a condition which threatens a moral disaster to humanity." For Southern Baptists, the Russian Revolution and the accompanying perceived spread of Bolshevism around the world proved the danger of democracy practiced by those unprepared for it. Weaver believed that the practice of democracy required responsibility, but more importantly, he also believed that "democracy is a safe method of government only when intelligent self-restraint is inspired by the knowledge and the fear of God. This type of democracy is ever found where Baptist principles prevail. In fact, the baptisticization [*sic*] of mankind is the basis of a permanent, beneficial democracy."[56] The post-war period was not only a Baptist age because of the spread of democracy. More importantly, it was a Baptist age because only Baptists taught the spiritual principles that could "make democracy safe for the world."[57]

Southern Baptists' most important anxieties about the dawning age revolved around the Interchurch World Movement because they believed that that organization epitomized the post-war obsession with democracy that was actually autocracy in disguise. Southern Baptist observers criticized the Interchurch World Movement as an autocratic organization whose goals better resembled those of the defeated Central Powers than those of the Allies. Baptists found absurd the idea that Christians who were more concerned with church union than with Baptist principles could be trusted to usher in what they considered a "Baptist age." One leader put it this way: "In a word, the program of the Inter-Church World Movement is to build up a Hapsburg Religious Empire. The denominations will not be crushed. On the contrary, they will be assigned their proper places and exploited to the limit of their resources."[58]

Rev. Clary, cited above, rejected the identification of interdenominational cooperation as the natural ecclesiastical expression of the spirit of the age. Instead he asserted, "Denominationalism is the democratization of Christianity. To state the idea in other words: Christianity minus all denominationalism would be little less than Roman Catholicism, formal and autocratic, regardless of any name it might bear. Under such domination the world would be in as deplorable condition religiously as it would have been civilly and politically had the Hun drive in France, March 21, 1918, succeeded."[59]

By defending their own rights as a denomination and, by extension, defending the rights of all denominations, Southern Baptists were doing the dirty work of keeping American Protestantism democratic. "As long as the spirit of democracy lives in the hearts of men there will be religious denominations in the world. As long as there are Baptists in the world the spirit of pure democracy will live."[60]

Additionally, many Southern Baptists accused the leaders of the IWM of being overly interested in money and in creating a machine that depended upon organization and bureaucracy to the point of neglecting prayer and spiritual energy. Southern Baptists admitted that they had already constructed a significant amount of "machinery," but they believed that their own organizations were powered by genuine spiritual energy. The IWM, on the other hand, was artificially propelled by a reliance on bureaucracy, money, and emphasis on "efficiency." In an editorial in the *Biblical Recorder*, Livingston Johnson made a veiled reference to the IWM when he noted that "many religious 'movements' of our day . . . have mapped out very elaborate and expensive programs, and have organizations as well nigh perfect as human wisdom can devise." In this respect, the IWM could be compared to the Germans, who were "far more efficient than the Allies." The edge that had given the Allies victory lay not in their organization, but in their spirit. In the same way, Johnson believed that Southern Baptists needed to remember that "machinery is worthless without power, and in the work of the Lord the power comes alone from the Holy Spirit. Machinery is good in its place but unless 'the spirit of the living creature is in the wheels' it is worse than worthless."[61] Anticipating that the sidelong comparison of the IWM to the German military might be lost on his audience, Johnson added another illustration, making the same point:

> Dr. D. E. Everett . . . had hanging on the wall of his office, a
> very suggesting picture. Two hunters had returned from the
> field. One had all the equipment of the modern huntsman. He
> had a hunter's jacket with his cartridge belt well filled with
> cartridge a fine breech-loading gun, two setter dogs, and a
> bag for game. The only thing he lacked was the game. The
> other was an old farmer with no coat, home-knit suspenders,
> flopped hat, muzzle-loading gun, and a very common looking
> dog; but he had a very fine looking string of birds. . . . The

picture needed no interpretation. . . . The breech-loading gun
was all right, but the man behind the gun was more important
than the gun.[62]

Also, as the IWM continued to execute its own program, many Southern Baptists counted the organization's persistent attempts to recruit Southern Baptists as a strike against it. Southern Baptist leaders felt that the representatives of the IWM should have left their churches and pastors entirely alone after the rejection of the movement by the 1919 Convention.[63] The IWM, however, continued to request information from Baptist churches in the South and to solicit their participation in its survey. "These people, unbidden, in fact after being told that they were not wanted by the Baptists, are intruding themselves and are thrusting their matter upon our own people much to their confusion and much to the hurt of our work. And their brazenness is amazing."[64] The editor of the *Florida Baptist Witness* had heard a rumor that IWM surveyors in Georgia were passing themselves off as employees of the new Baptist Seventy-Five Million Campaign, but whether this was the fault of the surveyors or a misunderstanding on the part of the Baptists that received them remains an open question.

J. B. Gambrell, observing this persistence, had no doubts about the goals of the IWM for Southern Baptists: "That they have planned and are pushing arrangements to utterly disintegrate and destroy the Baptist faith and order is as certain as human conduct can make anything."[65] Gambrell was probably overstating his case, but continuing Southern Baptist resistance to the Movement did not go unnoticed by other Southerners sympathetic to it. A December 1919 editorial in the *The Alabama Baptist* cited an editorial in its Methodist counterpart that painted Southern Baptists in a light that would soon become very familiar. "They seem to want no league, offensive or defensive, with anybody or anything unless it has the stamp of Southern Baptist on it," the editor wrote. "They are a strong, great people, but if they persist in their go-it-alone policy some of these days they are going to have a mighty lonesome feeling."[66] Editor Gwaltney of the *The Alabama Baptist,* one of the Convention's more even-handed editors, saw the attempt at coercion implicit in this statement, but forgave the Methodist editor on the grounds that "he must have been swept from his moorings by the threats of the Interchurch. This is the way some of those in high authority have talked to the editor of The Baptist [*sic*]."[67] Southern Baptists knew that many other Protestants were angry about their rejection of the IWM, but in the face of the Movement's persistence they felt that their own vocation (and size) justified their aloof stance towards it. As Curtis Lee Laws, one sympathetic observer, noted, "Even when they flock by themselves they are not lonely, because there are so many of them."[68]

Curtis Lee Laws's interest in the progress of Southern Baptist resistance to the Interchurch World Movement highlights the final reason that Southern Baptists feared the new organization. Southern Baptists slowly came to believe that the IWM was doctrinally suspect. At first, doctrinal criticism of the IWM was limited to the idea that IWM rejected specifically Baptist doctrines such as congregational autonomy. However, Baptists later began to suspect that the IWM was led by men whose positions on the "fundamental" evangelical doctrines were unsound.

Even before the 1919 Convention, where messengers voted to reject the IWM, L. R. Scarborough, president of Southwestern Baptist Theological Seminary, was warning Baptists against allowing interdenominational organizations to gain control of Baptist schools. Scarborough believed that "this is a day when Baptists are going to have to stand for the fundamentals of the New Testament as never before," but when he said this, he was mainly thinking of defending "Baptist principles, Baptist churches and Baptist movements."[69] This defense of "doctrine" was really just a reiteration of other Southern Baptist affirmations of denominationalism as the form of democratic religion.

Later, however, some Southern Baptists began to suspect that a number of IWM spokespeople held views that would be considered heterodox according to the canons of faith held in common by all of the Protestant denominations. An editorial published in the *Western Recorder* during the summer of 1919 leaves no doubt that at least one Kentucky Baptist had detected a connection between the IWM and "religious liberals." "They say that Christian people are rapidly coming together into a delightful agreement. Well, I see no harm in a complete union of all who are not grounded in true Bible doctrine and practice. It would be a good thing if all the religious liberals would flock together, and keep together." The author went on to articulate the connection between ecumenical tolerance and Modernist doctrine that Southern Baptist leaders would eventually recognize and publicly affirm.

> The cry for Christian union is mostly heard from those who
> have no great convictions to give up and who are not anchored
> to the sound fundamentals of Christ's religion. They have no
> real sacrifices to make. . . . If one would see a specimen of
> religious unionism, let him look at the leading religious paper

56

in New York, on whose editorial staff are some men of some very pronounced skeptical views. That paper is vehement in advocating "Christian union." At the same time, it is in free fellowship with Unitarians and the rankest kinds of heretics of various types.

The conclusion was simple and clear: "Do not be misled by the false voice of 'Christian union.' The mark of Cain is upon it."[70] Although such comments were rare in 1919, they would become more common in the years to follow.

Southern Baptist criticisms of the Interchurch World Movement were sweeping in their scope, and they permeated the media that Southern Baptists controlled. Southern Baptist response to the IWM was not limited to written and spoken criticism, however. When Southern Baptists framed their own program of fundraising, missions, and education to respond to the needs of the world after the end of the Great War, they framed it as a response to the IWM as well.

The Seventy-Five Million Campaign as an Offensive Action

In an editorial from an issue of the Texas *Baptist Standard* published before the 1919 Southern Baptist Convention, E. Y. Mullins counseled his fellow Southern Baptists to find a constructive way to meet the challenge of the Interchurch World Movement. While Mullins was aware of the "real dangers" attended by the ecumenical impulse, he felt that Southern Baptists could best respond by offering the world "a great triumphant note and a great and splendid program of missions and education and a going forward without fear to the performance of the great task."[71]

When the Convention met in 1919, it sounded the "great triumphant note" by approving a plan to raise seventy-five million dollars over the course of the next five years, a program that leaders eventually christened the "Seventy-Five Million Campaign." Convention leaders framed the Campaign as a response to the needs of the post-war world and in imitation of the recent fundraising campaigns of the other Protestant denominations, but they also framed it as an aggressive attempt to press back against what they felt was the potentially overwhelming tide of interdenominationalism that threatened to swallow Southern Baptist churches.[72] When the Convention committee charged with responding to the government's handling of religious work among the soldiers rejected the idea of

57

interdenominational cooperation, it explicitly cast the new Seventy-Five Million Campaign, which the Convention had already approved, in direct contrast with the discredited YMCA and the IWM. "Instead of wasting our time and confusing the minds of our people with fruitless discussion of impracticable proposals, let us make a program for ourselves so large, so progressive, so constructive, that it shall challenge the faith and imagination of our people."[73] One editor was more pointed about the reasons for adopting the Seventy-Five Million Campaign:

> The very force of Circumstances now puts Baptists on the defensive. To save our lives we can not avoid it. The great unionizing movements, general looseness in doctrine, increase in worldliness, and the tendency to make religion nothing more than mere respectability all make it necessary for sure-enough Baptists to give a reason for the faith that is in them. We are on the defensive. But *remember forever that the best defense is an attack.* In this matter certainly we must act on David Harum's golden rule: "Do unto the other fellow as the other fellow wants to do to you—and *do it first.* Only—we are never to adopt the underhand methods of "the other fellow."[74]

The new Campaign was specifically and publicly framed as a response to the Interchurch World Movement. By framing their own campaign of fundraising, missions, and education, Southern Baptists hoped to prove that a democratic, spirit-driven program could outperform the autocratic bureaucracy of the Interchurch World Movement.

Because Southern Baptists criticized the IWM as an "autocratic" institution, they were anxious to show through the Seventy-Five Million Campaign that their own "democratic" institutions could bring about results without capitulating to the IWM's "autocratic" methods. R. H. Pitt suggested that his fellow Virginia Baptists "show the world how a great religious democracy, with no ranks in its ministry, with no ecclesiastical councils or dignitaries to issue authoritative instructions, can none the less . . . march . . . to a great and glorious victory."[75] One month later, B. J. W. Graham, the editor of *The Christian Index*, made the same point. "Those of other faiths say that Baptists cannot put over a great campaign like this because of the democracy of their organization. Such a statement, however, is sheer nonsense." Graham illustrated his point with a typical military metaphor: "With our American democracy we put over campaigns in the getting together of an army and the raising of funds for welfare work among the soldiers quite as large, in proportion to numbers,

The Clock of the World

as this $75,000,000 campaign is for three million Southern Baptists."[76] Baptists were interested in raising seventy-five million dollars for missions and education, but they were just as interested in proving through the process of raising it that their polity was not inferior to that of other, differently organized groups.

As shown above, Southern Baptists believed that the IWM was an organization driven by money and an obsession with efficiency. In response to the IWM's perceived spiritual bankruptcy, Southern Baptists sought to show that the Seventy-Five Million Campaign was saturated by spiritual energy. When Southern Baptist leaders reminded their readers about the circumstances of the Campaign's birth during the months to follow, they always mentioned the spiritual power that seemed to pervade the 1919 Southern Baptist Convention. In fact, by the time J. W. Cammack discussed the origins of the Campaign in an October edition of *The Religious Herald*, the story of the Campaign's creation had started to assume the aura of a founding myth:

> The eighteen men who were appointed to represent the eighteen States in forming a report to present to the Convention outlining a forward movement felt that the most serious and responsible hour in all their lives had arrived. We went into the committee room and fell on our knees before God. No man dared suggest what that report should be until we waited with our souls prostrate before heaven and sought wisdom from the only source. The actual writing of the words in the report was referred to a small subcommittee and the one whose hand held the pencil which marked out the words in that statement here bears testimony that no human being may fairly claim to have "started" this campaign. That honor belongs solely to Him for whose glory Southern Baptists are laying their lives and their all on the altar in these strenuous days.
>
> The brief report was submitted to the full committee of eighteen and unanimously approved and a few minutes later presented to seven thousand Baptists who represented the entire South and of whom over 44,200 were delegates. After addresses by several of our representative men, and after prayer for divine guidance, the motion was put and the vote was as one voice. Does any Baptist believe that voice represented the voice of Satan? If so, let him "fall out" and have nothing to do with this business.[77]

59

When L. R. Scarborough described the same scene in his book *Marvels of Divine Leadership*, he emphasized the fact that the program was a creation of God partly in order to show that it was not the product of the sort of elite (and soulless) planning that Southern Baptist leaders saw behind the IWM:

> It cannot be said that anybody was prepared to suggest the outline of the larger task. No groups of men had gotten together and framed a program. No individual in the Convention can be named as the originator of the Campaign. The great movement seemed to come out of the very soul of the messengers, as they voiced the will of the people they came to represent. Nobody was surprised when the figures were set at seventy-five million. Many, especially among the laymen, were disappointed that it was not made one hundred million. There was a general demand of the people that something great be proposed and prosecuted to a glorious success. There is but one explanation of the inauguration of the great movement, and that is found in one word, "God." He was with us and led us, gave us leadership, gave us power. It was God's Convention and God's program. The Divine Spirit manifested Himself everywhere.[78]

The will of God, who had spoken through the gathered messengers of the SBC, was plain. Having heard God's voice, Southern Baptists could hardly refuse to participate in the Campaign.

The Seventy-Five Million Campaign as an Exercise in Imitation

Such insider interpretations of the Seventy-Five Million Campaign's origins only tell part of the story, however. Some Southern Baptists were suspicious of such accounts of the Campaign's founding, and extant evidence demonstrates that the Campaign was actually closely modeled after both earlier denominational fundraising campaigns and, more importantly, the Interchurch World Movement itself. Like the IWM, the Seventy-Five Million Campaign seems to have depended on the advance creation of a program by leaders who then submitted it to their constituency for their approval. It capitalized on patriotic and military language, and it utilized a number of promotional methods that the IWM had popularized. Finally, despite protestations of the fruitlessness of "efficiency," Southern Baptist leaders

60

began to expect an unprecedented amount of paperwork from their pastors and lay leaders—paperwork that was completed on forms secured from the Campaign's central office in Nashville and then filed away after its completion. While Southern Baptists rejected the Interchurch World Movement, they do not seem to have rejected many of its methods. In fact, SBC leaders adopted the chief goal of the IWM, although in a modified form: Southern Baptist leaders, true to the spirit of their times, were looking to shape the SBC into a strong, united organization that could then exert hitherto unknown influence both in the United States and around the world.

In the days leading up to the 1919 Southern Baptist Convention, a number of commentators in the Southern Baptist press mused about what might happen at the meeting. In the process, they revealed that the Seventy-Five Million Campaign was the result of somewhat more forethought than some later apologists would claim. L. R. Scarborough claimed that "the outlines of the program were not made before the Convention," but the public words of a number of Southern Baptist leaders in the days leading up to the 1919 meeting reveal that they had a very clear idea of what they wanted out of convention messengers.[79]

J. B. Gambrell, for instance, made the connection between the need to resist the Interchurch World Movement and the need for an enlarged missions program explicit in the Texas Baptist newspaper two weeks before the Convention met. "While we are carrying the issue raised by the New York unionizers to all our churches, we will be educating our Pedo-Baptist friends and brethren, deepening the conviction of our own people, and laying the predicate for an unparalleled mission appeal. . . . The coming Convention ought to clear the way for a campaign for indoctrinization [sic] and missionary enlargement."[80] Lee Scarborough, who would later claim that the Seventy-Five Million Campaign had sprung full-grown from the collective heads of the gathered messengers, had similar plans for the meeting. Noting that "the movement to federalize, unionize and interdenominationalize the churches" was a "peril . . . to the realities, verities and eternal fundamentals of Christianity," Scarborough asked that

> a great constructive Baptist program in every state, in every
> association, in every county, in every city, in every church, in
> every school, and in the heart and ministry of every preacher
> and missionary be put on, and a new program of evangelism
> should be made commensurate with the needs of the situa-
> tion and the challenge of the Unionists, and a new program of

61

education in the home, in the church, school, in religious education institutions, in our seminaries, in great conferences in
the foreign field and a new and world-wide Foreign Mission
program should be put on . . . all these causes call tremendously to Southern Baptists to put on a great forward movement. If Baptists are to win, they have not only to stand, but
they have to go. They will never win with a defensive warfare.
They must take the offensive.[81]

The connection between the Campaign and the threat of the IWM was
not the only aspect of the Campaign that Baptist leaders had foreshadowed in the days before the Convention. Eldridge Hatcher, the editor of
the Kentucky *Baptist World*, offered an outline of the fundraising methods that he hoped the Convention would adopt, suggesting "a South-wide,
simultaneous, concerted budget collection . . . during the next Convention
year such a drive could only be brought about later in the year." Eldridge
went on to outline many of the methods that such a budget collection
would require, including the creation of a new organization with "representatives in every state and in every community in the South," a special day on which preachers would present the program, and an "every-
member canvass" during which every church member would receive a
visit from a representative of the program.[82]

None of these authors left much to the lay imagination. Every aspect
of the resolution that called for the raising of seventy-five million dollars
was set out weeks ahead of time in the denominational press. As a result, one could be forgiven for doubting Southern Baptist leaders' claim
that the Seventy-Five Million Campaign was a spontaneous outpouring
of unexpected enthusiasm. Like the leaders of the IWM, Southern Baptist
leaders had high hopes for their constituent churches and sought to create
a program that would help those churches meet the perceived needs of the
post-war world.

While leaders shaped the program through informal means before
the 1919 Convention, they later gained a formal role. The Convention did
not establish any details about the Campaign's organization and methods
during its Atlanta meeting. In fact, the Convention voted to leave the whole
matter of the Campaign's organization and conduct to a small group. The
Convention approved a resolution that left it to the convention president
"to appoint a commission of fifteen members of the Convention" to handle
"the whole matter of laying plans and of launching and conducting this
campaign." Additionally, the Convention authorized the commission "to

The Clock of the World

employ any and all agencies which in its judgment may be necessary for the speediest and most successful accomplishment of this great task."[83] Even as the creators of the IWM had placed its planning in the hands of a "Committee of Twenty," Southern Baptists had tasked a commission of fifteen with planning the Seventy-Five Million Campaign.

Similarities between the IWM and the Seventy-Five Million Campaign did not stop with the Campaign's initial organization. Southern Baptists borrowed several methods of publicity from the IWM. For instance, Southern Baptist editors were fond of using patriotic and military language to encourage participation in the Campaign. Scarborough told readers of state Baptist newspapers that "the Baptist selective draft is in full operation."[84] B. C. Hening made a similar point when he noted that a failure of nerve on the part of Southern Baptists during the Campaign would show them "to be voluntarily and purposely deserters from this holy program for enlarging all our work and honoring our Master in a great way."[85] The editor of the *Biblical Recorder* even found himself having to apologize to sensitive North Carolina Baptists for the Campaign's use of the word "drive," explaining that "when we speak of the 'eight day drive,' we do not mean that any Baptist, or any church, is being driven; but that our great denomination . . . is to make a united effort to raise a large amount for the work of the kingdom of God, and that on a certain date a united drive will be made for victory." After all, "during the war which, God be praised, is now over, we heard much of the 'German Drives,' or 'The Allied Drive.' That did not mean that the army of whom the term was used, was being driven, but that they were driving the enemy."[86] The editor of *The Christian Index* even compared loyalty to the Campaign with loyalty to the State during the Great War, saying, "This campaign is testing the loyalty of every church, of every member and of every pastor, just as the world war tested the patriotism of every American citizen."[87]

Southern Baptists imitated other aspects of the IWM's fundraising campaign as well. Like the IWM, the Seventy-Five Million Campaign was designed to comprehend all aspects of denominational work, excepting only local church expenses.[88] Also, the Campaign commission planned and finally published a "survey of needs," similar to that the IWM had planned, detailing "all Southern Baptist causes and institutions in the home and foreign lands."[89] It employed volunteer "Four Minute Speakers" who served exactly the same purpose in the Campaign as they had in the IWM and in previous denominational campaigns.[90] Southern Baptist leaders also developed a new interest in the denominational press, emphasizing the importance of print advertising and, in many cases, pressing for denominational ownership of the state Baptist newspapers for the first time. Like the leaders of the IWM, Southern Baptist leaders were convinced that adequate publicity would all but guarantee a satisfactory outcome. "There are, too, thousands of our people who will never hear anything about this Campaign if knowledge of it is not carried to them in white paper and black ink. Those who see the paper go into the homes during August, will see the money coming out of them in December."[91]

While Southern Baptists had vigorously protested against the over-wrought "machinery" of the IWM, they applied a number of bureaucratic methods to the execution of their own program. Campaign leaders knew that they needed support from local church pastors and laypeople to raise funds, and true to bureaucratic form, they sought to elicit and direct that support from a central location. Eldridge Hatcher told his readers that "the royal staff at Nashville . . . simply sit[s] at the central office." While members of the newly constituted Baptist royalty "are at headquarters giving directions and laying plans and issuing summonses," though, "the real workers upon whom they depend are to be found in the different States—the pastors, associational directors, state officials, consecrated men and women: yea, no Southern Baptist can be found who is not needed in this campaign. Our whole Southern Baptist army must be mobilized. Like a prairie fire the conflagration must sweep throughout the States and kindle every heart."[92] For the first time, some Southern Baptists were making a living by telling other Southern Baptists what to do.

A significant portion of the "real work" Southern Baptists found them-selves doing came in the form of paperwork. Southern Baptist congregations had likely never been asked to produce such an amount of paperwork as the Campaign commission required of them. Scarborough required that local churches produce the names of those members who had been chosen to lead the Campaign in each local church. Asking that the "service rolls" be sent by September 15, Scarborough reminded his readers, "If you get in after that you will be 'late.' Don't be late."[93]

A similar notice in the *Florida Baptist Witness* revealed the detailed local organization that Campaign leaders required: "We need the names of the persons who constitute the 75 Million Campaign organizations in the local churches . . . we wish to send you your special literature and a lot of things, but we can't do it until you send us the names and addresses of the following persons in your church organization: (1) The church director; (2) the church organizer; (3) the church W.M.U. organizer; (4) chairman of boosters; (5) chairman team captains of five. Our work is

The Clock of the World

blocked off until we hear from you and get this information."[94] Leaders also sought to secure and keep records of pledges made during Victory Week. The central office sent churches enough pledge cards for Campaign participants to complete them in duplicate; one copy was to remain with the local church, while the other was to be permanently filed at state Campaign headquarters.[95]

Of all the goals and tendencies that the Seventy-Five Million Campaign absorbed from the Interchurch World Movement, however, the single most important was the dream of welding the churches of the Southern Baptist Convention into a single, indestructible missionary machine. When E. Y. Mullins outlined the reasons for raising seventy-five million dollars, he hinted at the goal that motivated the Campaign: to achieve a degree of unity of purpose once thought impossible for groups practicing congregational polity. "We need the unifying power of this great drive to consolidate us for the new age of opportunity and service. We must learn co-operation or go backward instead of forward."[96]

Mullins had learned to bridge the gap between the facts of congregational polity and the perceived need for Southern Baptist unity of action and purpose by casting dissent as a result of spiritual failure. Some Southern Baptist observers, however, feared that the movement toward denominational "consolidation" was ultimately irreconcilable with the very democratic principles that Baptists were seeking to defend. One insider critic, for instance, expressed his doubts about the wisdom of the emerging methods of the Seventy-Five Million Campaign before the 1919 Convention had even adjourned. M. Ashby Jones, an Atlanta pastor who had been involved with the YMCA during the war, defended the IWM from charges that it was attempting to roll America's Protestant churches into a single, doctrinally amorphous, ecclesial autocracy. At the 1919 Convention, he was the only person from the floor to voice any opposition to President Gambrell's opinions about ecumenism and the budding Campaign. In fact, during his speech Jones claimed that "in our efforts of centralized isolation we are going too far in the other direction. The whole tendency of this movement was to create out of the free churches of the South one church under the control of the Southern Baptist Convention."[97] Jones was not imagining things; at the Convention W. J. McGlothlin, the new president of Furman University, had said that "the Union which Baptists need is a union among themselves." Responding to this remark, the editor of the *Florida Baptist Witness* said that the Campaign provided the perfect opportunity for Landmark Baptists, Anti-Mission Baptists, and "Campbellite brethren" to "come home." Such a reunion would have cosmic benefits, ensuring that "the kingdom would come, and the knowledge of the truth would soon cover the earth as waters cover the deep."[98]

After the editor of the *Biblical Recorder* stated that the Baptist insistence upon democratic governance "does not apply to our present great campaign" because, "for the sake of efficiency, it was absolutely necessary to have some special agency, to which should be committed the momentous task of directing the campaign," one nervous North Carolina Baptist wrote to the paper to express his doubts about the wisdom of suspending the application of democratic principles to convention affairs for any reason.[99] To this observer, the Campaign was "born in the minds of a few leading Baptists, and then submitted to the Southern Baptist Convention at Atlanta, where the Convention endorsed the move." He was also suspicious of the fact that Convention leaders seemed to be claiming authority over local churches based on the unanimous approval of the messengers to the 1919 Convention. "Unless I am wrong," he noted, "no delegate can bind its home church without action from the church or authority to do so. So far as I can learn, the churches as a whole did not act on this, for the reason that it had never been presented to them." The author closed by expressing his fears that a compromise of democratic polity could eventually blossom into further problems down the road: "Large oaks from small acorns grow. Nothing is large in its beginning, but it is the gradual growing, and adding more to, that makes the full-grown. We should shun the very appearance of evil, and yet we are playing with our denominational church government, which gives us liberty and freedom, for which we have stood for so long, and for which our forefathers bled and died."[100]

At least in the mind of this single observer, the Seventy-Five Million Campaign's methodical innovations were chopping away the roots of the very system its leaders claimed to be defending. Southern Baptists were creating an in-house version of the IWM that would submit to denominational control, but some observers found the thought of denominational control almost as disturbing as the threat of runaway ecumenism.

Bureaucracy and the Southern Baptist Convention

Southern Baptists saw in the end of World War I roughly the same opportunities that other American Protestants did. Like their Methodist, Presbyterian, and Disciples of Christ brethren, Southern Baptists hoped to seize the post-war moment as an unparalleled opportunity for foreign mission expansion. At the same time, when many of these Protestants

66

began to identify the Interchurch World Movement as the means by which this goal could be accomplished, Southern Baptists balked, seeing in the IWM a reflection of the same sort of uncontrollable ecclesiasticism that they had experienced while working with the YMCA during the Great War.

Despite their distaste for the IWM, however, Southern Baptists pressed ahead with their plans to engage the post-war world on their own terms. Even while criticizing the Interchurch World Movement, Southern Baptist leaders borrowed many, if not most, of its methods as they framed their own in-house alternative, the Seventy-Five Million Campaign. In the process, these denominational leaders revealed that they had developed an affinity for the kind of bureaucratic control that the IWM represented. Additionally, these same leaders were also developing a sense that the SBC was itself more than a simple fellowship of churches; instead, it was to become a professionally led denomination whose resources would be efficiently marshaled by trusted leaders.

Southern Baptists were not the only Protestants in the United States who criticized, sometimes fiercely, the Interchurch World Movement. The rise of a historically identifiable Fundamentalist movement occurred during the same feverish period that saw the creation of the IWM. Although many Northern Fundamentalists opposed the IWM for different reasons than did Southern Baptists, each group saw a possible ally in the other. In the end, Southern Baptists chose to avoid the extremes of both Modernism and separatist Fundamentalism by affirming the doctrinal contentions of Fundamentalism as a part of Southern Baptist identity but rejecting its tendency to organizational criticism. The story of this tortured relationship between the Fundamentalists of the North and the leadership of the Southern Baptist Convention is the subject of the next chapter.

3

The Fundamentalization of Cooperation: Southern Baptist Reaction to the Fundamentalist Movement, 1919–1925

Isaac M. Haldeman, the pastor of New York's First Baptist Church during the rise and fall of the Interchurch World Movement, criticized the organization on many of the same grounds as did his fellow Baptist pastors in the South. In a pamphlet he distributed at the 1920 meeting of the Northern Baptist Convention, Haldeman charged that the IWM *"does not preach doctrine,"* but *"ignores it,"* *"is organized for the might of money"* raised by *"worldly"* methods, and chipped away at the rights of the individual Christian.[1] Southern Baptists who were conducting their own campaign against the IWM would easily have affirmed these criticisms of the new organization, but Haldeman made other accusations against the movement that would have confused his Southern counterparts. For Haldeman, the IWM was *"a post-millennial drive"* that *"substitutes the kingdom of Christ for the Church of Christ . . . by confounding the one with the other."*[2] Additionally, Haldeman charged that the IWM was in the business of promoting education, to which he asserted, "The Church is not here to educate men in the wisdom, knowledge and science of the world."[3]

Not every adherent of the wider Fundamentalist movement among Northern Baptists held to Haldeman's premillennial dispensationalism, however.[4] When *Watchman-Examiner* newspaper editor Curtis Lee Laws coined the word "Fundamentalist," he was only seeking to rally those Northern Baptists who sought to defend the "supernatural" content of Christian faith against Modernists who, subjecting Christian theology to a radical revision, naturalized it and emptied it of miraculous content. Far from issuing an international conservative call to arms, Laws simply envisioned a denominationally bounded movement that sought to preserve traditional Protestant doctrine within the NBC. While more radical Fundamentalists like Haldeman were developing ecclesiological attitudes that tended to dampen enthusiasm for denominational activities such as education and missions, more moderate Fundamentalists continued to support the missionary and educational programs of the Northern Baptist Convention.

Southern Baptists, observing the progress of the Fundamentalist controversy in the Northern Baptist Convention, struggled to respond appropriately. On the one hand, most Southern Baptists affirmed the theological conservatism that Fundamentalists taught. During the earliest years of the Fundamentalist controversy its leaders, like those of the SBC, were wary of the Interchurch World Movement. Southern Baptists welcomed Fundamentalist leaders to the South and accepted invitations to speak to Fundamentalist gatherings. In addition, Southern Baptist newspaper editors parroted Laws as he identified the affirmation of "supernaturalism" as the litmus test by which true Christianity could be revealed.

On the other hand, many radical Fundamentalists' tendencies toward denominational criticism and separatism repelled Southern Baptists. Because some of the more radical Northern Fundamentalists had adopted premillennial ideas, they began scaling back their own contributions to Northern Baptist denominational programs while calling for the creation of new methods to support foreign missions and alternative forms of theological education. Moderate, denominationally supportive Fundamentalists such as Laws consistently resisted these tendencies, but many Southern Baptist observers, for whom radical Fundamentalism was the most visible form of the movement, began to see in it the seeds of the destruction of the Seventy-Five Million Campaign. Southern Baptists resented radical Fundamentalist efforts to draw them into a nationwide Fundamentalist crusade that they felt tacitly implicated their own mission boards and seminaries. Additionally, while Southern Baptist leaders were genuinely committed to doctrinal conservatism, they rejected the possibility of a Northern-style Fundamentalist campaign by insisting that only mission board personnel and college and seminary boards of trustees investigate reports of aberrant theology among missionaries and seminary faculty. While Southern Baptist leaders warmly regarded Laws and other moderate Fundamentalists, they insisted that the Southern Baptist Convention, unlike the compromised Northern group, was capable of policing its own organizations without pressure from the grassroots.

Southern Baptist leaders responded to the pressures of the Fundamentalist movement among Northern Baptists by affirming the broad contours of its doctrinal contentions, then building those contentions into the fabric of the Seventy-Five Million Campaign and, ultimately, their articulation of Southern Baptist identity. By the same token, Southern Baptist leaders recast their own emphasis on denominational participation as a non-negotiable "fundamental," rejecting the interdenominational, separatist tendencies so common among radical Fundamentalists. As a result, Southern Baptists emerged from the Seventy-Five Million Campaign with a reinforced belief in the authority of the scriptures, the divinity of Christ, and the absolute necessity of denominational cooperation. In the minds of Southern Baptist leaders, denominational loyalty was becoming the sixth fundamental.[5]

Fundamentalism in the South:
A Historiographical Problem

Since the publication of George Marsden's *Fundamentalism and American Culture*, the idea that Fundamentalism was a phenomenon that germinated in urban, Northern soil has become a scholarly commonplace.[6] The extent to which contemporary scholars of American religion take this idea for granted obscures two facts, however. First, before Marsden's work appeared, scholars seem to have accepted the association between Fundamentalism and Southern religion as axiomatic.[7] For instance, in his 1964 monograph *Southern White Protestantism in the Twentieth Century*, Kenneth Bailey mingled mentions of J. Frank Norris's anti-Modernist fulminations and the Southern Baptist Convention's affirmation of personal evangelism. Bailey does not indicate that these phenomena are anything other than two sides of the same coin.[8] James Thompson's *Tried as by Fire: Southern Baptists and the Religious Controversies of the 1920s* shows increased sensitivity to the distinction between Southern Baptist conservatism and Fundamentalism among Southern Baptists, but the author still sees J. Frank Norris as "a logical starting point for examining Southern Baptist fundamentalism," confusing Norris's Fundamentalism with the home-grown anxieties of T. T. Martin and other Southern Baptist leaders.[9] Thompson also identifies Fundamentalism with premillennialism so tightly that his analysis excludes those more moderate Fundamentalists who declined to press the issue of eschatology.[10] Because scholars working before the publication of Marsden's *Fundamentalism* assumed that

71

Fundamentalism was native to the South, only one generation of scholars has had a chance to come to terms with this seismic shift in the study of Southern Protestantism.

Second, Marsden's identification of Fundamentalism with the urban North seems to have done little to stoke interest in the connection between Fundamentalism and Southern religion. During the last thirty years, remarkably little scholarly work has been published dealing with the relationship between these two phenomena. Of books that have been published in this area since 1980, the most informative is William R. Glass's *Strangers in Zion: Fundamentalists in the South, 1900–1950.* Explicitly building on Marsden's work, Glass shows that Northern-style Fundamentalists were "strangers in Zion" because Southern Protestants, while theologically conservative, were also loyal to their denominations and therefore wary of participating in alternative systems of foreign missions and theological education established by Northern Fundamentalists.[11] Glass's book is helpful and breaks new ground, but it also contains weaknesses that call for further study. First, Glass's analysis deals only with those Northern Fundamentalists radical enough to travel south in an effort to recruit Southerners to their cause. As a result, moderate, denominationally loyal Fundamentalists like Curtis Lee Laws and Frank Goodchild are excluded. Second, Glass identifies Fundamentalists with their educational and missionary institutions, assuming that Southerners were wary of Fundamentalism because they preferred their own denominational organizations over those supported by Northerners. This identification of Fundamentalism with its growing network of institutions obscures not only the extent to which Southern Protestants were passive objects of Fundamentalist action, but also the extent to which they were active observers of Northern developments, reading newspapers, absorbing theological arguments, and ultimately taking sides.

Strikingly, Southern Baptist awareness of the crises rocking the Northern Baptist Convention strongly influenced the process by which Southern Baptist leaders sought to unite their constituents under the banner of a single, increasingly centralized organization. While Fundamentalism was a centripetal force that tore at the unity of Northern Protestants, it became for Southern Baptists a catalyst for organizational development and an ingredient in the cement that held their denomination together. In other words, while these representative Southern Protestants did not endure a Fundamentalist controversy in their ranks during the 1920s, they were no strangers to the movement; the phenomenon of Fundamentalism made an indelible mark on their common life.

72

Southern Baptist Affirmation of the
Fundamentalist Movement

During the early 1920s, Southern Baptists struggled with a changing nation and with each other as they tried to come to terms with the theory of evolution. President William Louis Poteat of Wake Forest College openly admitted that the theory was taught in his classrooms, and the bitter criticisms against Poteat and later against E. Y. Mullins continued until a ceasefire was finally orchestrated in 1928.[12] In the midst of the struggle, Southern Baptists realized that an uncomfortable rift had developed between members of the Convention who held different opinions on the issue. For many observers of Southern Baptist life, the 1920s have been remembered as a period of fractious doctrinal conflict.

While the evolution conflict should not be ignored, the scholarly attention that has been paid to the evolution controversy tends to obscure two facts. First, although the evolution controversy overlapped with the Fundamentalist controversy, the two were separate phenomena. Many Americans (Northern and Southern) who neither knew nor cared about the internal theological controversies consuming the Northern Baptist and Presbyterian denominations found the evolution debate captivating.[13] By the same token, the theological controversies within the Northern denominations had little to do with evolution. Southern Baptist attention to Fundamentalism proper must be analyzed separately from the Southern Baptist evolution debate.

Additionally, and more importantly, while Southern Baptists endured prolonged controversy that stemmed from the nationwide evolution debate, they exhibited remarkable uniformity in their attitudes toward Fundamentalism as a movement to resist Modernism in the Northern Baptist Convention. At first, Southern Baptists found a particular point of contact with Northern Fundamentalists in their criticism of the Interchurch World Movement. Fundamentalists of more moderate sensibilities than I. M. Haldeman objected to the IWM, and a number of Southern Baptist observers explicitly connected the doctrinal laxity of the movement with a need for Christians to be more vigilant in their defense of traditional Christian truth claims. As a result, the earlier attention paid to the IWM helped prime Southern Baptists for later rhetorical support of the Fundamentalist movement. Additionally, editors from Texas to Virginia wrote editorials noticing the activities of the Fundamentalists and affirming their cause. The writing of these leaders reflects the heavy influence of Curtis Lee Laws's *Watchman-Examiner* in both their sympathies and their interpretation of the issues at stake in the controversy. Finally, Southern Baptist leaders often traveled north to speak at Fundamentalist conferences and Bible institutes, and Northern Fundamentalists found their way south for similar reasons.

The Southern Baptist rejection of the Interchurch World Movement was motivated more by Landmark-inspired fears of a tyrannical Protestant superchurch than by concerns about doctrinal redefinition among its supporting bodies. After the IWM had begun to collapse, however, some Southern Baptist observers began to articulate fears about the relationship between unionism and the decline of doctrinal conviction among American Protestants. In an article published in the North Carolina *Biblical Recorder* in 1920, W. C. Tyree charged that the new enthusiasm for Christian unity grew out of doctrinal indifference: "The coming together now of these denominations, which still differ about these doctrines, means that they are no longer regarded as important." Tyree did not believe that the churches were uniting based on doctrinal agreement but that they were uniting based on their agreement about "the moral and benevolent teachings of the Bible." Tyree did not object to focusing on the Bible's attention to moral and benevolent issues, but he did assert that the "situation must inevitably result in the elimination of the spiritual and supernatural features of our religion, and in its reduction to a mere ethical and benevolent system." For Tyree, church union could only result in reducing Protestantism to a theologically empty shell of organized benevolent action.[14]

In an editorial published in the Kentucky *Western Recorder* in late 1921, Victor I. Masters honed the same idea to a finer point. Seeing that the unionist impulse grew out of Protestant embarrassment about persistent doctrinal diversity, Masters believed that the Protestants participating in the IWM were attempting to downplay doctrine in order to curry favor with the wider world. As a result, unionism did not press groups to "take the Bible as the guide to closer unity of belief, but rather to play down and discredit all doctrinal teaching in favor of a least-common denominator liberalism." Then, moving beyond Tyree's cautious analysis, Masters confided to his readers that the devil was behind unionist tendencies to discredit Christian doctrine: "We live in a day of growing enmity to Christianity. . . . One of its favored approaches is that of discrediting of Christian doctrine. . . . If the devil is opposed to Christian doctrine, that in itself is fine presumptive proof that we ought to be diligent in studying it and teaching it."[15]

The Fundamentalization of Cooperation

Masters soon developed a reputation for doctrinal severity among Southern Baptist editors, a subject that will be discussed later. J. F. Love, on the other hand, rarely waded into the waters of doctrinal controversy without good reason. The corresponding secretary of the SBC's Foreign Mission Board, Love was one of those denominational leaders who stood to lose the most in a possible doctrinal scuffle within the Convention. As a result, he took measures to safeguard the FMB from doctrinal criticism in 1919, adopting a "Statement of Belief" which was then used during board examinations of all Southern Baptist foreign missionaries. Love faced criticism for his decision to adopt a doctrinal statement, but in a 1921 article that was reprinted in several Southern Baptist newspapers, Love connected the need for doctrinal guidelines on the mission field to the lax attitude that many "unionists" took toward doctrine. "Through the doors which the sentimentalists and anti-denominationalists have opened enemies of the gospel itself have entered. The sentiment which makes conscience dull on points of Christian truth imperils the Christian program, threatening first the things which are dear to a single denomination, they soon imperil things which are dear to all and the task of good men becomes not so much the saving of a missionary method as saving the missionary message."[16] Love's observations, along with those of these two other writers, show that Southern Baptists were, by 1921, successfully crossing the ideological line that separated the narrowly denominational concerns that had motivated the SBC to criticize the Interchurch World Movement from the more generally Protestant concerns that motivated the Northern Fundamentalists. While Southern Baptist identification with the Fundamentalist movement was never complete, by 1921 Southern Baptist leaders had come to realize that they had a stake in the Northern conflict.

Southern Baptist editors provided ample evidence of this identification in their frequent expressions of support for Northern Fundamentalists. P. I. Lipsey, the editor of the Mississippi *Baptist Record*, probably resided and worked miles away from the nearest Modernist, but he still lent his editorial weight to the Fundamentalists of the Northern Baptist Convention. Noting that "among Northern Baptists, there has been earnest discussion for several months on the subject of the Fundamentals," Lipsey summarized the discussion appearing in the pages of *The Baptist*, the new NBC news organ that the editor was apparently receiving and reading. In listing almost every issue being debated among Northern Baptists, including the inspiration of the scripture, miracles, the virgin birth, the divinity of Jesus, and the resurrection, Lipsey shows that he was at least superficially aware of the questions around which the conflict swirled. In addition, Lipsey made plain his own feelings about the conflict: "There is no place for evasion or equivocation in religion. For our part we have no fellowship with those who put a question mark about the absolute authority of the Bible as the word of God. . . . If the divine element is removed from our religion it is a delusion and a fraud."[17]

Lipsey's editorial mentioned H. C. Vedder, the church history professor at Crozer Theological Seminary. The editor commended Vedder for speaking his mind "out in the open," but condemned his attack on the substitutionary atonement.[18] Other editors also noticed Vedder's strong rejection of substitutionary atonement in the early months of the conflict and commented accordingly. A writer in the Louisiana *Baptist Message*, for instance, claimed that Vedder's "views are diametrically opposed to the orthodox and reverent teachings propounded in our Southern Seminaries."[19] For this author, Vedder's views completely eroded the foundation of evangelical Christianity, an opinion that duplicated Fundamentalist responses to Vedder's ideas. Even J. F. Love went into print to refute Vedder, noting that he had read Vedder's recent articles in *The Baptist*.[20] That Southern Baptists took an opportunity to defend the substitutionary atonement is not surprising, but these Southern observers were doing more than offering conservative opinions. Both Lipsey and Love explicitly mention *The Baptist* as the source of their information about the Northern conflict, showing that they were actively following Northern developments.

While the more genteel editors of the Atlantic coast were much less likely to comment on the Fundamentalist controversy than were their fellow editors to the west, they tended to affirm the Fundamentalists' contentions when commenting on doctrinal issues. R. H. Pitt, for instance, had already served on the staff of the Virginia *Religious Herald* for years by the time the Fundamentalist controversy broke in the North. Pitt was proud of the fact that Virginia was unfriendly territory for the heresy hunter, but even he had to admit that J. F. Love had good cause to be concerned about the doctrine that future SBC foreign missionaries taught.[21] Retaining his fear of formal creeds among Baptists, Pitt nevertheless admitted that the Foreign Mission Board "ought to guard, in their appointments and their administration, the fundamentals of Christian and denominational faith."[22] Pitt cites a story of an applicant for missionary service with another Baptist denomination who told his interviewers that Christ "is divine just as you and I are divine, no more, no less."[23] News of doctrinal change in the North was forcing even the most tolerant of ob-

76

servers among Southern Baptists into recognizing that one need not be a reactionary to discern the value of doctrinal boundaries.

Native Southern conservatism could easily explain Southern Baptist editors' predilection for the Fundamentalist movement, but evidence strongly suggests that these analysts of Baptist life received interpretive cues from Curtis Lee Laws and his popular newspaper, the *Watchman-Examiner*. Although the newspaper was based in New York City, Southern Baptists read it widely.[24] While the *Watchman-Examiner* was not founded in response to the NBC's creation of *The Baptist* and that newspaper's increasing identification with Modernism, after the end of the First World War the *Watchman-Examiner* increasingly identified itself with Fundamentalism and took up an editorial position opposite that of the official Northern Baptist news organ. In fact, it was in the pages of the *Watchman-Examiner* that Curtis Lee Laws first coined the term "Fundamentalist."[25] Throughout the conflict that he had helped to name, Laws offered his own interpretation of the disturbance, claiming, "The issue is supernaturalism, pure and simple."[26]

Southern Baptist editors endlessly repeated Laws's claim that the real issue separating Fundamentalists and Modernists was the retention of "supernatural" elements of the gospel. The editor of the North Carolina *Biblical Recorder*, for instance, told his readers that Modernist rejection "of the Virgin Birth is due to lack of faith in the supernatural, and the battle of the future will rage around the supernatural."[27] On another occasion, Z. T. Cody of *The Baptist Courier* repeated almost the same sentiment: "In some way, we do not know why, the 'virgin birth' has in modern days, become the centre for attack by those who balk at the supernatural . . . if one accepts the supernatural in our religion, we can see no reason why there should be special difficulty here."[28] In addition, some editors promoted Laws's interpretation of the Fundamentalist controversy by reprinting editorials from the *Watchman-Examiner* without comment. *The Florida Baptist Witness* of June 29, 1922 contains a *Watchman-Examiner* editorial in which Laws explains that "Fundamentalism . . . is a protest against that rationalistic interpretation of Christianity which seeks to discredit supernaturalism."[29]

Editors were not the only Southern Baptists who relied upon Laws to help them understand the meaning of the Fundamentalist movement. When Frank Burkhalter, the publicity director of the Seventy-Five Million Campaign, traveled to the 1922 Northern Baptist Convention and filed a report on the proceedings of that year's Fundamentals Conference with the state Baptist papers, Laws's presentation was the only one that Burkhalter

77

summarized. In that summary, Burkhalter repeated and affirmed the contentions about the conflict between rationalism and supernaturalism familiar to readers of state Southern Baptist newspapers.[30] Laws's influence over Southern Baptist interpretation of the Fundamentalist conflict among Northern Baptists would be difficult to overestimate.

Frank Burkhalter's appearance at the 1922 Fundamentals Conference foreshadows another aspect of Southern Baptist involvement with the Fundamentalists of the Northern Baptist Convention. Northern Fundamentalist leaders appeared in the South at conventions, as revival preachers, and as Bible conference teachers. By the same token, Southern Baptist leaders sometimes participated in Northern gatherings.

Curtis Lee Laws, himself a Virginia native, frequently traveled South for a number of different purposes. When the Southern Baptist Convention met in Chattanooga in 1921, a number of clearly pleased editors noted Laws's presence. For example, editor Cody of the South Carolina *Baptist Courier* noted, "Dr. Curtis Lee Laws, Editor of the *Watchman-Examiner*, was among the visitors to the Chattanooga Convention. His is the greatest Baptist paper we have."[31] Laws also went south in order to teach and preach. During the month after the 1921 convention, presumably during the same journey that brought him to Chattanooga, Laws offered the commencement sermon at Wake Forest College.[32] Two years later, Baptist papers reported that Laws was to share the platform with A. T. Robertson, a professor at the Southern Baptist Theological Seminary in Louisville, at a Bible conference in Shreveport, Louisiana.[33] Laws is also reported to have taught at a Bible conference at First Baptist Church in Miami, Florida. The editor appeared alongside John Roach Straton, dispensationalist S. D. Gordon, and William Jennings Bryan.[34]

Southern leaders often kept Fundamentalist company when they traveled North. Kentucky Baptist editor J. W. Porter appeared on the platform of the 1920 Fundamentals Conference in Buffalo, New York.[35] In 1921, both John Sampey and L. R. Scarborough appeared on the program of the following year's Fundamentals Conference in Des Moines.[36] In 1925, after the moderate Fundamentalists decided to establish their own seminaries in Chicago and Philadelphia, Scarborough traveled north again, this time to Chicago, to deliver a series of lectures at the new Northern Baptist Theological Seminary.[37] Such exchange between Southern Baptist leaders and Northern Baptist Fundamentalists would seem to indicate an easy identification between the two groups, but in reality Southern Baptists retained an anxious attitude toward Fundamentalism.

Southern Baptist Fear of the Fundamentalist Movement

As the Fundamentalist movement unfolded among Northern Baptists, participants soon realized that they were drifting into two groups. On the one hand, more moderate Baptist Fundamentalists like Curtis Lee Laws and Frank Goodchild simply claimed to "stand where loyal Baptists have always stood."[38] These moderates affirmed their belief in their own denomination and consistently rejected any suggestion that Fundamentalists should create their own schools and mission boards in order to circumvent compromised denominational institutions.[39] These moderate Fundamentalists were marked by a loyalty to their denomination that was almost as intense as their defense of conservative theology; as a result, they refused to abandon the boards and agencies of the NBC.[40] Additionally, moderates thought of the movement as an internal, denominational affair. Because the movement was aimed at reinforcing the Northern Baptist Convention and its agencies, moderate Fundamentalists tended to aim their appeal at other Northern Baptists.[41]

Almost as soon as the movement was underway, however, some Fundamentalists began to agitate for an approach to the problem of Modernism that was both more militant in spirit and more sweeping in scope than that advocated in the pages of the *Watchman-Examiner*. These radical Fundamentalists, frustrated with the anti-creedalism of many of the traditionalists in the Northern Convention and with moderate Fundamentalist willingness to compromise with moderate Modernists in order to preserve the machinery of the Convention, began to work independently of moderates like Laws. Separatist in ecclesiology and premillennial in eschatology, radical Fundamentalists tended to downplay denominational particularities and loyalty to the Northern Convention. Through the Baptist Bible Union, an organization they created in 1922, radical Fundamentalists such as William Bell Riley and John Roach Straton actively recruited participation from among Northern, Southern, and Canadian Baptists.[42] Over the entire enterprise hovered the specter of a possible denominational schism, a prospect made even more ominous by the financial burden the Northern Baptist Convention bore after the Interchurch World Movement collapsed.[43] Radical Fundamentalist creation of a separate missionary organization and support of alternative, nondenominational sources of theological education earned them the scorn of Modernists and denominationally loyal Fundamentalists alike.[44]

The claims and behaviors of the Baptist Bible Union's radical Fundamentalists understandably unnerved Southern Baptists observing the

79

Northern conflict. First, radical Fundamentalist hints that premillennialism should be made a "test of fellowship" bothered Southern Baptists, who differed among themselves on the issue of eschatology.[45] While Southern Baptist editors seem to have agreed that Southern Baptists were united in their belief in Christ's second coming and that premillennialism was an acceptable theological position for a Baptist to hold, they believed individual Baptists should enjoy liberty in determining their own beliefs in the matter.

Second, the Fundamentalist tendency to call for redress of doctrinal grievances through mass meetings and unplanned resolutions introduced on the floor of the NBC unnerved Southern Baptist leaders. When John Roach Straton attempted through a resolution to keep Brown University president and Modernist leader W. H. P. Faunce from speaking at the 1923 Northern Baptist Convention meeting, the Fundamentalist leader was shouted down.[46] Editor R. H. Pitt thought that this was a clear example of Fundamentalists hurting their own cause by their outrageous behavior.[47] At best, such behavior was impolite and garish by Southern standards, and at worst it implied that the structures of the Northern Convention were so corrupt that its leadership could not be trusted to address the legitimate concerns of their constituency. Because similar accusations had been made against Southern Baptist leaders in the past, the contemporary leadership of the SBC found this tendency threatening.

Third, Southern Baptist leaders reacted strongly when the Baptist Bible Union released a confession of faith whose preface claimed, "The Baptist people of the earth are at the present time in sad confusion and their fellowship is torn by increasing controversies. Practically every convention, state and local association and almost every mission station and local church, is the subject and scene of strife."[48] J. W. Mitchell, the editor of the Florida Baptist Witness, responded typically when he countered that "in the Southern Baptist Convention . . . there is absolutely no confusion, but on the other hand, the sweetest fellowship prevails."[49] Southern Baptists like Mitchell were offended at being lumped in with doctrinally-compromised Northern Baptists.[50] Through watching the Northern conflicts, Southern Baptist leaders had learned that doctrinal insinuations like those the BBU was making had immense financial implications, and Baptist leaders in the South resented radical Fundamentalist declarations of nationwide crisis that had the potential to endanger Southern Baptist fundraising efforts.

Fourth, and most importantly, Southern Baptist leaders were offended at radical fundamentalist tendencies to neglect the cooperative efforts of the Northern Baptist Convention. R. H. Pitt responded to the BBU confession of faith in the same way that J. W. Mitchell and almost every other Southern Baptist editor had, but he augmented his comments by warning that the authors of the Baptist Bible Union statement were going "to contribute as far as their influence goes to the spirit of disintegration and confusion."[51] Pitt's assertion went directly to the heart of the matter in the eyes of Southern Baptist leadership. While doctrinal conflict raged in the North, Southern Baptist leaders struggled to transform Seventy-Five Million Campaign pledges into cash. Already unable to meet their financial obligations, these leaders saw in the critical tendencies of the radical Fundamentalists the potential death-knell of the Seventy-Five Million Campaign. William Bell Riley, a leader among more strident Northern Baptist Fundamentalists, for instance, made it plain that his church had refused to participate in the Northern Convention's New World Movement because "it could not give conscientiously to the educational work of the Convention, the colleges and seminaries constituted as they are."[52] Further, Riley pleaded his church's inability to give to the denomination at a time when it was heavily involved "in the building and educational directions."[53] Riley thought he would vindicate himself with this explanation, but Southern Baptist leaders were simply unprepared to accept any excuse for failing to give to a program that so closely mirrored the Seventy-Five Million Campaign.[54] When paired with radical Fundamentalist insinuation of aberrant theology among Southern Baptists, Riley's publicized behavior bore the potential to derail the Campaign by leading contributors to believe that the recipients of their generosity were promoting questionable beliefs. Riley's expressed preference for investing in his own church over the programs of the denominations must also have grated on the nerves of Southern Baptist leadership.[55]

Southern Baptist leaders eventually came to distrust William Bell Riley, but they developed a full-fledged loathing of radical Fundamentalism's Southern representative, J. Frank Norris. While Norris's exploits among Texas Baptists, bizarre even by radical Fundamentalist standards, have become something of a "twice-told tale" among Baptist historians, a few details need be repeated here for the sake of clarity. During the 1920s, Norris spent the better part of his time accusing Baylor University professors of hiding their belief in evolution and criticizing the Seventy-Five Million Campaign as the best possible example of the fact that "the main thing the denominations were after today was not souls, but money."[56] Norris's very public refusal to give to the Campaign and accusations of doctrinal irregularity closely mirrored William Bell Riley's strategy in

Minneapolis, but Norris's position in Texas and explicit criticism of specific Texas Baptist institutions made him especially obnoxious to Southern Baptist leadership in Texas and across the South.

Due to the respect he enjoyed among Texas Baptists and his position as the General Director of the Seventy-Five Million Campaign, it naturally fell to L. R. Scarborough to defend both Baylor and the Campaign from Norris's accusations. The tone of the conflict between these two men was eerily reminiscent of the Hayden and Bogard controversies of the turn of the century; Scarborough painted Norris as being a denominational obstructionist even as Norris harped on the aggregations of money and power that he claimed characterized the leadership of both the Texas state organization and the SBC.[57] Scarborough successfully defended Baylor and the Campaign, but not without cost. While Norris seems to have enjoyed the conflicts of the 1920s, Scarborough emerged from them professionally intact but emotionally bruised. Although Scarborough was certainly no Modernist, he absorbed through his conflicts with Norris a deep-seated fear of radical Fundamentalism. Scarborough, whose ardor for the Southern Baptist Convention has been labeled an "obsession," could see in Norris-style Fundamentalism nothing but a threat to the ongoing institutional work of the Baptists of the South.[58]

What remains unclear in the existing literature on Norris, Scarborough, and the conflict between them is the extent to which Scarborough's intense distaste for radical Fundamentalism metastasized to the rest of the Southern Baptist Convention because of his leadership in the Seventy-Five Million Campaign. As the General Director of the Campaign, Scarborough often wrote articles to be syndicated to the various Baptist newspapers of the Southern Baptist Convention, but during the conflict with Norris Scarborough's articles often had as much to do with the threat of radical Fundamentalism as they did with contributions to the Campaign.

One representative article, "The Weakness of the Fundamentalists," is typical in its criticisms. After affirming the fundamentalist struggle among Baptists in the North, where "they have a situation different from what Southern Baptists have," Scarborough chides the Fundamentalists of the South for overemphasizing premillennialism. Then, moving on to the substance of his criticism, Scarborough paints his opponents with the Interchurch World Movement brush. "They are alien immersionists; they receive members from other pedo-Baptist sprinkling churches without re-baptism. . . . In the main, they are inter-denominationalists." Although Scarborough accuses Texas Fundamentalists of being infected with ecclesiological heresy, he admits that "the Northern Fundamentalists, in the main, were opposed to the Inter-Church World Movement." While showing that Scarborough knew that not all Fundamentalists were cut from the same cloth as Norris, this also shows that Scarborough saw the split between moderate and radical Fundamentalists as running along the Mason-Dixon Line. Like most other Southern Baptists, Scarborough supported the Fundamentalist project as long as it stayed within the confines of the Northern Baptist Convention.[59] Fundamentalism in the South, on the other hand, was a threat to organized Baptist denominational work. Quivering between the lines of the article, and stated explicitly in more than a few others, is Scarborough's identification of radical Fundamentalism with those rebels of the Baptist past who refused to participate in denominational activities while accusing denominational leadership of greed, megalomania, or doctrinal weakness.[60]

Articles like "The Weakness of the Fundamentalists" ran in Southern Baptist state newspapers almost constantly during the Seventy-Five Million Campaign, and many state editors echoed Scarborough's sentiments.[61] Although motivated primarily by the bad blood between Norris and Scarborough, Baptists read these articles from Albuquerque to Baltimore. Some of these Baptists knew that Scarborough's criticisms of Fundamentalism were really just "his way of getting at the Rev. Frank Norris," but others must have taken Scarborough's accusations at face value.[62] The unusual result was a denomination whose members clung to conservative theology while harboring varying levels of suspicion for the organized Fundamentalist movement.

The fear of radical Fundamentalism eventually overshadowed the natural Southern Baptist affinity for the moderate conservatives gathered around Curtis Lee Laws's leadership. Laws constantly reminded Southern Baptists that his own wing of the movement was not affiliated with the radicals and their Baptist Bible Union, and editors seem to have taken him at his word.[63] At the same time, while moderate Fundamentalists refrained, for the most part, from soliciting Southern Baptist assistance in their struggle, radicals continued to clamor for Southern Baptist attention. While they never repudiated their support for Fundamentalism as a defensive movement in the North, many Southern Baptist leaders tended somewhat unfairly to view Fundamentalism through a lens created by people like Norris and Riley. Furthermore, the word "fundamentalist," which Laws himself had coined in 1920, had become so suspicious through its treatment in the Southern Baptist press that Southern Baptists rarely failed to qualify it when they used it.

83

J. E. Dillard, the book editor for *The Alabama Baptist*, for instance, found himself having to explain himself at length when a reader asked him whether he was a Fundamentalist or a Modernist. "If by Fundamentalist you mean the group of men who hold the literal, verbal inspiration of the whole Bible and therefore to its inerrancy and infallibility in all matters grammatical, historical, ethical, scientific, social, political, etc., as well as all matters religious, and who desire to discover all who do not believe as they do and would disfellowship them and drive them from the denomination . . . then I am not a Fundamentalist." On the other hand, Dillard claimed that he could be considered a Fundamentalist if that word was defined as "one who believes the Bible is the revelation of God and his will to man, and unfolding of the great plan for the salvation of individuals and of society." Strikingly, Dillard performed a similar operation with the word "Modernist," saying that he could, under the right circumstances, accept that label as well. At the end of the day, however, Dillard seemed to have wearied of the need to be labeled. "I am just a plain truth seeker. I believe in God, I am not scared. I am not angry."[64]

Only one month later, a minor controversy cropped up in the pages of the Florida state Baptist newspaper. Len Broughton, a popular, conservative Southern Baptist pastor, criticized the editor of the *Florida Baptist Witness* for saying that Lincoln McConnell, another Southern Baptist pastor, was a "Fundamentalist." Broughton had no quarrel with McConnell, and agreed that his "intimate friend" was qualified to wear the label. Instead, the pastor resented the use of the word itself among Southern Baptists, charging that its appearance could only indicate that "in our Southern Convention territory there must have come about, some way, a division of our forces into Fundamentalists and non-Fundamentalists" and that "only the few believe, while the many do not believe." For Broughton, this was absurd. "Everybody knows that Southern Baptists stand flat-footed upon the rock of revealed truth as we have it in the Bible. . . . Why then, I repeat, label one man a 'Fundamentalist' and not his co-laborers in the same way?" The word had obtained such divisive connotations as to make it too dangerous to use. "Am I a Fundamentalist? If so, with the fewest exceptions, every Baptist preacher and teacher in our great Southland is the same, and there should be no such designations as imply otherwise."[65]

Len Broughton's assertion that the pastors of the SBC were almost universally free from the taint of Modernism was not arbitrary, nor did it stand in an ideological vacuum. The idea of a special South, a place shielded from the vicissitudes of Northern industrial upheaval and reli-

The Fundamentalization of Cooperation

gious decay, would provide Southern Baptist leaders with the raw material out of which they could construct a new identity for the Southern Baptists.

The "Scarborough Synthesis": A New Identity for Southern Baptists

Briefly stated, the new identity that Southern Baptist leaders synthesized under the informal leadership of L. R. Scarborough emphasized the distinction between Southern and Northern Baptists by drawing on then-widely accepted ideas of Southern exceptionalism and then framed the Southern Baptist Convention as a guarantor of conservative doctrine. Scarborough went one step further when he defined the Southern Baptist doctrinal consensus as including cooperation with other congregations as a "New Testament doctrine," thus excluding and stigmatizing radical Fundamentalists who failed to give to the Seventy-Five Million Campaign for ostensibly doctrinal reasons. Although Scarborough's proposal to define cooperation as an article of faith received a mixed response from Southern Baptist editors, leaders at all levels of Southern Baptist life participated in a program to promote the Campaign and other denominational programs in venues that necessarily juxtaposed Convention activities with evangelism and doctrinal preaching. By the time the 1925 *Baptist Faith and Message* appeared, the idea that loyalty to Christ required denominational participation was already so commonplace among Southern Baptists that no one seemed to notice the document's unusual inclusion of a new article on "Co-Operation."

In the wake of the Civil War, Southerners forged a new sense of identity out of the need to cope with the embarrassment of military defeat and the hardships of Reconstruction. The "Lost Cause" ideology that dominated Southern self-reflection from just after the end of the Civil War until at least the end of the First World War offered an image of the South as (among other things) a spiritually-sensitive land of homogenously Protestant virtue.[66] Southern Baptists were among those who accepted this idea of the meaning of Southern experience, as a book written in 1920 by Victor I. Masters illustrates. Before his radicalizing move to the editor's chair of Kentucky's *Western Recorder* in 1921, Masters served as superintendent of publicity for the Southern Baptist Convention's Home Mission Board. *The Call of the South*, the last book Masters wrote during his tenure at the Home Mission Board, plainly illustrates the shape of Southern Baptist appropriation of "Lost Cause" ideas about Southern identity.

85

Masters's South was marked by a "sense of solidarity" growing out of its Civil War experiences and scarcity of foreign immigrants.[67] While the North, flooded by immigrants, had begun to change so quickly that it could no longer remember its past, the South was an "old" place where history still mattered.[68] Populated by those who could still recall either the Civil War itself or, at the very least, the privations of living in a region wrecked by war, the people of the South had cultivated a spirit that would prove more valuable to the nation than any amount of economic development. That "spirit . . . a certain depth of soul which the South has acquired through the bitterness of trials which purged it of dross and have healed it of hate" would "conserve the spiritual dynamic with which God has equipped us for building in our own section a great Christian civilization" and eventually aid in achieving "the same end in the other sections of our beloved country."[69]

Masters concretely spelled out the shape of the salvation that he hoped the South could provide to the rest of the nation:

> Southern religious bodies have held on to the supernatural in religion and to the inerrancy of Scripture revelation with a tenacity which is a blessing to other sections, where rationalism and liberalism have done much to rob Christian faith of its vital power. If God shall give us to see the day of our opportunity, so far from being infected by the disease of doubt which has laid hold of many, we of the Southern religious bodies shall with increased devotion and determination cling to the faith once delivered to the saints, which alone can avail for humanity's needs.[70]

A spiritual seed bank, Masters's South stood as a spiritual repository ready to replant the rest of the nation after the cultural and religious upheavals that had so devastated sections of the nation that might have been expected, at one time, to look after their own spiritual interests. Like Winston Churchill musing on the moment when the New World would step forth to rescue the Old, Masters wondered if the churches of the South would wake up to their call to rescue America from itself.

> There are deep-thinking Northern men who are watching the South with hope, wondering if we shall rise to our God-given opportunity in the nation. They desire to know if our unmixed Anglo-Saxon blood, our unvexed Americanism and evangelical faith, will so equip the South with spiritual comprehension

The Fundamentalization of Cooperation

and motive that it shall not only be able to save itself, but have a blessed overflow to help the North and the West in their struggle against new and strange forces, which are seeking to choke America's political and religious testimony to a hungry and weary world.[71]

Masters was beginning to develop a reputation as a controversialist, but *The Call of the South,* including its chapter on "The Revolt Against Doctrine," seems to have raised little or no protest from his readers. When news about the Fundamentalist controversy began to spread more widely throughout the South, Southern Baptist leaders were already prepared to respond at least in part by breathing a sigh of relief that they were "not as other men are."

A number of Southern Baptist leaders would probably have preferred to leave their response to the Northern conflict at that, but lay fascination with the Fundamentalist conflict would force them to deal with the conflict more directly. Even had Baptist editors chosen not to cover the movement, secular newspaper coverage would have guaranteed that lay Baptists would hear about the Fundamentalist controversy. Although lay interest in Fundamentalism cannot be confirmed directly, editorial use of Fundamentalist themes to grab attention reveals that those who wrote for the Southern Baptist press knew that mentioning Fundamentalism attracted the attention of readers much more effectively than did discussions of evangelism or stewardship. In 1920, for instance, the Texas *Baptist Standard* published on its first page "Five Fundamentals of Evangelism." Although the brief article makes no explicit reference to the original "five fundamentals," the tone is similar as it insists that "the whole Bible [is] the Word of God" and that "all men without Christ are lost." On the other hand, the article shows that at least one anonymous author had learned that it was possible to use Fundamentalism to attract attention to an article on a well-worn topic.[72] By 1924, Frank Burkhalter, the publicity director of the Seventy-Five Million Campaign, had apparently learned the same lesson. In an article titled "Do Southern Baptists Believe God's Word," Burkhalter assured his audiences that they did, but quickly moved into a pitch for the Seventy-Five Million Campaign, asking whether they believed "to the point of launching out in faith upon . . . the many precious promises God has given us in that Word."[73] Burkhalter had learned the same lesson as the Texas author of the "Five Fundamentals": Fundamentalism gathers attention from readers. Presumably, this indicates that the rank-and-file pastors and laypeople who read these newspapers

Southern Baptist Reaction to the Fundamentalist Movement

were interested in Fundamentalism and likely would not allow their leaders to let sleeping dogs lie.

Scarborough and the other leaders of the Southern Baptist Convention, then, had little choice but to address fears of Modernism directly. After the appeal to regional exceptionalism, the first element in their response to Fundamentalist concerns was to affirm the conservative doctrine of moderate Fundamentalism but to frame the Southern Baptist Convention as the organization that would guarantee its preservation. As a result, Southern Baptist leaders were able to affirm the need to protect traditional Protestant doctrine even while defending the legitimacy of the Southern Baptist Convention against its radical Fundamentalist critics.

In an article appearing in several Southern Baptist newspapers in May 1923, Scarborough sought, once again, to discredit the Baptist Bible Union in which J. Frank Norris participated. Angered by the BBU's call for the formation of a new denomination, Scarborough retorted that "Southern Baptists are against modernism in any form and through their present organization in their associations, churches, and state and general conventions can take care of the incoming of modernism."[74] While Modernism was a genuine problem, Scarborough was certain that the organizations making up the SBC were themselves capable of stemming the tide. "Southern Baptists are a constructive set. They are the true fundamentalists. They do not accept modernism in any form. They stand practically four-square against any form of evolution that destroys the integrity of the Bible or the deity of Christ; they also stand against any movement that would destroy the integrity and witness of Christ's churches."[75] The idea that the Southern Baptists were the "true Fundamentalists" was apparently an important idea to Scarborough, as he repeated his claim that "Southern Baptists are the original Fundamentalists" in an article published the following month.[76]

In a letter to the editor of the Arkansas *Baptist Advance*, one Missouri Baptist summarized Scarborough's position and demonstrated that at least one common Southern Baptist had absorbed Scarborough's attitude.[77] After castigating the Modernists and averring that the Fundamentalists "mean well but . . . are not helping," this rank-and-file reader claimed that Southern Baptists represented a "third class" in the conflict. "They are the salt of the earth. They will go on and 'saw wood' and save the day. They have their feet planted on the Eternal Rock of Ages. They will sound out the fundamentals of Christianity to the ends of the earth."[78]

SBC leaders wanted to distinguish themselves from the Fundamentalist movement partly by avoiding open denominational conflict. South-

The Fundamentalization of Cooperation

ern Baptist leaders sought to convince their constituency that the Convention, along with its mission boards, colleges, and seminaries, was capable of monitoring the beliefs of its own employees without constant, disruptive, direct action on the part of concerned Baptists. As early as 1922, Editor Gwaltney of *The Alabama Baptist* was forced to defend himself against accusations that he was trying to "silence" discussion on the matter of evolution in his newspaper. In response, the editor said, "There are boards of trustees appointed by Baptist conventions whose business it is to employ teachers for Baptist schools. These trustees are the people to dismiss them when they are found unorthodox or otherwise unsuited for their places." Gwaltney did not fear the possibility of dismissing teachers who had reached unacceptable doctrinal conclusions, but he did believe that such discipline should be carried out by appropriate authorities and not by an angry mob.[79] Such a strategy made a Northern-style Fundamentalist uprising less likely while encouraging trust in the SBC and its institutions.

Other leaders repeated Gwaltney's call for increased confidence in trustees. Later that year, in response to the trustees' firing of a Modernist professor at William Jewell College, the editor of the Tennessee *Baptist and Reflector* reported favorably on the trustees' action. "*The . . . action of the Board of Trustees of William Jewell College, Missouri, is indication of the general attitude toward heresy on the part of Baptist Colleges of the South. They can evidently be trusted to take a decided step whenever and wherever it is necessary.*"[80] In 1924, after a similar incident during which Mercer University's trustees released a biology professor who did not "seem to believe anything that pertains to the Christian religion," several editors expressed nearly identical sentiments.[81] J. W. Mitchell asserted that "the management of Mercer deserves the thanks of the denomination for their action in this matter. . . . We venture the assertion that the fine action on the part of Mercer, is going to be the beginning of the end of all rottenness that is found existing in our Baptist schools."[82] Although the politically astute Louie D. Newton, editor of *The Christian Index*, explicitly tried to leave "controversial matters aside," he expressed unqualified support for Mercer's trustees in their removal of the errant Biology professor. When Newton became aware of the professor's beliefs, he was "thoroughly convinced . . . that he should retire at once." At the same time, however, Newton reminded his readers that "we have worked as constructively and patiently as we knew how to work." Instead of using his position as editor to "throw the denomination into excitement," Newton implied that he preferred to work through Mercer's

89

trustees who "should have the direction of the institutions and agencies to which they are appointed" and in which Baptists should feel "the fullest confidence."[83] Even when Modernism surfaced in the faculties of Baptist schools, editors stood their ground and supported the dismissal of offending faculty so long as duly elected trustees carried out the dismissals.

Importantly, Scarborough himself endorsed this method of dealing with Modernism in Southern Baptist schools. In an article in the Oklahoma *Baptist Messenger*, Scarborough admitted that "there may be a few, a very few" teachers in Southern Baptist schools who were drifting theologically, but that the answer to this problem lay not in following "destructive misrepresentatives of the truth." Instead, Scarborough called on the Baptists of Oklahoma, stoked to a fever pitch by the looming battle over the proposed *Baptist Faith and Message*, to work for change in Baptist schools by appealing to those entrusted with the schools' administration. "Wherever and whenever removals or resignations are in order, prompt and courageous action should be taken by proper authorities." Scarborough sympathized with the determination of laypeople and common pastors to "rid their school of this taint of poison," but insisted that this be done constructively. By the same token, if the rank-and-file of the Southern Baptist Convention were expected to work for change through duly designated authorities, those in charge of the schools, "the presidents, faculties and trustees, must be constantly conscious of our responsibility in building our schools loyal to **Christ and His revealed truth**."[84] Scarborough was ready and willing to investigate legitimate doctrinal complaints, but he was unwilling to tolerate Norris-style carping.

Southern Baptist leaders did not want lay Baptists to fight Modernism by directly criticizing schools and other denominational agencies, but they did offer one avenue by which Southern Baptists could advocate for sound Baptist theology. Modernism was best opposed not through political maneuvering but through active support of Southern Baptist missions and education, channeled through the Seventy-Five Million Campaign. In a 1921 article, Scarborough connected support for the boards and agencies of the Southern Baptist Convention with the need to press back the tide of Modernism quite explicitly:

> No organization on earth could by any possible means get
> Southern Baptists to pledge even ten thousand dollars to
> support men who would teach and preach what these Mod-
> ernists believe and teach. They would not pay their sacred
> pledges made already if they had reason to believe that the

90

money would be spent in supporting preachers and teachers who would not willingly subscribe to a faith in Christ's deity, the integrity and inspiration of the Bible and that the main business of Christ's churches is to win souls. . . . The question is whether we will make our pulpits, our mission boards, our schools and seminaries agents to propagate the Gospel given us by Christ through the inspired hands of His apostles, or to propagate garbled mutilated gospel given and inspired by the "dead hands" of German Rationalism, Darwinian Evolution, socialistic reformation. Let's dedicate our lives, guard our schools, save and give our money to train our youth for the proclamation of a creed given by the "crucified hands" and send it out into the world.[85]

J. W. Mitchell also believed that the best medicine for the disease of Modernism was "steadfastness and zeal" and "a passion for souls." He stated, "We need not be troubled about these matters so long as we keep busy, bend our energies and give our money, looking to the advancement of the cause and the coming of the Kingdom."[86] In order to make the same point, the *Baptist Advance* of February 28, 1924 printed a Moody Bible Institute cartoon in which seven aspects of "the faith which was once delivered unto the saints" were contrasted with "Modernist theology." Between these two theologies a chasm was placed, indicating that there was "no middle ground" between the two. The editor's caption summed up the posited relationship between the Campaign and the situation illustrated by the cartoon: "SEVEN GREAT FUNDAMENTAL BIBLE TRUTHS THAT ARE BEING PREACHED AROUND THE WORLD THROUGH THE 75 MILLION CAMPAIGN WHICH ARE REASONS WHY ALL OF US SHOULD PAY OUR PLEDGES."[87] A dollar given to the Seventy-Five Million Campaign was a dollar given to the support of right doctrine in an age of apostasy.

If Scarborough incorporated the defense of sound doctrine into the identity of the Southern Baptist Convention, he also incorporated support for the activities of the SBC into his definition of sound doctrine. In an attempt to turn the tables on J. Frank Norris, Scarborough defined cooperation as a Baptist doctrine, as important as any other "fundamental" doctrine. In the process, Scarborough set up the second element in the emerging Southern Baptist synthesis.

As early as November 1921, Scarborough was willing to say, "If men go separately and do not work together, or if churches go independent of each other in this movement for the world's redemption, they violate the most sacred doctrine of Christ's teaching and imperil the whole program of Jesus Christ. This doctrine of co-operation is a fundamental doctrine. The progress of doctrines depends on the doctrine of co-operation; and disloyalty to this doctrine of co-operation is the most vicious and menacing disloyalty in the program of Jesus Christ."[88] Later that year, Scarborough repeated this opinion before the gathered Baptist General Convention of

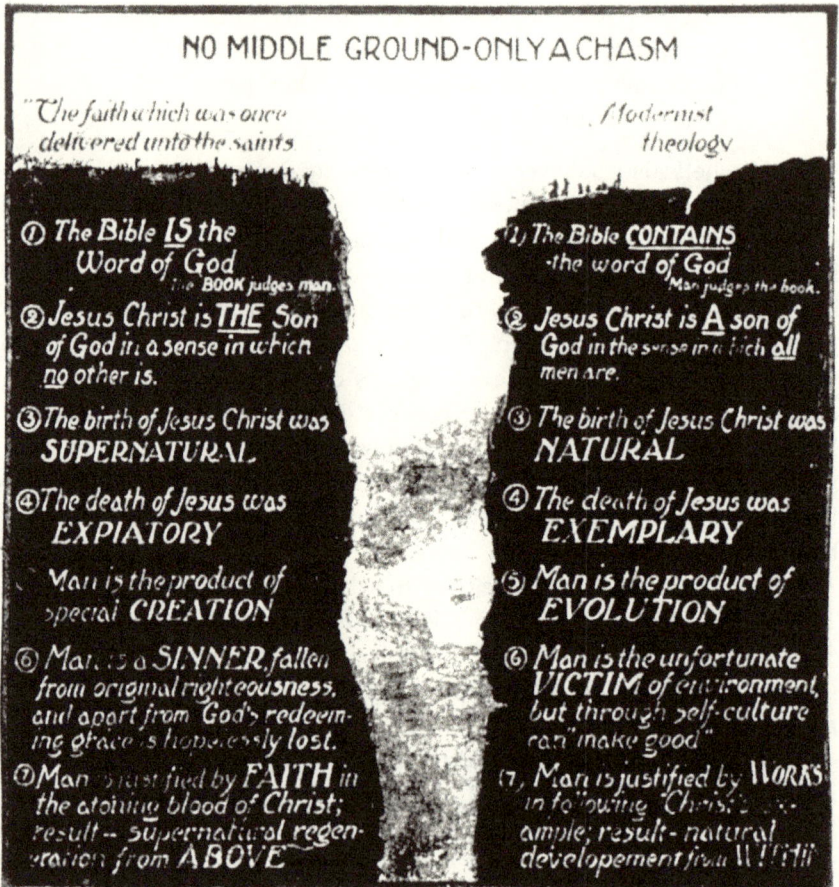

NO MIDDLE GROUND—ONLY A CHASM

"The faith which was once delivered unto the saints"

Modernist theology

① The Bible IS the Word of God
The BOOK judges man.

② Jesus Christ is THE Son of God in a sense in which no other is.

③ The birth of Jesus Christ was SUPERNATURAL

④ The death of Jesus was EXPIATORY

⑤ Man is the product of special CREATION

⑥ Man is a SINNER, fallen from original righteousness, and apart from God's redeeming grace is hopelessly lost.

⑦ Man is justified by FAITH in the atoning blood of Christ; result—supernatural regeneration from ABOVE

① The Bible CONTAINS the word of God
Man judges the book.

② Jesus Christ is A son of God in the sense in which all men are.

③ The birth of Jesus Christ was NATURAL

④ The death of Jesus was EXEMPLARY

⑤ Man is the product of EVOLUTION

⑥ Man is the unfortunate VICTIM of environment, but through self-culture can "make good"

⑦ Man is justified by WORKS in following "Christ's example; result—natural development from WITHIN

The front page of the February 28, 1924, *Baptist Advance* (detail). When this cartoon appeared in the November 15, 1923, edition of the *Advance*, it was attributed to the "Moody Institute," even though the organization's full name is Moody Bible Institute. Permission to reprint graciously provided by Arkansas Baptist Newsmagazine, Inc.

92

BAPTIST ADVANCE

FOR CHRIST, THE CHURCHES AND CO-OPERATION

Volume XXIII.　　　　LITTLE ROCK, ARKANSAS, FEBRUARY 28, 1924.　　　　Number 9

Preaching for Preachers to Preach

* * *

SEVEN GREAT FUNDAMEN-
TAL BIBLE TRUTHS THAT
ARE BEING PREACHED
AROUND THE WORLD
THROUGH THE 75 MILLION
CAMPAIGN WHICH ARE
REASONS WHY ALL OF US
SHOULD PAY OUR PLEDGES.

NO MIDDLE GROUND-ONLY A CHASM

"The faith which was once delivered unto the saints."　　　Modernist theology

① The Bible IS the Word of God.　　　The Bible CONTAINS the word of God

② Jesus Christ is THE Son of God in a sense in which no other is.　　　Jesus Christ is A son of God in the same sense in which all men are.

③ The birth of Jesus Christ was SUPERNATURAL.　　　The birth of Jesus Christ was NATURAL.

④ The death of Jesus was EXPIATORY.　　　The death of Jesus was EXEMPLARY.

⑤ Man is the product of special CREATION.　　　Man is the product of EVOLUTION.

⑥ Man is a SINNER, fallen from original righteousness, and apart from God's redemptive grace is utterly lost.　　　Man is the unfortunate VICTIM of environment but through self culture is ever rising.

⑦ Man is saved by FAITH in the atoning blood of Christ, resulting in supernatural regeneration from ABOVE.　　　Man is justified by WORKS which result in ethical development from within.

Preachers, Preach this Preaching!

$1,550,000 Added to Baptist Denominational Property in Arkansas in a Little Over Four Years of Campaign!

ABOVE ALL DEBTS, $1,550,000 IN CLEAR-CUT GAINS IN NEW BUILDINGS, ENDOWMENT AND EQUIPMENT HAS BEEN ADDED TO PERMANENT PROPERTY AND POSSESSIONS OF THE BAPTIST DENOMINATION IN ARKANSAS SINCE THE 75 MILLION CAMPAIGN WAS LAUNCHED! READ THESE MOST GLORIOUSLY ENCOURAGING ITEMS:

THERE HAVE BEEN ADDED TO:

1. OUACHITA COLLEGE—		4. MOUNTAIN SCHOOLS	150,000
(1) Property and Equipment	$ 240,000	5. HOSPITALS	325,000
(2) Endowment (actually paid or ready to be drawn upon right now)	375,000	6. ORPHANS' HOME (estimated)	15,000
		7. CALEDONIA ACADEMY	15,000
2. CENTRAL COLLEGE—		8. BEQUEST	55,000
Property and Endowment	165,000	9. ASSEMBLY GROUNDS (above obligations)	15,000
3. JONESBORO COLLEGE—			
(Deeded to Home Mission Board)	195,000	Total	$1,550,000

NOTE.—$238,000 would pay all obligations against all these institutions except our two hospitals. Our hospital property is worth more than $325,000. We have reckoned it worth that above all obligations.

THUS $1,550,000 (NET) IN UNENCUMBERED PROPERTY HAS BEEN ADDED TO BAPTIST DENOMINATIONAL INSTITUTIONS IN ARKANSAS IN THE FOUR YEARS OF THE 75 MILLION CAMPAIGN! HOW THIS GLORIOUS NEWS OUGHT TO ENCOURAGE US TO PAY OUR PLEDGES!"

"LET THE PEOPLE KNOW!"　　　　　　J. S. ROGERS, General Secretary.

The front page of the February 28, 1924, *Baptist Advance*, showing the juxtaposition of Seventy-Five Million Campaign promotional material with anti-Modernist material from Moody Bible Institute. Permission to reprint graciously provided by Arkansas Baptist Newsmagazine, Inc.

Texas. "There is not only danger in heretical teachings in theology and in ecclesiology, but there is danger of heresy being taught and practiced in non-co-operation as well. I believe that there is a doctrine of co-operation. . . . It is fundamental, too. . . . It is a doctrine of co-operation in the divine mind."[89]

The fullest expression of Scarborough's thoughts on this matter, however, were laid out in a 1922 article, syndicated to the various Southern Baptist newspapers, titled "Is Cooperation a New Testament Doctrine?" In this article, Scarborough noted that Christian liberties are "all . . . within the circle of Christ's eternal and sovereign Lordship." Just as Christ commanded all Christians to be baptized after conversion, he also commands all Christians to cooperate in the church's work in the world: "Can a church member refuse to join with his fellow church members in a plain command of Christ in carrying the gospel to all the world and justly plead alibi and a justifiable defense and exemption on the ground of his freedom and personal liberties? This is anarchy in Christ's kingdom." By the same token, churches that failed to cooperate with other churches were "worse than dead." This was the practical application of Mullins's "consensus of the competent," whipped into a frenzy by a rash of radical Fundamentalist criticism and the stress of a failing fundraising campaign.[90] Like Mullins, Scarborough believed that unwillingness to cooperate with other Christians and churches for the sake of the extension of the Kingdom was a sign of spiritual weakness.

Unlike Mullins, however, Scarborough wanted to give the doctrine of cooperation unprecedented recognition. While Scarborough battled Norris in Texas, a group of Northern and Southern Baptists was toying with the idea of framing and releasing a joint confession of faith. The effort eventually failed, but the idea of a confession of faith wafting through the air caught Scarborough's attention.[91] Noting that no existing Baptist (or Anabaptist) confession of faith included the "doctrine of cooperation," the seminary president suggested that the new confession include a nineteenth article enjoining denominational participation.[92] While admitting that no one should cooperate with "any movement that clearly seeks to dethrone Christ, vitiate His teachings, or emasculate His churches," Scarborough wanted to draw a clear line between "our cooperant and cooperating individuals and churches and those who oppose, hinder, criticize and block the mighty missionary, education and benevolent program of our people." Exasperated by his conflict with Norris, Scarborough was ready to label non-cooperation as heresy formally, no less than the denial of any other cardinal doctrine.

94

Editorial response to Scarborough's suggestion was mixed. Some editors affirmed the importance of cooperation while expressing skepticism toward the idea of writing it into a confession of faith. The editor of the Louisiana *Baptist Message* commended Scarborough's article to his audience but admitted that he was "a little dubious that the writer has gone a whit too far."[93] More pungently, V. I. Masters noted that he was "firmly for co-operation, but not with a club."[94] Other observers, however, welcomed Scarborough's contention with open arms. One Texas Baptist, writing in the *Baptist Standard*, agreed, "Co-operation brings a rich grace, while non co-operation is a deadly heresy."[95] The most enthusiastic response, however, probably came from J. S. Compere, the editor of the Arkansas *Baptist Advance*. Working amid still-painful memories of the Bogard crisis, Compere offered his unqualified approval:

> Dr. Scarborough has recently written an article on "The Heresy of Non-Co-operation" and he said last Thursday that he believes any Baptist who refuses to co-operate in the work in which his church in engaged is not a sound Baptist. The editor of the Advance has been saying for a long time that a Baptist has no more right to refuse to co-operate in Baptist work than he has to get drunk or commit adultery. Dr. Truett said he would as soon be numbered with those who get drunk and reel on the streets as to be numbered with those who break the fellowship of Baptists or cause them to refuse to co-operate. . . . If a new Baptist confession of faith is to be formulated (as it seems that there will be) we believe an article on co-operation should be included in the confession. We believe no Baptist should be considered sound or in good standing if he refuses to co-operate in the work of Baptists.[96]

More than a year later, Compere's attitude had not changed. Those who "make a big noise" about their orthodoxy without giving to their denomination's cooperative efforts were an "abomination in God's sight."[97]

Editors and other observers may have had mixed feelings about Scarborough's assertion that denominational cooperation was a "fundamental," but they all seem to have participated in the publicity program through which they sought to convince Southern Baptists that cooperation with the Southern Baptist Convention was as crucial to true Baptist faith as was belief in the inspiration of the scriptures. Often labeled a program of "Information and Inspiration," the efforts of Southern Baptist leaders to garner support for the Seventy-Five Million Campaign rested heavily on the efforts of the Southern Baptist newspaper editors whose job it was to provide information to Baptists who would then necessarily be "inspired" or "enlisted" by this information.[98] Baptists so inspired or enlisted would, in turn, offer financial support to the Campaign. In addition, Southern Baptist leaders appropriated gatherings such as associational meetings, revivals, and Sunday worship services as venues in which the Campaign should be promoted. The framing of the Campaign as an object worthy to be juxtaposed with acts of evangelism, exhortation, and doctrinal teaching helped to solidify cooperation's status as a "fundamental" doctrine.

Southern Baptist leaders began musing in print about the importance of the state Baptist newspapers very soon after Victory Week ended. E. Y. Mullins himself averred that "the most fatal of our present-day weaknesses is our failure to support our denominational press. . . . Until we solve this problem we will fail to solve the others. If we remain weak here we will remain weak elsewhere."[99] In a congregationally oriented denomination whose members were relatively poor and whose pastors were largely uneducated and bivocational, leaders saw that the chief obstacle to the Campaign's success was poor communication between the Nashville leadership and the common pastors and laypeople. They almost universally embraced increased support and emphasis upon the state Baptist newspaper as a remedy. A number of these papers were already the property of the various state conventions, and after Victory Week a number of other state conventions bought their respective papers as well, placing privately owned papers in a small minority.[100]

A few observers objected to this trend, wondering aloud how state convention-owned newspapers could ever retain an ability to criticize those organizations when necessary, but theirs was a voice crying in the wilderness.[101] In the new Progressive Southern Baptist Convention, leaders increasingly took it for granted that the place of the newspaper was to articulate the goals of the various state conventions and those of the SBC, forming pastors and laypeople into loyal supporters of the program.[102] One writer in *The Baptist Record* claimed, "For the layman to be in sympathy with the kingdom movements he must have the information contained in his denominational paper. For him to follow the right kind of pastoral leadership he must have this information. For him to develop into a well-rounded Christian he must have it."[103] E. Y. Mullins offered more detail but made roughly the same point:

> We ought to be patient and careful and discriminating in working out our problems. This need is based upon the nature of a

96

religious democracy. We can only solve our problems slowly, because every solution rests upon conviction and not upon authority. We must create the necessary conviction. Again, a religious democracy depends greatly upon wise leadership, by reason of the fact that it has no ecclesiastical authority. As I have so often said, the power of the denominational press, in a religious democracy, is simply incalculable for good or evil. More than any other agency, "ye editors" and the correspondents and writers of articles bear the burden of responsibility in leadership.[104]

Mullins believed that Baptist democracy could only function if the consciences of messengers to state and national conventions had been rightly formed by their ecclesiastical betters.[105] The "consensus of the competent" rose directly from the convictions of Christians participating in the Baptist democratic process, but Mullins and other leaders realized that wise use of the denominational press created those convictions necessary for the continued functioning of Southern Baptist denominational machinery. Thus, the decisions of Baptist bodies could be fully democratic even while reflecting the strong influence of Convention leadership operating through Baptist publications. Tellingly, Mullins hoped that Baptist newspapers would help prepare messengers for upcoming Convention meetings by providing them with a "digest of important matters" prepared by the Executive Committee.[106]

Newspapers were not the only media leaders used to promote the Seventy-Five Million Campaign and other Convention activities. They also asked preachers to mention Convention programs during sermons at revivals, associational meetings, and weekly worship services. Scarborough himself, in an article intended to promote a "soul-winning campaign" as an adjunct to the struggling Seventy-Five Million Campaign, reminded his readers about those things that should take place at any Southern Baptist revival. Scarborough noted that in addition to emphasizing prayer and appropriate training for workers, the preachers should stress the importance of the denomination's activities. Every revival should set aside "a denominational day in which the whole program of Baptists is set out in the spirit of evangelism." Scarborough also wanted preachers to stress the "doctrines of stewardship and tithing" and to "get subscriptions for our Baptist papers." In fact, Scarborough thought that every new convert baptized at one of these revivals "should be enlisted in the 75 Million Campaign and a two years' subscription should be secured from him during the meeting in which he is saved."[107]

Editors and other leaders joined Scarborough in calling for the promotion of denominational goals in settings traditionally intended for worship, evangelism, and doctrinal instruction. The editor of the *Western Recorder* believed that the associational meeting, already an "intensely missionary" gathering, should be a place where "missionary information" and "missionary inspiration" are offered to all participants. Furthermore, as in Scarborough's portrait of a perfect revival, the Kentucky editor believed associational meetings should be places where "some one should present the claims of the Recorder and a number of our people concern themselves in securing subscribers. In all our acquaintance, we do not know a man or woman who is earnestly interested in our mission work who does not read a religious paper."[108] Recruiting subscribers for the newspapers was missionary work, because these newspapers were the most important means of gathering support for missions.[109] The gatherings of individual congregations were also viewed as an opportunity for program promotion. John Sampey, future president of Louisville's Southern Baptist Theological Seminary, wrote, "Pastors should refer frequently in sermon and in private conversation to our missionary and educational programs. We should preach and teach missions as we have never done before." Even more, Sampey believed that new subscribers should receive congregational recognition, and that churches "would do good to have a testimony meeting as to the value of the campaign in promoting the spiritual life."[110]

By 1925, Southern Baptists had become accustomed to hearing the doctrine of cooperation preached and taught alongside other "fundamental" doctrines. Revivals, associational meetings, and Sunday sermons became means of mass communication between the denomination and its constituents, and Baptist newspapers defended SBC programs as stridently as they warned about the dangers of Modernist heresy. Editors may have been squeamish about labeling cooperation a "New Testament doctrine," but it seems they were willing to treat it as such. Many preachers and pastors doubtless followed the advice of their denominational leaders and did the same thing. As a result, this second part of Scarborough's newly synthesized identity for the Southern Baptist Convention became as firmly ensconced in the denominational consciousness as the first—the idea that the SBC itself was a bulwark against Modernistic doctrine, disproving the need for any outside organization to serve this function. When the denomination chose to adopt an official confession of faith in the middle of the decade, they would approve a document that reflected these two ideas.

The Baptist Faith and Message:
A New Identity for Southern Baptists

As Southern Baptists attempted to cope with both the imminent failure of the Seventy-Five Million Campaign and the quandary of Fundamentalism, they also dealt with the distinct problem of evolution as an explanation of human origins. Some editors such as R. H. Pitt, L. L. Gwaltney, and Livingston Johnson cautiously tolerated those Christian science teachers who were persuaded of the theory's legitimacy, while others, most especially V. I. Masters and C. P. Stealey, saw evolution as an intolerable form of Modernism.[111] The very public debate over the theory, stoked by attacks from Norris and William Bell Riley, became so heated by the 1924 meeting of the Southern Baptist Convention that many messengers clamored for a resolution roundly repudiating evolution. E. Y. Mullins was only able to redeem the situation by suggesting that a committee be formed to frame a confession of faith that would be considered at the next meeting of the SBC.[112]

The fireworks surrounding the following year's discussion of the resulting document revolved around the disagreement between two members of the committee: C. P. Stealey, editor of the Oklahoma *Baptist Messenger* and staunch antievolutionist, and Mullins himself. While Mullins had avoided any direct reference to evolution in the document, a revision of the New Hampshire Confession of Faith, Stealey insisted that the article on "The Fall of Man" be modified to include such a reference. After an intense debate on the floor, Stealey's amendment failed, and the *Baptist Faith and Message* was adopted as originally offered.[113]

Mullins and Stealey were only two members of a seven-person committee, however, and their worries about explicitly mentioning evolution were not the only concerns that shaped the finished product. The committee also included L. R. Scarborough, and an inspection of the 1925 confession reveals that the seminary president incorporated his own denominational concerns into the document. In fact, the 1925 *Baptist Faith and Message* could easily be described as a codification of the "Scarborough Synthesis."

In articles written to discuss the *Baptist Faith and Message* to readers in the wake of its adoption, Scarborough described the document as accomplishing both of the tasks that jointly constituted the new identity that he had framed for his denomination over the course of the Seventy-Five Million Campaign and the tussle with J. Frank Norris. First, Scarborough believed the document proved that Southern Baptists were united theologically and that the denomination itself was able to police its own doctrinal boundaries. Scarborough promised his readers that the "document now approved and recommended by the Southern Baptist Convention" made "definite, constructive statements of our belief on the following great doctrines–the inspiration of the Bible; the virgin birth, the deity, holy life, atoning death, bodily resurrection and personal return of the Lord Jesus Christ. . . . No Modernist can accept any of these doctrines."[114] Framed by the Convention's best minds and approved by the gathered body, the document represented the theology of the entire Convention and did not simply reflect the views of a noisy Fundamentalist minority.[115] Scarborough also sought to steady Southern Baptist nerves regarding evolution. Although the Convention did not explicitly mention evolution in the *Baptist Faith and Message*, it did include a separate statement about science and religion that rejected the theory. In discussing this approach to defusing the evolution controversy, Scarborough noted that Dr. R. A. Torrey, the well-known Fundamentalist leader, had told him that the Convention's statement on science and religion "ought to satisfy any Fundamentalist in the world."[116] Scarborough also implied that the new articles of faith of the infant Eastern Baptist Theological Seminary were comparable in language and strength to the *Baptist Faith and Message*. The new confession, along with the denomination whose theology it represented, was up to moderate Fundamentalist standards. The new confession proved that it was possible in the South to accomplish the doctrinal ends of the Fundamentalist movement without resorting to radical Fundamentalist methods.

The *Baptist Faith and Message* itself revealed the other plank of the "Scarborough Synthesis": the insistence that denominational cooperation was a "New Testament doctrine." Although the document was based on the New Hampshire Confession, the committee had added several articles covering topics not included in the original document. Two of these, articles on "Stewardship" and "Co-Operation," reflect the same viewpoint on these subjects that Scarborough had advocated throughout the Campaign. When the latter of these two articles notes that "members of New Testament churches should co-operate with each other, and the churches themselves should co-operate with each other in carrying forward the missionary, educational, and benevolent program for the extension of Christ's Kingdom," it echoes the basic outline of Scarborough's article "Is Cooperation a New Testament Doctrine?"[117] Scarborough's insistence that cooperation was a fundamental doctrine of the faith, originally viewed by many Southern Baptists as idiosyncratic, had found its way into the denomination's first confession of faith.

Scarborough was not shy about announcing the meaning of the article's inclusion. Describing those Fundamentalists dissatisfied with the new confession, Scarborough noted that they "do not want a settlement but only an issue. . . . You cannot satisfy these men. They are obsessed. They have a brain spasm. They are opposed to the articles of faith the Convention has approved" because "it contains an article on New Testament Cooperation."[118] The *Baptist Faith and Message*, then, was designed to exclude Modernists on the left and radical Fundamentalists on the right, leaving in the middle "orthodox, evangelistic, working Baptists." While the Convention was otherwise engaged, Scarborough slipped his own idea of what Southern Baptists ought to be into their new confession of faith.

The Challenge of Fundamentalism

In 1919, J. B. Gambrell, the president of the Southern Baptist Convention, asked "whether for this hour and this opportunity the 7,000,000 American Baptists–white, black, yellow, Northern, Southern–all of us–can not get together on a distinctive Baptist program and put out our united strength, then, through existing Baptist organizations, to make Christ's Great Commission effective around the world."[119] Gambrell, who claimed that "it is nothing to me whether a Baptist lives in the North or the South," would have been disappointed in the denominational developments that followed his death in 1921.[120]

Southern Baptist leaders struggled with evolution during the early 1920s, but they also attempted to cope simultaneously with financial difficulties stemming from the failure of the Seventy-Five Million Campaign and political turbulence rippling from the doctrinal controversies rumbling among Northern Baptists. Theologically conservative themselves, Southern Baptist leaders openly affirmed the doctrinal contentions of moderate Northern Fundamentalists but feared the divisive tactics that characterized the more radical Fundamentalists who formed the Baptist Bible Union in 1922. Already at the end of their financial rope, Southern Baptist leaders were unwilling to embrace those Fundamentalists who had already publicized their willingness to withdraw financial support from denominational programs and to encourage others to do the same. That the loudest advocate of this more divisive form of Fundamentalism, J. Frank Norris, was based in Texas and focused his criticism on Texas institutions made it inevitable that the task of refuting him would fall to a fellow Texan. Southwestern Seminary president L. R. Scarborough rose to the challenge, successfully averting a major schism in Texas Baptist life but confounding in the process his role as anti-Fundamentalist polemicist with his more formal appointment as General Director of the Seventy-Five Million Campaign. As a result, Scarborough's anti-Fundamentalist fulminations seeped into articles written in support of the Campaign and printed throughout the South, spreading a suspicion of Fundamentalism throughout the entire Convention.

By that time, the phrase "Southern Baptist" no longer described a regional but otherwise indistinct branch of a larger American religious phenomenon. Instead, the phrase had begun to designate an emerging tradition whose leaders had married the structures of their denomination so tightly to their definition of orthodoxy that they could almost describe participation in that denomination as a means of grace.[121] When Martin Marty described the Southern Baptist Convention as the "Catholic Church of the South," his phrase might have come close to capturing the dream articulated by Scarborough and other Southern Baptist leaders during the early 1920s.[122]

Fundamentalism was not the only challenge that Southern Baptist leaders faced during the Seventy-Five Million Campaign, however. Many Baptists failed to participate either out of ignorance or out of motives that were more reminiscent of John Taylor than J. Frank Norris. As a result, leaders found themselves attempting to motivate Southern Baptists to give through a variety of methods. Nonparticipating Baptists were stigmatized and threatened in the Baptist press while more cooperative pastors and laypeople were rewarded through public praise. In both cases, Southern Baptist leaders were groping for a way to exercise meaningful leadership over a burgeoning denomination of churches that insisted on maintaining a non-coercive polity. The next chapter will more fully explore how Southern Baptist leaders attempted to balance Baptist congregational polity with the Progressive impulse toward centralized control.

4

Carrots and Sticks: Reward and Coercion
in the Seventy-Five Million Campaign

The Seventy-Five Million Campaign was conceived on a grander scale than any Southern Baptist denominational movement had been before. Baptists pledged more than ninety million dollars to the Campaign, and denominational leaders, impressed by the enthusiasm with which the program was conducted, seem to have assumed that the entire amount pledged would be paid gladly and on time. J. W. Porter, editor of the *Western Recorder*, made this explicit during the Campaign's first phase. When a "good brother" mentioned to Porter that organizations such as the Anti-Saloon League always needed to write off a significant number of the pledges made to them and that Southern Baptists would eventually need to do the same, Porter confidently replied, "In our case the subscriptions were made directly to the Lord's work. And though it is true that every debt is binding, it is also true that a peculiar sanctity attaches to a debt that is due to God. . . . In our judgment it manifests a sad lack of confidence in our brethren to even suppose, for a moment, that they will not meet their thrice sacred obligations. For our part we shall never believe they will default until the close of the five-year period shows a deficit."[1] The way in which denominational officials moved to appropriate Campaign monies even before they had materialized showed that Porter was not alone in deeming the Campaign pledges reliable. Livingston Johnson noted in the *Biblical Recorder* that beneficiaries of Campaign funds in North Carolina had, in some cases, "contracted obligations as if the whole of the five-year pledges" were already available.[2] Mission workers across the state refused to reduce their requests for funds even when asked, resulting in mission appropriations far greater than the amount that leaders could reasonably have expected.[3] The apparent success of the Campaign led to a rash of spending that threatened to bury Southern Baptist denominational work underneath a mountain of debt.

Unfortunately, the years following the Great War did not bring un-mitigated prosperity. The close of hostilities brought economic depres-sion to the United States, and low cotton prices hurt farmers of the still-agricultural South. A number of Southern Baptists seem to have pledged in the heat of post-war excitement more than they were later willing to pay, while many rural Southern Baptists seem never to have expressed any interest in the Campaign in the first place. As a result, funds trick-led in to the coffers of the Campaign at a rate far too slow to sustain the spending of Southern Baptist institutions.

In response, Southern Baptist leaders, recognizing the need to create "a tender, honest, religious conscience . . . on the matter of paying these pledges," turned to a number of methods as they attempted to encour-age pastors and laypeople to support the Campaign.[4] Although leaders had attempted to reward and coerce pastors and church members even during the period leading up to Victory Week, the financial crisis that loomed during the later years of the Campaign made these attempts more frequent and more acute, despite the difficulties inherent in Baptist polity. Hemmed in by a ferociously guarded tradition of congregational auton-omy and therefore unable to reward or discipline wayward preachers and laypeople directly, leaders sought indirect means of denominational influ-ence. Baptists who buttressed the embattled movement by paying pledges and encouraging others to do the same were rewarded by being publicly commended in the Baptist press or by being promised various material and spiritual benefits. On the other hand, Southern Baptist leaders tried to convince uncooperative Baptists to participate using a wide variety of co-ercive methods intended to "haunt a man and drive sleep from his pillow if he fails when he could pay."[5] Pastors who opposed the Campaign met suggestions that their employment be terminated, while laypeople faced abusive language, threats of church discipline, and intimations that they were attracting the wrath of God, a displeasure that might bear frighten-ing eternal implications.

Reward and Coercion: Why They Matter

The growing tendency among Southern Baptist leaders to use systems of reward and coercion during the Seventy-Five Million Campaign is sugges-tive on its own. Viewed in the light of Baptist tendencies toward bureau-cratization during this period, however, these inclinations point toward

Carrots and Sticks

the increasing centralization of the Southern Baptist Convention during the third decade of the twentieth century.

Bureaucracy emerges as a method of administering rationally justified rules or laws fairly among a group of people too large to be dealt with on an informal, personal level.[6] While bureaucracies tend to control their employees by applying systems of reward, providing their employees with prestige, social standing, and a regular, fixed income, bureaucracies tend to enforce their rules and laws upon outsiders using coercion.[7] It is important to note that coercion need not be physical; it can also take "sacerdotal" forms.[8]

Since bureaucracies require a steady flow of cash in order to reward their employees, the development of bureaucracy presupposes a "money economy" and a "stable system of taxation."[9] Additionally, because bureaucracies are responsible for administering the rules or laws of a given organization, enforcing the laws of taxation naturally falls within a bureaucracy's circle of responsibilities. Bureaucrats, then, help raise their own salaries by enforcing the rules that channel funds into their sponsoring organizations.

During the Seventy-Five Million Campaign, Southern Baptist leaders began to speak about the Convention and its people in ways that showed they had adopted a bureaucratic model of church polity. First, editors and other leaders began to assume that pastors and laypeople were, in at least a limited sense, obligated to the denomination and subject to the direction of Convention leaders. In a discussion of J. Frank Norris's claim that a number of Baptists would soon abandon their home denominations in a "bull moose bolt," the editor of the *Florida Baptist Witness* bemoaned the fact that a man like Norris could set himself against the SBC when he "gets his living out of the denomination."[10] While Norris was no saint, the fact that Editor Mitchell could identify a local church pastor, paid by his own congregation, as one living off the largesse of the denomination shows that Baptist church polity, at least in one editor's mind, was undergoing significant revision. Mitchell revealed a similar attitude when he castigated churches for carrying inadequate fire insurance on their buildings: "The edifice of a Baptist church, ethically speaking, belongs to the Baptist denomination. The local church worshipping in the edifice has legal possession of the property, and is responsible for the property. . . . In a very real sense the church using such a property is simply the representative of the denomination, and its members would have no moral or ethical right

105

to sell such property and to pocket the money."[11] In Mitchell's hands, congregational autonomy had become a legal technicality. Ethically, the local church was now a denominational franchise.

Denominational leaders also emphatically rejected the idea that contributions to the Seventy-Five Million Campaign were donations or gifts.[12] Instead, leaders claimed that payments on pledges represented the discharge of an obligation variously described as a debt, a tax, or rent. Z. T. Cody, editor of *The Baptist Courier*, quoted with obvious approbation the words of a woman who had been hard pressed to pay her doctor following a trip to the hospital: "I think it is just as important to borrow money to pay our pledges to the 75 Million Campaign as to borrow money to pay doctor's and hospital bills."[13] In light of news that some Baptists facing financial difficulty were not planning to pay their pledges, Cody made a similar point in a later editorial, claiming that "the pledges are a recognition of dues rather than from a mere charity motive. This completes their identity with debts. They can be put in no other class."[14] Thinking along similar lines, Livingston Johnson of the *Biblical Recorder* compared the honoring of Campaign pledges to the payment of rent. "If our people could only realize their solemn duty as stewards of the Lord, and that he is Landlord He should receive His rent before any other claims are met, there would be no doubt in the world about our paying every penny of our pledges this year."[15] When viewed in light of the less-than-pleasant relationship that many poor Southern farmers endured with their creditors and landlords, these comparisons take on a slightly sinister hue.

Perhaps the most striking comparison made by those emphasizing the obligatory nature of Campaign pledges was that made between pledges and taxes. "The State requires of each of its citizens a certain per cent of his possessions as taxes to maintain the government, and the citizen, knowing that that amount must be paid, puts it aside for that purpose. If a citizen of heaven were to deal as fairly by the Lord as he does by his State, he would set aside a certain per cent of his income for the cause of Christ, and would not take that into account for any other purpose."[16] Editors and other leaders did not often juxtapose the Campaign with government taxation; critics of the Campaign would invoke the idea of taxation much more often than would denominational officials.[17] Still, that editors were willing to hint at taxation as a model for denominational finance reveals their increasing tendency to view the denomination in bureaucratic terms.

106

The Peculiar Shape of Southern Baptist Bureaucratization: A Historiographical Note

American Protestant denominations of all stripes tended toward centralization during the early decades of the twentieth century, from the radically congregational Churches of Christ to the Episcopal Church.[18] In this sense, Southern Baptists were indistinguishable from their competitors. At the same time, however, the influence of the Fundamentalist controversy shaped the direction of the bureaucratization process in those denominations that it affected. In his book *Yet Saints Their Watch Are Keeping: Fundamentalists, Modernists, and the Development of Evangelical Ecclesiology, 1887–1937*, author J. Michael Utzinger describes how the Fundamentalist controversy reacted to and was driven by the movement toward centralization.

The second half of Utzinger's text revolves around several key assertions. First, Utzinger notes that the movement toward denominational centralization provoked denominational conflict within the Northern Baptist, Northern Presbyterian, and Disciples of Christ denominations because conservatives believed (with some justification) that the new structures were administered by and served the interests of Modernists. As a result, Fundamentalists attempted to organize themselves in order to exercise some control over denominational institutions, such as mission boards and seminaries, which they believed had fallen into Modernist hands through newly created denominational bureaucracies.[19]

Second, the author shows that the tension between conservatives and liberals within these denominations became acute due to the denominational financial crises precipitated by the failure of the Interchurch World Movement. Because loans underwritten by several mainline denominations had financed the IWM, its collapse placed denominational leaders in the unenviable position of having to divert funds from denominational budgets to amortize loans used to launch the defunct organization. Utzinger claims that the financial pinch that followed this turn of events forced previously coexisting parties to begin competing for funds, creating conflict between Modernists and Fundamentalists.[20]

Third, Utzinger finds that the two-party model that scholars have traditionally used to explain the Fundamentalist controversies fails to consider the multitude of generally conservative but irenic and denominationally supportive clergy and laypeople who were more interested in preserving the structures of their denomination than in pressing a particular theological agenda. The author claims that the compromises that eventually settled the conflicts succeeded because moderate Modernists, moderate Fundamentalists, and this third "party" of denominational loyalists were able to hammer out solutions that preserved denominational structures while leaving consciences free.[21]

Among Northern Baptists, the 1919 formation of a "Board of Promotion" significantly modified Northern Baptist polity by creating an organization responsible for collecting contributions from churches and parsing them out to schools, mission boards, and other denominational organizations.[22] Nascent Fundamentalists were immediately suspicious when the Board was placed in charge of collecting and distributing the anticipated one hundred million dollars to be gathered by the Northern Baptist New World Movement, because one-third of the money was going to educational institutions. If it was bad that institutions like Crozer and the University of Chicago taught heterodox doctrine, it was even worse that the denomination had established a finance program that virtually required support of those schools as a condition of denominational participation.[23] Importantly, the program that Fundamentalists provided at their pre-Convention conferences rarely focused on individuals and churches, but on denominational institutions. Fundamentalists were willing to allow other Baptists to worship and believe as they chose, but they were unwilling to allow Modernists, through their increasing influence within the denomination's still-new hierarchy, to use conservative money to advance Modernist ends.[24]

After years of doctrinal wrangling and parliamentary maneuvering, Northern Baptists hammered out a compromise that set no doctrinal parameters beyond defining baptism as the "immersion of believers."[25] Excluding extreme Modernists and radical Fundamentalists, by 1926 the Northern Baptist Convention had succeeded in putting the Fundamentalist controversy behind it for the sake of missions, but only at the cost of unofficially banishing theological language and reasoning from its discourse at the national level. Paul Harrison noted the persistence of this phenomenon thirty years later when he wrote that "leaders [within the bureaucracy of the American Baptist Convention] . . . must maintain a theological neutrality. . . . An administrator is not a theologian, and religious belief must remain an adjunct to the attainment of the goals which he has been directed to achieve."[26]

The way doctrinal conflict influenced the institutional development of the Disciples of Christ had even direr consequences. Although the conservatives of the Disciples of Christ were not (strictly speaking) Fundamen-

talists, they began during the early twentieth century to show some genuine affinities for their counterparts in other denominations. The *Christian
Standard*, the newspaper around which they rallied, carried articles by
William Jennings Bryan, positive mentions of the World Christian Fundamentals Association, and at least one advertisement for the Scofield
Reference Bible.[27] By the same token, Progressives within the Disciples
of Christ were in many ways indistinguishable from Modernists active
in other denominations. In fact, Progressive Disciples helped lead the
early development of the Divinity School at the University of Chicago.[28] Between these two groups was a large number of "moderate restoration-
ists," committed to the "Restoration plea" but equally supportive of the denomination's emerging bureaucratic structures as the necessary means
for putting the plea into action.[29]

When the denomination's International Convention, only recently authorized to conduct the denomination's business, considered consolidat-
ing a number of the denomination's organizations into a United Christian
Missionary Society for the sake of streamlining fundraising efforts, conservatives balked almost immediately.[30] One conservative pastor associated the proposed organization with the Progressive Campbell Institute,
claiming that the creation of the UCMS would necessarily deepen the
already-disproportionate influence that Institute members held over Disciples institutions. After the UCMS became a reality in 1919, the debate
surrounding it only became more acrimonious when some conservatives
claimed that missionaries of the Society practiced "open membership"
in their churches in Asia, allowing new Christians to join their churches
without being baptized by immersion. While Progressive Disciples already
affirmed the practice of open membership, conservatives adhering to
what they considered to be a strict application of restorationism principles
found it unacceptable. Although whether and to what extent missionaries
actually welcomed unimmersed members into their churches remained
unclear, the Society's Board of Managers sought a compromise solution in
which missionaries were asked not to practice open membership but were
allowed to freely retain their own opinions in the matter.[31]

Predictably, conservatives found such a solution, imposed by the leaders of the UCMS rather than created on the floor of the Convention, intolerable. Not only did they interpret the action of the Board of Managers
as a smokescreen meant to protect the practice of open membership and
the Progressives that promoted it, but they also rejected constant "calls
for unity in organization . . . in spite of diversity of belief on cardinal

109

doctrines."[32] As in the case of the Northern Baptist Convention, denominational leaders had sought to hold the Disciples together by making theology a matter of private opinion.

In this case, however, the strategy proved unsuccessful. For the first time in 1927, conservative Disciples held their own meeting, called the North American Christian Convention, immediately following their final attempt to extract from the International Convention an unequivocal condemnation of the practice of open membership.[33] Although churches participating in the NACC remained nominal members of the original denomination until the Christian Church (Disciples of Christ) was created in 1968, observers agree that in practice they had passed the point of no return. The final break with the Disciples of Christ in 1968 was only a formal recognition of a split that had resulted from the tumultuous conflicts of the 1920s.[34]

The process of bureaucratization managed by Southern Baptist leaders during the Seventy-Five Million Campaign occurred even as theological conflicts threatened to split Northern Baptists and the Disciples of Christ. Through his influence, however, L. R. Scarborough was able to convince many newspaper editors and leading pastors that money given to the Campaign would only support institutions sound in the faith. In fact, the "Scarborough Synthesis" was itself the seminary president's method of preventing within the Southern Baptist Convention the same kind of conflicts that so disturbed other, similar denominations. By removing the fear that funds given to the Campaign would be used to subvert traditional Baptist doctrine, Scarborough ensured that the growth of the denomination's bureaucracy would continue apace without noisy interruptions from Fundamentalists. As Southern Baptist leaders persuaded pastors and laypeople to place funds into denominational hands, then, they attracted support from a variety of Southern Baptists, including many editors and pastors that feared Modernism as much as any Northern Fundamentalist. The support that leaders received planted the seeds of a robust program of centralization, one in which local churches were explicitly designated as denominational property and the wrath of God was called down upon those who failed to cooperate.

Target Behaviors of Denominational Leaders

Denominational bureaucrats sought to collect promised funds from rank-and-file Southern Baptists, but full payment of Campaign pledges was only one behavior that Southern Baptist leaders sought to encourage among Baptist pastors and laypeople. Intuitively, leaders knew that the Campaign's success relied on Southern Baptists embracing the entire emerging bureaucratic apparatus, and they never missed a chance to encourage Southern Baptists to do those things that would draw them into a closer orbit around the denomination. As a result, Baptist leaders sought to promote an entire constellation of denominational activities using reward and coercion.

Leaders sought to persuade Southern Baptists to redeem their pledges, and a significant portion of the cajoling found in Southern Baptist newspapers during this period is directed towards this goal. At the same time, leaders recognized that the local church pastor stood as the "key man" for promoting the Campaign among lay Baptists.[35] Baptist leaders consequently directed significant energy toward encouraging local church pastors to promote the Campaign, ensure that the pledges of their church members be paid in full and on time, and persuade church members to participate in any other denominational activity that leaders suggested. One loyal Baptist pastor put it this way:

> It goes without saying that the preacher is the key man in
> building the denominational spirit in a church. Few greater
> misfortunes can come to a church than to have a man for a
> pastor who is willing for his church to settle down to isolation
> and separation from the world. It is a scandal for any church to
> have a petty, stunted, self-opinionated snob for a pastor. The
> Gospel is the message of the capacious, lofty-souled, broad-
> minded, big-hearted Son of God, and it will shrivel on the lips
> of a little pesky man. The soul of the church he ministers to
> will be atrophied, and its sympathies will die.[36]

Pastors who faithfully led their congregations into closer relationships with the Convention were rewarded, while pastors who were viewed as obstructionist (such as the hypothetical butt of this pastor's remarks) bore the brunt of official criticism.

Baptist leaders also sought to convince pastors and lay leaders that it was important to separate money collected for the Campaign from money intended to fund the local congregation. By the concluding year of the Campaign, leaders had apparently learned that some churches had taken money paid on pledges and spent it on local projects. Scarborough wrote against this practice in a series of articles that appeared widely in the Southern Baptist press. His language was characteristically strong: "We can not only rob God in failing to give the tithe and offerings; but we can

111

rob God's causes by misappropriating funds and diverting them from one cause to another."[37] The stigma that leaders sought to attach to this practice is clear.

Additionally, Southern Baptist leaders sought during the latter years of the Campaign to convince pastors and laypeople to recover the vocabulary of "stewardship" and habits of regular tithing.[38] During the 1919 push for pledges, Scarborough and the Campaign's army of Four Minute Speakers relied on a strategy of eliciting pledges from Baptists through exciting public speaking, a method drawn from the peculiar practice of Texas Baptists and derided by some as a "whoop-em-up" method of fundraising.[39] Long before the end of the Campaign, some observers had begun to suggest that this method of gathering support for the Campaign lay behind the failure of many Baptists to redeem their pledges. L. L. Gwaltney, an editor whose opinions were generally oriented eastward, complained, "Whoop-up methods will no longer get the results. Even Texas Baptists, who in days agone, have set the Southern Convention so many worthy examples of the 'whirlwind campaign' seem no longer able to stir the rank and file of their people by such methods."[40] Furthermore, Baptist leaders were learning that institutions requiring a steady flow of funds could not be financed through methods that provided resources in irregular fits and starts.[41] Stated differently, Southern Baptist leaders were learning that bureaucratic institutions require bureaucratic methods of funding.

Southern Baptist leaders responded to this realization by reframing the Campaign as an obligatory part of Baptist stewardship and by resuscitating the concept of the tithe. Editors published countless letters and editorials pressing both ideas, authors often paying homage to stewardship and tithing in the same article. The 1921 meeting of the Southern Baptist Convention approved a new Campaign to recruit a half-million tithers, while the entire year following the 1923 Convention was explicitly dedicated to the causes of stewardship and tithing.[42] The editor of the *Baptist and Reflector* admitted that the introduction of tithing and stewardship as the methodological underpinning of the Campaign was a late modification, but defended it as necessary in preserving the Campaign and the success of future fundraising efforts:

> It often occurs that construction engineers build a new railroad bridge while the trains continue to run, new pieces gradually taking the place of the old parts until finally an all steel structure stands where there was a wooden one before. Without interruption in the traffic and operation of the 75 Million

Carrots and Sticks

Campaign in the time which remains of it, the principles and practices of Christian stewardship can be put under it and at the same time we can make ready for the oncoming movements among Southern Baptists. Campaigns are like trains— they come and go; but stewardship is the bridge which spans the chasm between what we have and what we need to do—it is a permanent improvement and is that over which any and all campaigns must move if they reach their destinations.[43]

Introducing the ideals of stewardship and tithing into the bloodstream of the Campaign months after Victory Week seems to have been a matter of embarrassment for some Baptist leaders, but this did not prevent them from rewarding Baptists who accepted the new emphases or castigating those who resisted.

Leaders also sought to rearrange the financial methods of local churches during this period, hoping to make congregations more efficient sources of denominational revenue. To this end, leaders encouraged churches to adopt budgets. Leaders believed that a budgeted church would pay its pastor more regularly, making the pastor a more reliable denominational ally. They also believed that it would increase the likelihood that funds earmarked for the Campaign would find their way into the hands of Convention boards and agencies rather than funding local church projects. One Texas pastor who led his congregation to adopt an annual budget noted, "At the end of the first year we had made a very substantial increase, even paying off a large slice of the debt and increasing pastor's salary." The following year the church was able to retire its debt, and money intended for the "work of the denomination . . . was paid on time and . . . sent to Dr. Groner."[44] Leaders were willing to dangle the possibility of a higher salary before pastors as an enticement to place their churches on a budget but were equally willing to criticize pastors who refused.

Leaders dedicated themselves to making sure that Southern Baptists redeemed their pledges, but they soon found that even a pledge paid in full was a mixed blessing if it came designated to one or another of the boards and agencies of the Convention. Leaders also found that designated gifts threatened to nourish some Southern Baptist organizations while starving others. Boyce Taylor, a conservative Kentucky Baptist pastor, actively encouraged his flock to designate their offerings to the Foreign Mission Board, asserting that "we don't believe in the social service program of the women" and claiming that "our Home Board is leaning too much to the material and the temporal rather than the spiritual and eternal."[45] Taylor also expressed doubts about the Relief and Annuity Board, a skepticism that the curmudgeonly J. J. Taylor shared.[46]

To leaders committed to the idea that denominational "efficiency" depended upon channeling denominational funds through a central, united budget, such talk was little better than outright rejection of the Campaign. Trained leaders, not individual Christians, should be responsible for writing the budget of the denomination. As influential Baptist Selsus E. Tull wrote, a budget "goes to pieces just as soon as the plan is thrown open for individuals to break with the whole program and to support it only in spots." Tull's advice to grassroots Baptists was not to "kick out of harness" but instead to give to the entire program.[47] Furthermore, the tendency to designate gifts not only damaged the centralizing motive behind the Campaign, but also undercut leaders' explicit desire to use the tug of foreign missions as a means to raise funds for other, less popular activities. In early 1923, Frank Burkhalter, the Southern Baptist Convention's director of publicity, noted a suggestion that "the call of home and foreign missions be made the dominant note of the spring program in behalf of the Campaign" and suggested that "when home and foreign missions are aided all other causes fostered by the Campaign will be assisted, for each cause shares in every undesignated dollar contributed to the Campaign."[48] The following year, a contributor to the *Baptist Standard* claimed that the high regard in which Southern Baptists held the task of foreign missions had been the most important reason for the Campaign's "success." The author warned against deemphasizing foreign missions: "If foreign missions were eliminated from our program, I candidly believe the whole program would be largely a failure. It is the New Testament appeal of foreign missions that has largely carried some of the other causes."[49] Southern Baptist leaders reacted strongly against designation in light of the perceived danger it would cause the Campaign, praising those who sent their money undesignated and criticizing those that did not.

Finally, Southern Baptist leaders sought to increase circulation of the various Baptist state newspapers by encouraging all Southern Baptists to subscribe and by asking pastors to serve as the newspapers' local agents. Outside of word-of-mouth promotion, the newspaper was the only method of communication between the denomination and its constituency, and leaders greatly emphasized increasing its circulation as a means of connecting thousands of small, scattered churches to the goals of the centralizing denomination. In the April 12, 1923 issue of the Arkansas *Baptist Advance*, a cartoon appears in which a farmer, marked "PASTOR,"

114

milks a cow, marked "CHURCH." In the first frame, the cow fails to give milk because, as the caption says, "He will not pour the feed into her unless she first pours down the milk." The feed box, marked "NO BAPTIST ADVANCE," represents the pastor's failure to provide the state Baptist newspaper to his people before they start giving more money. In the second frame, the farmer/pastor has provided the newspaper to every home by including it in the church budget, and as a result the cow/church has filled several buckets with the "richest milk"; these buckets, marked "OLD PREACHERS," "ORPHANS HOME," "FOREIGN MISSIONS," and so on, represent the church's generosity not only to its own pastor, but to denominational enterprises as well.[50] In the corner of the page, a cartoon of a balding man in a vest and tailcoat rushes to the right. He has his own caption: "A bright idea has struck this pastor! He is going to put the Baptist Advance in the Budget!"[51] During the Campaign period, Southern Baptist leaders would reward pastors who helped to expand circulation of the newspaper and reserve harsh words for those who did not.

Rewards for Compliant Baptists

During the early 1920s, Southern Baptist leaders tried to encourage a wide variety of pro-denominational behaviors among their pastors and laypeople. More important, however, were the methods by which they sought to elicit those behaviors. In true bureaucratic fashion, Southern Baptist leaders seized opportunities to reward those pastors and laypeople that complied with denominational requests. Approaching obedient Baptists as "insiders," leaders attempted to guarantee financial security, professional stability, and social prestige to Southern Baptists who supported the centralizing goals of Southern Baptist leaders.

First, leaders promised a higher salary to pastors who used their pulpits to buttress the Campaign. Under a congregational polity, leaders were powerless to directly control pastors' salaries, but leaders did insist that pastors attending to denominational needs would receive more money for their pastoral efforts. More to the point, editors encouraged congregations to raise the salaries of "loyal" pastors.

R. H. Pitt, editor of *The Religious Herald*, made such a plea in a 1921 issue. Pitt noted that the Baptist pastor, "key-man for all our denominational problems," was the only person that could guarantee the collection of Campaign pledges. Furthermore, he stated that the pastor was the front-line apologist for the Campaign, going "up against the inertia, the lethargy, the prejudices, the narrowness, the obstinacy, the worldliness of

Reward and Coercion in the Seventy-Five Million Campaign

Page 16 of the *Baptist Advance*, April 12, 1923. Southern Baptist pastors were encouraged to provide their congregations with the state Baptist newspaper to increase congregational contributions to denominational activities. Leaders promised pastors that this would increase pastoral salaries as well. Permission to reprint graciously provided by Arkansas Baptist Newsmagazine, Inc.

many of his people." As if that was not enough responsibility, Pitt asserted that the pastor's leadership was also essential to the continuing health of the *Herald*, and he called on churches "to cherish their pastors, to provide for them so considerately and generously that they may be left free from corroding care and enfeebling anxieties, free to perform the heavy tasks which continually challenge them."[52] The "tasks" for which pastors must be "left free" were, for Pitt, exclusively denominational. Pitt's allusion to "enfeebling anxieties" reflects denominational leaders' anxieties regarding the relative ineffectiveness of pastors who were forced to support themselves through a second job. Providing adequate pastoral compensation not only encouraged pastors; it also made them more effective allies of the denomination.

Other leaders stressed that increased pastoral salaries were a natural result of loyalty to denominational aims. In 1925, *The Baptist Record* carried a story about a church in Louisiana of which eighty-two percent of members tithed and each member gave regularly to the church's budget. Presumably, a significant portion of those receipts was bound for denominational objects, because the pastor was noted for his support of the "denominational program. Hence, you need not be surprised that his salary is $6,000.00 a year, for he seeks first the kingdom of God by placing emphasis on missions."[53] Along the same lines, an article in the Tennessee Baptist newspaper told its readers "How Enlistment Put A Moribund Church On Its Feet."[54] The church in question was struggling with its finances until an enlistment worker from the state Convention taught the church about stewardship and led them to adopt a congregational budget. Far from resisting preaching on the subject of money as the deacons had expected, the people "savagely drank in the Scriptural teaching." After the worker had taught the church "what the Lord had to say about pastoral support" and "sacred financing of his work," he helped the church put its finances in order. With a budget in place, the church was able to pay off its lingering debt and "decided that they could pay the deficit . . . pay the pastor $12,000 instead of the $1,000, and still take care of their other expenses." The ensuing revival even "resulted in forty-four additions to the church by baptism."[55] While some pastors might have seen church finance as a zero-sum game in which money sent to the denomination was siphoned away from his own salary and other local expenses, denominational leaders sought to show pastors that faithfully supporting denominational objects actually made it easier to raise one's own salary. A contributor to the *Florida Baptist Witness* was explicit: "It is hard to get some of the pastors

117

to give the work of the denomination a fair hearing for the reason that they are afraid that their people will not be able to pay what they have promised on the preacher's salary. My own experience is that the pastor who preaches missions and gives the work of the denomination a fair chance will come nearer getting his salary than he will otherwise. . . . The pastor who preaches faithfully the whole gospel shall live of the Gospel."[56] Denominational leaders were certain that pastoral salary rates could only benefit from cultivating the denomination.

Leaders also knew, however, that Baptist pastors held their pulpits precariously. Besides failing to provide a full-time salary, many rural churches also kept their preachers in a perpetual state of professional suspense by refusing to abandon the traditional practice of offering pastors an "annual call." Churches unhappy with a pastor's suggestion that a congregation might adopt a budget or increase its financial commitments to the denomination could simply decline to renew a pastor's contract at the end of the year.[57] Leaders needed to find ways to counteract this conservative influence among pastors. F. S. Groner, the corresponding secretary of Texas's executive board, moved tentatively towards quelling pastoral anxieties about the relationship between length of pastoral tenure and denominational involvement by suggesting that *the longest pastorates in Texas are those where, as a rule, there is the largest [Baptist] Standard mailing list in proportion to the number of members.*[58] In other words, pastors kept their jobs for longer periods of time in churches where laypeople were connected to the denomination through the state newspaper. Leaders were much more likely, however, to suggest that pastors estranged from or opposed to the denomination were likely to find themselves without jobs, a tendency more appropriately discussed in the next section.

Southern Baptist leaders used the prospect of higher salaries and longer tenures to encourage pastors to support the Campaign and its institutional paraphernalia, but they were also interested in advancing the denomination's cause among its wider constituency. Because laypeople, with a few exceptions, did not receive their livelihood from the denomination, leaders also practiced other methods to elicit lay support of the Campaign. Laypeople and pastors that paid their pledges were featured in Baptist newspapers either through short articles or by having their portraits printed, while churches that made good on their collective pledges were sometimes printed in "honor rolls." Finally, and most importantly, Southern Baptist newspaper contributors frequently claimed that payment

118

of pledges would result in great crop yields, a deeper relationship with God, or some other reward.

Leaders were aware that many of the rank-and-file Baptists who made up the churches of the Southern Baptist Convention were poor. When the general poverty of the region collided with the economic fallout of the Great War, leaders scrambled to remind readers of Baptist newspapers that even the poorest Baptist could, with enough sacrifice, afford to redeem his or her pledge. Editors printed a number of short articles commending widows, orphans, the dying, and the mentally ill who had, despite difficulties, managed to fulfill their Campaign obligations. Through printing these stories, leaders rewarded those about whom they wrote and hoped to inspire other marginal Southern Baptists to show similar sacrificial support for the Campaign. In 1920, for instance, the *Baptist and Reflector* printed a short but "thrilling" story about a ninety-two-year-old woman who spent two days picking cotton in order to pay the second installment of her pledge.[59] Later, as the Campaign ended in 1924, Frank Burkhalter told with approval the story of a widow who sold "some of her furniture" in order to pay her pledge.[60] Leaders seem to have offered these stories without any sense that their subjects might have gone too far. Orphans under denominational care were also given opportunities to sacrifice. L. R. Scarborough himself wrote in 1921 about the means by which the children in the Buckner Orphans' Home in Texas paid their pledges. "The boys in the home keep their pledges paid up through money they make trapping rabbits and chopping and picking cotton. To accomplish the same purpose, the girls do tatting and sewing," the superintendent explained. Even those too young to work paid a pledge: "The little folks . . . save up the small amounts given them by visitors and pay their pledges with it." The Orphans' Home even paid forty dollars into the Campaign on behalf of the forty babies in the orphanage nursery.[61]

Leaders sought the support of Southern Baptists who were at the end of their financial ropes, but they also remembered those struggling with illness and death. The editor of *The Religious Herald* printed a story about a woman whose mother told her on her deathbed that her "daddy was losing his mind." Before long, the children of the family indeed had to send him to "the Pineville Asylum for the Insane," where he "spent the balance of his days, fourteen long years." Although he suffered from the sense that he was irrevocably damned, the woman's father continued to take a special interest in the work of the Convention and read the "good books and Bibles and the Baptist paper" his daughter sent him. Upon reading

Reward and Coercion in the Seventy-Five Million Campaign

about the Seventy-Five Million Campaign, the man asked to forego his winter suit in exchange for the ability to give a pledge to the Campaign. His daughter pledged fifty dollars to the Campaign in his name and, even though he passed away before the conclusion of the Campaign, she promised to "pay it all if I have to sell all the chickens on the place to do so."[62] Almost two years later, the editor of the *Baptist Standard* offered another story, terse but disturbing, about "Miss Elizabeth Bacon of El Paso, Texas, a young school teacher." When this young woman found out that she was terminally ill, she "asked for her checkbook and wrote a check for $50 to finish paying her subscription of $250 to the 75 Million Campaign, saying that she could not go out to meet God with her pledge unpaid."[63] Leaders loved to commend Southern Baptists in print for this kind of dedication, but this schoolteacher's fear of dying without having paid her pledge reflects the darker side of the Campaign to be discussed in the next section.

Southern Baptists whose Campaign compliance was more conventional than that of people facing illness, death, or serious privation were often given more perfunctory notice in the newspapers. One method by which leaders did this was the "honor roll." Newspapers printed lists of churches whose payments were current as a way of rewarding those churches and gently nudging churches that had fallen behind.[64] Tennessee's Corresponding Secretary noticed that "a number of brethren are disappointed because their churches were left off the first honor roll. In some instances they thought they were up, when they were just a few dollars behind. One case of this kind was Broadway, Knoxville. They lacked less than $100.00 and the treasurer immediately mailed check [*sic*] for the amount they were short for the three full years."[65] At least some Southern Baptist churches were sensitive enough to such publicity for the honor roll to be an effective means of encouraging compliance. In addition to publishing lists of churches, the newspapers also printed portraits of pastors and laypeople that had been particularly loyal to the Campaign, either individually or in groups.[66]

Finally, and perhaps most importantly, Southern Baptist leaders sought to convince laypeople and pastors that paying one's pledge and otherwise supporting the Campaign would bring material blessings. Some contributors cast the promise of benefit for those fulfilling their financial obligations in general terms, but others made more specific claims. Livingston Johnson's call for tithers in North Carolina fit into the first category. "We are firmly of the opinion that if one gives a tenth out of love for God and with sincere desire to honor Him, God will make the nine-tenths go as far as the ten-tenths would go if all used for one's self," Johnson

120

Page 16 of the *Baptist Advance*, December 13, 1923 (detail). Baptist editors rewarded compliant pastors like Rev. Weaver by printing their portraits in the paper along with short accounts of their denominational contributions. Permission to reprint graciously provided by Arkansas Baptist Newsmagazine, Inc.

Rev. F. P. Weaver, Sidney, a good soldier of Christ Jesus, can preach so the acorns will fall, spiritual, true to our whole program, a mountain preacher of the first type.

wrote.[67] In an article on the increasing Southern Baptist interest in tithing, J. F. Love was probably thinking roughly the same thought when he wrote, "It warms my heart to reflect upon the copious blessing which God will bestow upon these 500,000 men and women and the churches of which they are members when they have done this thing. . . . God will . . . fulfill His promise and open the windows of heaven and pour out upon us blessings in abundance."[68] Other authors were more specific about the benefits that Southern Baptists could hope to receive if they remained faithful to their Campaign pledges. The editor of the South Carolina Baptist newspaper had an entire laundry list of benefits to be expected by those who practiced "systematic and proportionate giving." Editor Cody believed that practicing stewardship would "bring spiritual blessings and promote growth in christian [*sic*] character" as well as encourage "frugality among our people and . . . the diversification of crops on the part of our farmers, which is recognized as an economic necessity."[69] Other authors were even more explicit. One Mississippi Baptist pointed out that "somehow it is easier for churches which pay up their pledges to build houses," and Frank Burkhalter offered a news story in which a tithing businessperson found

121

SOME MORE of OUR GOOD PREACHERS and FAITHFUL WORKERS

Rev. J. L. Henderson, the new pastor at Eureka Springs. He is a good one, fine and true.

Rev. J. L. Barrett, new pastor at Mulberry. He is a pusher, strong preacher, and true to all that's Baptist.

Deacon L. T. Dennis, Walcott, who has been secretary of Sunday School at Mt. Zion Church, Greene County, for 30 years; joined this church 60 years ago; been church treasurer 30 years, is 80 years of age; never misses a Sunday; pays $50 a year on 75 Million; has taken Baptist Advance from its first issue, and stands for the whole Baptist program. He is a great Baptist.

Rev. L. P. Thomas, Hackett, a good pastor, spiritual, true to the whole program, a worker, a fine soul.

Rev. H. E. Harris, pastor at Parkin. He is a goer, choice soul.

Rev. Ralph Bishop, pastor at Wesson, graduate of Ouachita, spiritual, strong, and a fine soul.

Rev. E. P. Minton, Jonesboro, one of the foundation builders, really a great preacher; 50 years in the ministry; universally loved, true and orthodox.

Rev. T. M. McGee, Kennett, a veteran of the cross, good preacher of Christ Jesus, loyal always.

Rev. T. F. Landreth, England, a veteran preacher, country pastor, great old stand-by.

Rev. F. F. Weaver, Sidney, a good soldier of Christ Jesus, can preach so the acorns will fall, spiritual, true to our whole program, a mountain preacher of the first type.

Rev. D. N. Keck, Fayetteville, one of our good country pastors, loyal and true.

Rev. L. G. Miller, Maynard, one of our coming young preachers, strong, a man of promise, true to the program.

Page 16 of the *Baptist Advance*, December 13, 1923. Baptist newspapers printed portraits of pastors and lay leaders who consistently supported the Seventy-Five Million Campaign or cooperated with the denomination in other ways. Permission to reprint graciously provided by Arkansas Baptist Newsmagazine, Inc.

that he had enough money in his bank account to help a young person pay his final years' tuition.[70]

P. I. Lipsey, the editor of the Mississippi *Baptist Record*, was not expressing an idiosyncratic opinion, then, when he suggested, "If you do whatever God asks you to do, God will do whatever you ask him to do."[71] In fact, the belief that God judged and rewarded behavior in concrete, material ways was a significant feature of the Southern Protestant religious outlook. Southern Protestants were unwilling to accept the Civil War and its outcome as divine judgment on slavery, but they did not thereby reject the idea of God's providential intervention in history. Southern denominations tended instead to ascribe Southern defeat to the greed and worldliness of the South, or perhaps to their inadequate efforts at converting their slaves to Christianity.[72] Southerners may not have agreed amongst themselves that the Civil War was sent as a punishment for their sins, but the idea that God sends ill fortune to the wicked escaped the war intact. In 1905, for instance, a committee of the Southern Presbyterian General Assembly asserted that a recent rash of train accidents stemmed directly from the railroads' insistence upon operating on the Sabbath. "So long as the nation shows such utter disregard for His authority," the committee reported, "so long may we expect the continued repetition of these and other so-called accidents."[73] Southerners were comfortable with the idea of providence in the early twentieth century, and they were aware that God sent disease, drought, and financial ruin as surely as He sent health and security.

Coercion for Uncooperative Baptists

In light of Southern beliefs about God's willingness to cause suffering for those who disobey His will, it is hardly surprising that Southern Baptist leaders tried using these beliefs to coerce Southern Baptists into participating in the Seventy-Five Million Campaign and other related denominational movements. Just as leaders treated cooperative Southern Baptists as insiders by offering them rewards, leaders treated uncooperative Southern Baptists as outsiders, making a wide variety of assertions about the ill fortune that awaited the noncompliant. The threats that Southern Baptist leaders made toward those whose behavior was unacceptable to them often mirrored the rewards offered to compliant Baptists. In place of financial and professional stability, pastors were threatened with decreased income and job loss. Leaders warned laypeople about the damage that greed would do to their crops, and all Baptists were counseled about the dangers of facing the last judgment with an uneasy conscience. Leaders served this buffet of threats in a heavy stew of abusive language left over from the recent World War.

Just as leaders assured Southern Baptist pastors that teaching on missions and promoting the Campaign were keys to receiving a higher salary, they also tried to convince preachers that failing to promote denominational aims would result, at the very least, in a decreased salary. L. E. Barton, writing in the *Baptist Advance*, told pastors that their salary was one of the "great issues dependent on [their] success or failure in reaching your church for a worthy offering." Barton strongly implied that low pastoral salaries were mainly the result of "a dearth of teaching concerning missions and stewardship."[74]

Barton's emphasis on promoting missions as a means to a higher salary was tame, however, compared to the often-repeated assertion that pastors standing in the way of the Campaign and other denominational movements would find themselves unemployed. A. T. Robertson, remembered by his students as a favorite professor of Greek and New Testament at Southern Seminary, also left a trail of pungent language scattered through Baptist newspapers in the early 1920s. One of the first to realize that uncooperative preachers might well stand between the denomination and Campaign pledges, Robertson noted that churches were anxious to part ways with pastors who did not support the Campaign and expressed his unqualified approval of their sentiments:

> The 75 Million Campaign, like the great World War, has revealed the slackers in the ministry with a powerful searchlight. The state director of the campaign in one of the Southern States told me that in a dozen churches in his State leading laymen had asked him to recommend to them loyal preachers who can be counted on to lead the churches in the new era of service. These churches all have pastors who proved slackers in the campaign. The onward movement of the churches will throw these pastors out of a job. The preachers who have stood guard at the door of the churches to keep the denominational agents away will soon find that they are without a job. The laymen in the churches have lost confidence in the preacher who is a slacker. He has been weighed and found wanting. In a ministers' conference Monday I heard a minister say that in his association one of the pastors refused to present the apportionment to the church or to allow any agents of

124

the campaign to come and speak. But all the same the laymen in the church reading the denominational paper and unwilling to be found a slacker church because of a slacker pastor, took the matter in hand and went over the top in spite of the pastor. Needless to say, that pastor's usefulness is over in that church and community.[75]

As strong as Robertson's language was, it was not unique. The editor of the *Baptist Advance* used, if possible, even stronger language: "When a pastor decides that he is called of God to act as guardian of the pocketbooks of his people to keep them from giving away their money for the support of the work of Christ's kingdom, or when he decides that his commission requires him to discourage all efforts to get the members of his church to give support to the general work of the Kingdom, he ought to be 'fired.' No church ought long to tolerate such a pastor, and it will ruin any church that does tolerate him."[76] A year later, J. F. Tull wrote in that same journal that the pastor failing to recognize that "times have changed" had only two choices: he "must either find out how to adjust himself to the present day pastorate, or make up his mind to go to the scrap heap."[77]

In each of these cases denominational leaders sought to influence churches, through the denominational press, to release pastors who did not support the Campaign. In at least one case, however, an editor told of a pastor who had lost his job not due to congregational anger, but due to the displeasure of God.

> It is easy to believe that the Heavenly Father refuses to honor those who refuse to honor him. Here is a true case in point from the experience of a Baptist pastor in one of our leading Southern states, as related by one who was familiar with all the facts in the case:
> This minister who failed to tithe was the pastor of three churches which paid him a salary of $1,800, the largest salary drawn by any minister in that association. When the Woman's Missionary Union sought to enlist the members of the churches in the practice of tithing this minister not only preached against the plan but also talked against it. Of course he did not tithe his own income. Within two years two of his churches had discontinued his services, leaving him only one church to draw from, and that church paid only $700. In the language of another, "Make your gifts according to your income or the Lord may make your income according to your gifts." [78]

Reward and Coercion in the Seventy-Five Million Campaign

Leaders were not above attempting to convince churches to dismiss pastors who stood between the denomination and laypeople's money, but they also sought to convince pastors themselves that God could intervene and relieve them of duty, with or without denominational help. In both cases, denominational leaders used the threat of unemployment to attempt to coerce reluctant pastors into supporting the aims of the Campaign.

Leaders directed coercion at a wider audience as well, and abusive language was one of their most striking coercive methods. Although directed specifically at preachers, A. T. Robertson's commentary on the fate of pastors who did not support the Campaign demonstrates how Southern Baptist leaders used abusive language to pressure Southern Baptists into carrying out the plans of the denomination. During the Campaign period, Southern Baptist leaders at all levels liberally applied a variety of slurs and epithets to Baptists they deemed uncooperative. L. R. Scarborough, reaching into an obvious source for combative language, alluded to the Bible when he accused "a leader that doesn't lead" of being "the abomination of desolation standing where it ought not as spoken of by Daniel the prophet."[79] On other occasions, Baptist leaders reached into the rural farm experiences that many of them shared with their constituents. Contributors to Baptist newspapers were especially fond of referring to Baptists who complained without contributing as "kickers." Just like stubborn mules, some Baptists would never learn to work as part of a team.[80] In another case, the *Baptist Messenger* published a cartoon of two calves tied together, each trying to eat from buckets of feed placed so far apart that they could not both eat at the same time. The calves eventually learn that they can only get what they need by working together rather than against each other.[81]

While language drawn from the Bible and rural experience could be strong, the most striking abuse of all was adapted from the slang of the Great War. When leaders used words such as "slacker" and "disloyalty," they not only tapped into the energy that the war had produced but also recalled memories of violence against those who had dodged military service or failed to buy enough war bonds. Like A. T. Robertson, other Baptist authors would refer to pastors who opposed the Campaign as "slackers." As one pastor wrote in the South Carolina Baptist newspaper, a man who would "side step and evade responsibility" and "refuse[s] to get under the burden but let the other brother do the paying for him . . . is a slacker."[82] The editor of the Southern Baptist newspaper serving southern Illinois clarified the connection between the necessity of participating in the war effort and the importance of the Campaign:

126

The citizen who was not for the great war work, heart and soul, was called a slacker! Our people literally poured out their money that the war might be won. What shall be said of the Baptist who will not help in this great "Baptist 75,000,000 Dollar Campaign?"

Is it any better to be a slacker in the work of God's kingdom than it is in the service of one's country? Surely, it is not, God should be first in everything.[83]

The use of the word "slacker" implied more than simple laziness; in the immediate post-war period it still carried implications of compromised patriotism and criminal neglect of duty.

Perhaps even more disturbing is the fact that some leaders were willing to label unhelpful pastors and laypeople as "deserters." Before the pledges had even been made, B. C. Hening reminded North Carolina Baptists that success in the Campaign required only one thing: "All we need is the WILL. . . . Not to have the WILL is to be voluntarily and purposely deserters from this holy program for enlarging all our work and honoring our Master in a great way."[84] Only a few months later, R. H. Pitt made essentially the same point: "There must be unity. We must make it unanimous. Each of us must do his full part. Each of us must be found in his place. We must have no shirkers, no slackers, no cowards, no deserters."[85] W. E. Gwatkins, writing in *The Baptist Message*, offered the most graphic possible comparison of uncooperative Baptists and wartime deserters, stating, "Next to loyalty to Christ is loyalty to Christian men and women. I owe it to the man who is giving his strength, his blood, his life by my side in the battle line, to be the soldier that he is, at least, to do my best. How dare I shirk and desert the ranks, when my brothers are pouring forth their very strength and blood for victory? The man who deserts the ranks in the front of the enemy is shot to death with musketry. He deserves to be."[86] It would be difficult to accuse one of desertion more starkly.

The connection Gwatkins makes between dissent from the Campaign and the execution of deserting soldiers illuminates what must have been implicit in Southern Baptist use of war language, of which the word "slacker" can serve as a representative example. When this word was originally used during the Great War, it implied the possibility of the use of violence, either official or unofficial, to enforce compliance. "Slackers," or men that avoided enlisting in the army for "less than conscientious" reasons, were hounded by government officials at best and targeted by the War Department for courts marshal at worst.[87] Government action against draft dodgers reached their high water mark in March 1918 when the federal government, acting in concert with police departments and civilian vigilantes, began rounding up thousands of young men in a series of "slacker raids."[88] These raids, which continued almost until the cessation of hostilities in Europe, gathered men suspected of draft dodging into local jails without charging them with any crime. On other occasions, zealous civilians would take and hold suspected slackers and send telegrams to their local draft boards inquiring after their status. Responses would sometimes take weeks.[89]

The meaning of the word "slacker" quickly expanded to include any American that failed to do their wartime duty. Bernard Baruch, the chair of the War Industries Board, told one lumber worker who had proved unwilling to meet government requirements, "You will be such an object of contempt and scorn in your home town that you will not dare to show your face there. If you should, your fellow citizens would call you a slacker, the boys would hoot at you, and the draft men would likely run you out of town."[90] Even failing to buy enough war bonds could earn you the suspicion of your peers, or at least that of the local Council of Defense.[91] In April 1918, the South Dakota Council of Defense circulated a letter to the county councils declaring that citizens who failed to buy their assigned quota of Liberty Bonds "come under our classification as 'slackers' and where they can afford to take certain amounts of bonds can justly be suspicioned as being in opposition to the policy of our government." During the war, state councils set up "kangaroo" courts and other means of coercion aimed at those who did not purchase enough Liberty Bonds.[92]

When Southern Baptist leaders accused Campaign non-participants of being "slackers," they were not poking fun or being playful. They were using language directly connected with government use of coercion. Although Southern Baptist leaders endlessly described the Campaign as a method of "cooperation," their enthusiastic use of wartime language shows that they were willing, if necessary, to build the denomination's future on a foundation of grudging obligation.

The Southern Baptist tendency to rely on wartime language implied negative consequences for those who failed to participate in the Campaign and other allied denominational programs. As in the case of pastoral employment, however, Southern Baptist leaders also explicitly listed negative consequences that Baptist laypeople would suffer if they did not engage in the Campaign. Again, many of these threats mirrored the rewards promised to laypeople that supported the Campaign.

128

Traditionally, Southern Baptist churches had used discipline to enforce evangelical standards of behavior and orthodoxy.[93] During the Seventy-Five Million Campaign, however, a number of voices began to call for local churches to discipline members whose giving had fallen short of denominational standards. The author of a letter to the editor of the *Biblical Recorder* made this point subtly but well:

> All our churches need to exercise discipline. I am getting tired of hearing preachers and papers knocking people for their failure to meet their pledges, and what they ought to do or what we think they should do. I have been about as negligent in my duty in carrying out church laws as any other member in my church, and for a while, I suggest that we, as a Baptist people, stop boasting of being the biggest in numbers, and be a body of people practicing what we preach.
>
> Let us drive out as nearly as possible and come clean handed, and then we won't need to beg, plead, and state in our church conferences that we are behind with our pastors, missions, orphanages, or any other objects.[94]

When A. T. Robertson made this same point, however, he was characteristically plain: "I have asked many audiences at Northfield, at Winona, at Montreat, and in many pulpits of various denominations if any one had ever known a church member excluded from church on the charge of covetousness. I have yet to receive one affirmative answer . . . we let pass the idolatrous covetousness of 'Deacon Skinflint' which cries to heaven. . . . One needs tact, to be sure, in handling the covetous church member, but he also needs courage. . . . Judgment must begin at the Throne of God, but it should begin. Thank God, a new day has come."[95] The extent to which churches took up Professor Robertson's advice is unknown, but he was unequivocal in calling for discipline to be applied to Baptists giving too little of their income.

The most important means that Southern Baptist leaders used to coerce Baptists who were tempted to duck their Campaign obligations was the threat of material or spiritual loss. Just as leaders promised that compliance would bring material and spiritual blessings, they sought to convince their constituents that God would punish those who failed to support the aims of the denomination.

Southern Baptist leaders often connected agricultural shortfalls with failure to pledge or failure to pay pledges. Finley Tinnin, the editor of the Louisiana *Baptist Message*, noted that while farmers had money in the

Reward and Coercion in the Seventy-Five Million Campaign

bank, they were failing to catch up on their pledges. As a result, God had "taken a BIG COLLECTION from the farmers of the parish we have in mind. The same ground that produced one bale of cotton last year failed to produce even one-fifth of a bale this year, and in many instances, the farmers will fail to realize enough to pay for the fertilizer they put out in the Spring." There was only one way to interpret the low yields: "God . . . is a Collector Whom we can never dodge or cheat!"[96] The gentle Livingston Johnson of the North Carolina *Biblical Recorder* agreed that agricultural disappointment could be directly linked to the failure of many Southern Baptists to redeem their pledges.

> We are now within less than two months of the Convention, and we have raised not more than one-fourth of the amount due on the 75-Million pledges. . . .
>
> It is true we have had a disastrous year in most parts of the State so far as crops are concerned, and crops are the basis of our prosperity. . . . May it not be that God has permitted much of the crops to be destroyed in order to show us our unfaithfulness as His stewards? He certainly dealt in this way with His people in olden times. What right have we to say that He does not use the same methods to remind us of our remissness in duty?[97]

Johnson was more careful than his western counterpart, but he clearly thought that crop failure could be God's judgment on Southern Baptist greed.

Southern Baptist newspapers also carried other, more sensationalistic stories pointing to God's ability to collect what was rightfully his from Baptists greedy enough to try to withhold it. One story circulated in which "a woman who refused to give after hearing a sermon on giving has her pocketbooks [*sic*] stolen just after leaving the church. On making the discovery, she said, 'The parson could not find the way to my pocket, but the devil did.'" Editor Tinnin of *The Baptist Message* borrowed this story from the *Western Recorder*, but added his own interpretation: "That was one time that we are glad the devil was on the job. It served her right."[98]

These were harsh words from a denominational representative, but they proved tame in light of a story written by Frank Burkhalter in 1923. In it, he asserts, "If we do not use our means for the glory of God He removes our resources from us." Burkhalter tells of a man so "stingy" that he failed even to provide adequate church clothing for his mother. Over time, he amassed a small fortune, but when asked to give to the Campaign, he refused to give the $1,500 asked of him, instead offering one-third that amount. Upon selling his business and moving to another state to spend the winter, the miser met a couple of men that held themselves out as bond brokers. They offered to sell him for forty thousand dollar bonds that would soon be worth twice that much but, when the man had signed away half of his savings, "two other masked men came in the room, took the check and the bonds and disappeared." The two "bond brokers" took him out to search for the thieves, eventually telling him to give up and offering him train fare for the ride back to the city in which he was robbed. "When this man who had refused to share his prosperity with God got back to the big city, where he went to spend the winter in ease and realized that he had been buncoed out of more than half his money, he committed suicide." Burkhalter was unflinching in his certainty that the man had brought his misfortune on himself: "If he had honored God with his means, as a faithful steward, he would have been spared all this worry, humiliation, disgrace and sin, and would have been richer, happier and more useful at the same time, having had a share in extending God's Kingdom in the world."[99] It is hard to escape the conclusion that Burkhalter hoped to instill fear of a similar fate in the hearts of his readers.

If Southern Baptists could be made to fear death as a result of their negligence towards the Campaign, they could feel terror at the prospect of facing the final judgment with unclean hands. Southern Baptist leaders repeatedly implied (and sometimes explicitly declared) in their writing for Southern Baptist newspapers that Baptists who failed in their duty to the Campaign would face spiritual disaster at God's "judgment bar."[100]

Some intimations of the spiritual consequences that resulted from failing to give, especially those penned before the stress on the Campaign became acute, were relatively gentle. Layman I. H. Hunt seemed as worried about the effect of greed on his prayer life as he was about his eternal fate. "Even though paying my pledge may involve slight temporary sacrifice, I am going to pay, for I cannot be happy unless I can commune regularly with God, and I find I cannot face my Heavenly Father with a good conscience until I have first met my obligation to His work as represented in my pledge to the Campaign."[101] Frank Leavell was similarly gentle when he emphasized not damnation, but the prospect of eternal joy for those who were faithful in their tithing. "The millionaire and the miser alike must give an account of their stewardship. . . . Conscientious tithing is preparation for that day. Happy is he to whom the Lord will say, 'Well done, thou

131

good and faithful servant: Thou hast been faithful over a few things, I will make thee ruler over many things.'"[102]

Other leaders were more explicit about the final consequences of failing to give to the Campaign. The normally reticent J. F. Love, whose Foreign Mission Board was by then struggling under more than one million dollars of debt, clearly believed that the severest consequences could await those who withheld funds from the denomination. "The years are not many when three million Southern Baptists will stand before the White Throne to give account of the deeds done in the body. I fancy that among the deeds for which we shall give answer or there receive encomiums of Heaven, will be the deed of paying our campaign pledge." For Love, failure to answer the call of the world's need could only result in "condemnation."[103] The editor of the *Florida Baptist Witness* agreed. Despite the fact that Southern Baptists were spending much of their income on "pleasures and luxuries," they still maintained that they were unable to make good on their pledges. As a result, "when we will have to give an account of our stewardship . . . it may be our Lord will no longer count us worthy of handling that which belongs to Him."[104] Southern Baptist editors had begun to articulate a soteriology that was lurching away from salvation by grace in favor of salvation by stewardship. Sensing this ambiguity, Scarborough himself said, "An unco-operating baptized man is not any account. Why he won't burn because he is saved, and we would be afraid to ask God to take him to heaven."[105] Baptists who dissented from the Campaign, failing to rise to their leaders' new soteriological standards, were left in low-church limbo.

The famous pastor of First Baptist Church, Dallas, George W. Truett, may have offered the most striking example of Southern Baptist attempts to instill a fear of divine judgment within uncooperative Baptists. The pastor told the story of a "very wealthy woman" who had "used her great wealth for her own self. . . . Never was it known for her to give a cent to the relief of anybody. She never made a contribution for God's causes." When her doctor told her that she was dying and would "be gone before the sun sets," she "drew the sheets about her face and screamed, 'Oh how I dread to meet God to account for the way I have lived!'" In offering his own commentary on this anecdote, Truett moved not to reassure his audience that "grace did much more abound" but to confirm the woman's fears: "Well may she dread that meeting! She will have to give an account to him for the use of all she had . . . don't let your property control you. . . . It is a stewardship."[106] Truett, along with many other Southern Baptist spokespeople, believed that poor stewards had good reason to fear the last judgment.

132

Coercion, Reward, and a New Baptist Polity

Frequent invocation of God's final judgment among Southern Baptist leaders may have reflected the apocalyptic nature of the Seventy-Five Million Campaign's failure. The unwillingness of denominational workers to scale back their activities, when combined with the failure of many Baptists to make good on their pledges, threatened to trap the Convention's agencies inside a labyrinth of debt. Leaders responded by turning to a system of reward and coercion to ensure that churches, pastors, and laypeople would meet their financial obligations. In the new Convention, pastors would be farmers whose first duty was to milk their congregations for cash, churches would become income-producing franchises of the denomination, and, as Mullins hinted in *The Axioms of Religion*, denominational workers would be bishops in all but name, leaders whose job was to increase the "efficiency" of local churches and to spread the gospel of stewardship and denominational loyalty.

Most Southern Baptists who adopted this new gospel received it as mediated by their pastor or by their state Baptist newspaper. A few Southern Baptists, however, were immersed in the new bureaucratic ideal much more thoroughly through their matriculation at a Southern Baptist college or seminary. The next chapter explores how the bureaucratization of the Southern Baptist Convention shaped the denomination's educational institutions.

133

5

The Right Arm of Our Power:
Southern Baptist Higher Education and
the "Scarborough Synthesis"

During the Seventy-Five Million Campaign, Southern Baptist leaders sought to point their denomination to a new identity that took into account both the doctrinal conflicts raging among Northern Baptists and their own felt need for a more rationalized institutional structure. L. R. Scarborough and others asserted that Southern Baptists, through their institutional apparatus, should take it upon themselves to preserve and defend Christian doctrine from Modernist modification. At the same time, Southern Baptist leaders tried to insulate the Convention from Fundamentalist fractiousness by emphasizing that orthodox Baptist doctrine necessarily included a "doctrine of co-operation." Radical Fundamentalists who recklessly critiqued their denominations and failed to support them financially, then, had as little place in the councils of the new Southern Baptist Convention as did their Modernist targets.[1]

During the Seventy-Five Million Campaign, Southern Baptist educational institutions predictably became loci for applying Southern Baptists' new, emerging identity. By the beginning of the twentieth century, most state Baptist conventions in the South had within their territory at least one denominationally related college. Southern Baptists also moved toward a more formal relationship with their first theological seminary, located in Louisville, Kentucky, while Baptists in Texas sought a similar relationship with Southwestern Baptist Theological Seminary after it separated amicably from Baylor University in 1907. During the Seventy-Five Million Campaign, leaders newly emphasized the role of these schools as guarantors of doctrinal orthodoxy. Although Southern Baptist leaders reserved some doubts about the teaching in their colleges, they affirmed that the denomination, through boards of trustees, was competent to cleanse schools of heterodoxy when it was found, thus guaranteeing that Southern Baptist colleges would continue to offer an education untainted by Modernism. In particular, leaders emphasized that professors espousing Modernist theology would be dismissed and lent their support when boards of trustees did just that. This emphasis on institutional defense of right doctrine reflects the first prong of the new identity that Southern Baptist leaders offered to their constituents: the "Scarborough Synthesis."

Even as they asked their schools to closely monitor what was taught in their classrooms, Southern Baptist leaders began to strengthen the organizational bonds that connected Baptist colleges and seminaries to the denomination. Until the early twentieth century, Baptist colleges and schools had been semi-autonomous, independently soliciting funds and for the most part determining their own policies.[2] Under the centralizing and denominationalizing influence of the Seventy-Five Million Campaign, however, leaders called for the denomination to provide colleges with funds adequate to their task, designating them as institutions essential to the denomination's mission. By the same token, leaders expected to get their money's worth out of the schools that they supported. Southern Baptist leaders feared "nondenominational" Christian education and therefore began to insist that their educational institutions, now the recipients of Campaign funding, tie their students to the denomination as tightly as possible. Leaders indicated that Southern Baptist seminaries and colleges should stress the importance of training students in both denominationally sponsored ministry methodologies and denominational loyalty. Students, including future laypeople, were to be trained to serve a role in the denomination as a part of their standard course of study, learning about the denomination's programs for young people and methods of missionary support. Baptist institutions, such as Southern Baptist Theological Seminary and Carson and Newman College, offered at least muted responses to the denomination's call for a denominationalization of their curricula, but the curricula of Baptist women's institutions revealed a sharp turn towards denominational education. For example, Bessie Tift College, a Baptist women's college in Forsyth, Georgia, began to emphasize the methods of the Woman's Missionary Union as strongly as it did the liberal arts. By the same token, the Training School of the Woman's Missionary Union, located adjacent to the denomination's seminary in Louisville, also moved to include more denominationally oriented training in its curriculum, including preparation for full-time careers in which women would either work for the WMU itself or advocate for and administer the denomination's programs in their employing local church.

This emphasis on denominational loyalty and employment reflects the second prong of the "Scarborough Synthesis."

Northern Influences on Southern Baptist Educational Change, 1920–1925

Southern Baptist leaders entered the Seventy-Five Million Campaign period knowing that the orthodoxy of the teaching in their schools and colleges was not a foregone conclusion. During the latter third of the nineteenth century, the denomination's only theological seminary was twice shaken by conflicts over the religious opinions of its faculty. In 1879, the trustees of that institution accepted the resignation of Crawford Toy, an Old Testament professor who had run afoul of his colleagues by teaching modern, German methods of biblical criticism and affirming Darwin's theory of evolution.[3] While the Toy controversy was an internal matter settled by seminary faculty and trustees, the *fin de siècle* conflict over William Whitsitt's assertion that Baptist origins could be traced not to John the Baptist but to the Protestant Reformation ignited a firestorm within the Convention. Like Toy, Whitsitt was ejected from the faculty of Southern Seminary, but only after a struggle that drew lively participation from newspaper editors, pastors, and laypeople.[4] As a result, leaders among Southern Baptists learned that a professor's membership in a Baptist church was no guarantee that she or he would teach only what was acceptable to a Baptist constituency. Ironically, then, Southern Baptists harbored a latent suspicion of their own educational institutions even as their leaders developed an ideal of denominational solidarity that dictated they offer regular and increasingly substantial financial support to those same institutions.

When the Fundamentalist/Modernist controversy broke out among Northern Baptists, however, Southern Baptists looked North and saw that Baptist theological education on the other side of the Ohio River was both the epicenter of the Modernist movement and, in many Baptists' opinions, an example of just the sort of education that Southern Baptists had sought to avoid.[5] In particular, many Southern Baptists were suspicious of the curriculum at Pennsylvania's Crozer Theological Seminary and, even more importantly, the Divinity School at the University of Chicago.

Southern Baptist suspicion of Crozer revolved around that institution's professor of church history, Henry Vedder. A public defender of theological Modernism, Vedder raised Southern Baptist eyebrows when he denied, among other things, the doctrine of substitutionary atonement.

Editors and other leaders quickly moved to condemn his opinions in print. Z. T. Cody of *The Baptist Courier* claimed of Vedder's opinions on the atonement, "We do not remember ever in life to have read or seen anything from a Baptist minister or a theological teacher that was more abhorrent than this, or that was more subversive of Scripture teaching and of our historic Baptist faith. And yet Dr. Vedder is an honored professor of a theological seminary! . . . it would certainly be untrue to claim that he is an evangelical Christian, to say nothing of his being an orthodox Baptist."[6] J. F. Love, the Corresponding Secretary of the Foreign Mission Board, made the same point, saying that Vedder's denial of substitutionary atonement struck at the "controlling doctrine of our evangelistic preaching."[7]

The conclusion of Love's article showed that Southern Baptist concern with the theology taught at Crozer went beyond a mere theological quibble. "Crozer Theological Seminary," Love continued, "makes annually its overtures to young preachers in Virginia to attend the institution in which Dr. Vedder is a prominent and distinguished teacher."[8] A Virginia observer confirmed Love's point in the same newspaper a year later, noting that in the most recent class of Crozer graduates, Virginians outnumbered residents of any other state save Pennsylvania, the school's home.[9] As a result, Southern Baptist leaders feared that heterodoxy in Pennsylvania could easily cross the Mason-Dixon line into Southern territory. As Livingston Johnson put it, "If our preachers who go to Crozer become receptacles for poisoned gas, and pour out the same from their pulpits, in case they should come back to the South we may expect to have to meet the stream of German rationalism that is sweeping over the North."[10]

Adding insult to injury was the fact that many Southern Baptist students chose to attend Crozer because that institution had financial resources that the seminary in Louisville lacked. As a result, some Southern Baptist leaders seem to have used Crozer's heterodoxy as a means of steering Southern Baptist students towards Louisville. Livingston Johnson complained that while Crozer's president denied sending agents to Southern Baptist colleges, the financial incentives that the seminary offered to Southern preachers, including money in sums "that Louisville could not duplicate," were still a threat when combined with the theology taught in the school.[11] J. F. Love also noted, "The financial help which Crozer Seminary can give a young preacher is no compensation for the weakening of his faith."[12] Instead of sending students to Crozer, concerned leaders insisted that college professors send their students to the seminary in Louisville. Johnson, the editor of the North Carolina *Biblical Recorder*, even suggested that any Wake Forest professor who refused to steer his students toward Louisville and away from Crozer be released from the faculty.[13]

If Crozer provided Southern Baptists with an example of a denominational seminary slowly weakening its bonds with the evangelical faith, the Divinity School of the University of Chicago revealed the fate of a school that had come completely unhinged from its confessional roots. From its founding by Baptist millionaire John D. Rockefeller, the University and its Divinity School had been set on a course that would earn the suspicion of Southern Baptists. The institution's first president, Baptist Hebrew scholar William Rainey Harper, dreamt of a democratic university through which religious scholarship of the highest quality would be brought to bear on an integrated system of ecumenical Christian education that stretched from the local congregation into graduate study. It was this very insistence upon translating the rarefied results of religious scholarship into congregational vernacular that propelled the University and its Divinity School into the trenches of the Fundamentalist controversy.[14] Southern Baptists seem to have had little information about the University that was not gathered from secondhand sources, but when Northern Fundamentalists complained of the theology taught at the University, Southern Baptists listened. For the most part, they uncritically repeated Fundamentalist complaints.

Although editors sensed that the University of Chicago and its most important professional school had begun to distance itself from the Northern Baptist Convention by the early 1920s, they still saw it as a constituent part of the Northern Baptist Convention and reacted to it accordingly, interpreting it as an internal threat to Baptist life.[15] An anonymous author in the Arkansas *Baptist Advance*, upon learning of a Southwestern Seminary professor who planned to travel to the University of Chicago for a summer of study, wrote, "I see no good to come from theological teachers in our Southern seminaries spending the summer in the University of Chicago to study . . . in an atmosphere that is rife, rank, reeking and rotten with the noxious fumes of the Rev. Dr. 'scrap of paper' Von Rationalism."[16] Three years later, an author in *The Baptist Record* expressed almost the exact same sentiment:

> Would any of our people encourage any teacher in any of our
> institutions of learning to teach in the Chicago University,
> which is the fountain head of evolution and modernism?
> Would we say to them, spend a few months imbibing their
> teaching and inhaling the atmosphere of that school? Oh but

139

you say when one of our teachers go up there he will give them the truth and help purify the institution. That would be like a man going down in the sewer and wading around and when asked his purpose would say, "I am down here purifying things." When any teacher in any of our institutions begins to consort with the Chicago University it is time to let him go forever.[17]

Chicago was not just a dangerous institution; it was the very center of the Modernist movement, saturated with heterodoxy and therefore irredeemable.

As a result of their own experiences with educational institutions and their observation of Northern developments, then, Southern Baptist leaders found themselves in an awkward position. On the one hand, leaders knew that theological education was a risky business, as colleges and seminaries all too often turned out to be hotbeds of heresy. On the other hand, leaders needed to support their schools, despite any doubts about them they might have had, in order to continue to provide an alternative to Northern educational institutions infected with heterodoxy.

The Delicate Orthodoxy of Southern Baptist Educational Institutions

During the Seventy-Five Million Campaign period, Southern Baptist leaders generally dealt publicly with this tension by assuring their constituency that their schools taught sound doctrine and simultaneously reminding themselves, Baptist faculties, and the laypeople that paid the bills that aberrant teaching would be excised quickly and effectively. State conventions and the editors that served them had different levels of tolerance for the doctrine of evolution, but most leaders insisted that Southern Baptist schools must be, and for the most part were, free of Modernist teaching.[18]

P. I. Lipsey, editor of *The Baptist Record*, wrote in 1921 that while Baptist schools had no business teaching "destructive critical theories" or undermining the faith of students with "rationalistic unbelief," he believed that "in most of our Southern Baptist schools the above requirements are met."[19] After the end of the Campaign period, L. R. Scarborough endorsed the security of teaching in Southern Baptist schools with stronger words, writing that a "great constructive answer to modernism is found in the sound, gospel, orthodox . . . Baptist schools in the South . . . these are filled by lovers of the truth as revealed in the New Testament. . . . These

The Right Arm of Our Power

. . . professorships form a mighty, impregnable bulwark against the tides of modernism."[20]

At the same time, however, leaders were clear in their assertion that the orthodoxy of Baptist colleges and seminaries was not automatic but was instead the product of denominational vigilance. In particular, leaders charged trustees with the task of keeping Southern Baptist schools free of heterodoxy. After visiting the 1921 Northern Baptist Convention meeting, Scarborough himself warned the denomination, "We should watch our schools with a constructive, loving watchfulness, seeing that they are controlled by the people instead of by self-perpetuating boards."[21] Scarborough, along with other leaders, actually supported the existence of boards of trustees at Baptist schools, but believed that they should be the means of denominational control of the institutions rather than "self-perpetuating" guarantors of their independence. Six months after Scarborough's trip to the NBC, Livingston Johnson of North Carolina summed up the Southern Baptist consensus on the role of college and seminary trustees: "We cannot have an absolutely uniform standard of loyalty or conformity to certain beliefs and policies. . . . This leads me to say that the trustees of an institution should be the judges of its standard of loyalty. . . . I believe the denomination should control its institutions. . . . The control is exercised through boards of trustees. . . . The trustees elect members, but the election must be ratified, or confirmed, by the Convention." Trustees were advocates of the denomination as well as the school, and in the event of a conflict of interests, they were required to press the interests of the denomination instead of the wishes of the faculty or administration. "A board of trustees becomes the nexus between the institution and the denomination. . . . They are acting for the denomination and should see to it that the institution committed to their care is loyal to those things for which the denomination stands."[22]

Southern Baptist leaders relied upon trustees as a way of forestalling Fundamentalist-style grassroots conflict in the denomination, but their concern for keeping their schools free of Modernism was as real as their distaste for popular agitation.[23] R. H. Pitt of Virginia, for instance, explained that the bad habits of Fundamentalists should not be an excuse for a failure to supervise Baptist colleges.

> The fact that some of those who are most vociferous and clamorous in behalf of sound teaching are merely accidentally prominent or have made themselves so for unworthy motives may be deplored by the sound, conservative elements among our

141

people, but will not shake their loyalty. Nor must those, who discover these defects in the noisy and ambitious leaders, suffer any resentment toward them to interfere with the plain discharge of their duty to God and to their brethren in seeking the correction of wrong and injurious teaching in any of our institutions.[24]

When trustees dismissed professors for Modernistic teaching at William Jewell in 1922 and Mercer in 1924, every editor that took notice of the trustees' actions approved, including Louie D. Newton, the genteel editor of Georgia's *Christian Index* and an assiduous avoider of controversial topics.[25]

Newton, along with many other Southern Baptist editors, generally took care not to air their own dirty educational laundry in public for the same reason that they insisted that trustees, and not the Baptist public at large, defend Baptist educational institutions from heresy.[26] Public accusations of heterodoxy involving Baptist schools invariably led to decline in financial receipts and a weakening of the gossamer bonds that held the denomination's institutions together. A letter to the editor of the Tennessee *Baptist and Reflector* expressed this succinctly: "That in union there is strength is an axiom that admits of no question . . . if our church papers print every criticism that any one feels impelled to make the usefulness of our schools will be lessened to a great extent. This open forum method, as democratic as it may seem, will probably do more harm than good."[27] One North Carolina Baptist claimed that the fight in that state over President Poteat's teaching of the theory of evolution "crystallized in many young men going off to other States and into schools of other denominations; and as admitted in the Convention, a loss of one hundred thousand dollars in the contributions for education and missions."[28] Editors knew that the financial health of their institutions depended not only on their ability to publicize their need for funds, but also on their ability not to publicize their failings. In short, Baptist leaders struggled to strike a balance between the need to keep their schools honest while taking care not to jeopardize their sources of denominational funding.

Keeping Loyal to Schools while Keeping Schools Loyal

Leaders hesitated to endanger the wellbeing of their schools during the Seventy-Five Million Campaign because the Campaign itself promoted Baptist schools as a strategically important aspect of the Southern Baptist

142

Convention's mission. Editors working during the Seventy-Five Million Campaign increasingly called for Baptist schools to be drawn from the periphery of the denomination's work into the very center. E. Y. Mullins, writing in 1920 before his election as president of the Southern Baptist Convention, articulated the ideas that lay behind the rising tide of interest in Southern Baptist education:

> The Campaign has brought on a new Baptist era in the realm of education. This has been one of our great weaknesses in the past. We have not seen the close relation between education and all the rest of our work. Our missionary and philanthropic impulses have been fine, and we had been doing something to equip our schools and colleges; but we had only held in a vague and uncertain way the vital relation between the power which education brings and the altruistic impulse behind all our missionary endeavor. Henceforth we shall see and appreciate more fully than ever before the meaning of education in our denominational progress. It is the right arm of our power.[29]

Southern Baptists had always had an interest in education, but only during the Campaign, according to Mullins, had Baptists begun to discern the connection between education and denominational effectiveness. During an era in which strong state-sponsored colleges and universities appeared in the South and met the need for basic postsecondary education, denominational education was destined to focus increasingly on denominational needs.[30]

The growth of state universities in the South had at least one other major effect on denominational colleges: the two classes of institutions competed for the same pool of students. This was doubtless what L. R. Scarborough had in mind when he wrote, "Loyalty to the denomination carries with it loyalty to Baptist schools. I think Baptist parents ought to patronize, not only with their prayers and money, but with their children our Baptist schools. . . . There they will get as good literary training as in any other school and they will get all of the religious influence and spiritual development and growth in denominational loyalty."[31] Scarborough and Mullins were painting the same picture of the relationship that the Baptist school had with the denomination, but from two different perspectives. Scarborough sought to show that the denomination had the same duties toward its schools as it had toward its mission boards and other institutions, while Mullins articulated the new Southern Baptist

Southern Baptist Higher Education and the "Scarborough Synthesis" fascination with the things that colleges and seminaries could provide to the denomination.

The Tie that Binds: Denominational Schools as Nurseries for Denominational Loyalty

Bureaucratization of government or, by extension, of any other large social institution influences educational institutions to modify their instruction to meet that institution's need for employees with specialized skills and training.[32] Schools whose original goal was to produce "cultivated" men and women who were familiar with the arts and sciences found themselves modifying their curricula in order to prepare their students for their place in the emerging bureaucracy.[33] During the Seventy-Five Million Campaign, Southern Baptist leaders demonstrated this tendency as they pressured their postsecondary institutions to provide a more "denominational" education in which all students, including laypeople, would be formed in an environment saturated with loyalty to the Convention and prepared to do the work that the denomination and its various organizations required.

Baptist leaders began calling for a "denominationalizing" of Southern Baptist colleges and schools even before the collection of Seventy-Five Million Campaign pledges in December 1919. In the context of the postwar conflict between the nascent Interchurch World Movement and the Southern Baptist Convention, L. R. Scarborough identified the YMCA and YWCA, commonly active in Baptist colleges, as a fifth column of the church union movement. Scarborough believed that these organizations sought to turn Baptist young people away from their denomination, eventually moving "to interdenominationalize Baptist education in the South, and through our schools to interdenominationalize our Baptist churches." In response, Scarborough asserted that "our mission boards and educational institutions should provide all that is needed for the promotion of the life and mission interests in Baptist schools, in such a way that these Baptist schools could control these movements."[34] The seminary president believed that Baptists had to provide for students an in-house alternative to the YMCA and YWCA in exactly the same way that the Seventy-Five Million Campaign would provide a home-grown alternative to the Interchurch World Movement.

Not every plea for a "denominationalization" of Baptist schools grew out of a fear of ecumenism, however. Some Baptist leaders called for reform in the life of their colleges for the sake of positively stated organizational goals. Thomas Watts, Sunday School and Baptist Young People's Union secretary for South Carolina, wrote during the summer of 1919 that while the denomination's schools rendered a great service to the denomination, it could not yet be said that they provided "a complete denominational training." For Watts, such training would have to include at least three things. First, colleges would need to provide courses in the Bible that would include instruction in "denominational truths and ideals," ensuring that students would be "riveted as with steel to the denomination." Second, Watts believed colleges should be required to provide young people with "knowledge of Baptist organization and usages in both the local churches and in the general bodies." In particular, young Baptists should "learn how to conduct the financial affairs of a church, something of the precise responsibilities and precise duties of church officers and especially concerning the relationship of the churches and their memberships to the denominational missionary, educational, social, and benevolent enterprises." Finally, Watts believed that the Baptist Young People's Union, "an organization specifically set in the denominational machinery for the training of our young men and young women, should be very highly appraised by our schools and given the widest opportunity in dealing with the life of the student body, in directing their Christian activities, and in the promotion of training, courses in missions, denominational teachings and Christian service in the local church and everywhere."[35] Given that Southern Baptist leaders during this period tended to see pastors, church treasurers, and other church officers as denominational functionaries, in place to ensure that the denomination received its due from local congregations, Watts's words disclose a desire to make Baptist colleges and seminaries training grounds for denominationally loyal lay workers.[36]

Writing in early 1920, J. E. Dillard made a similar point, but extended his thoughts into the church's need for professional leaders. "In the new day there must be great stress laid upon definite Christian service," Dillard wrote. "Not only should there be evangelistic services conducted in all of our schools, but there should be calls for volunteers for definite Christian work, and suitable provision should be made to care for those offering themselves."[37] In the context of the Seventy-Five Million Campaign, during which L. R. Scarborough made a point of "calling out the called" by inviting young people to dedicate themselves to the pastorate, mission work, or "other phases of special service," Dillard's emphasis on "definite Christian work" indicates a desire that Baptist schools would not only educate all of their students in Baptist theology, polity, and methods, but would also take special care to train some students for full-time, professional involvement in religious activities.[38]

During the early twentieth century, Southern Baptists were beginning to imagine a number of new professions that fell within the scope of full-time religious work. W. T. Connor, a professor at Southwestern Baptist Theological Seminary in Fort Worth, Texas, noted this movement: "We no longer consider that the ministry is the only line in which a man can devote himself to special religious work. I think this is a good indication. . . . We are seeing that a man may give himself to religious work without being an ordained preacher. There is a great field opening up for men to give themselves to educational work in the churches, to Gospel music, church secretary work, and other lines. These people need to be trained for this work. This calls for separate schools to give them training or for distinct lines of work in the schools that we already have." Connor seemed to think that Baptist schools could be both a training ground for volunteer lay workers and a center for preliminary training in these emerging forms of religious work: "The young men and women that are trained in our colleges should study the Bible. . . . They should be given some knowledge of our denominational work and training in methods of doing religious work. . . . This training in the colleges should be not only for the preachers there, but for all the students; and possibly some of the colleges might give special training along the lines of religious education and possibly something in Gospel music."[39] Furthermore, Connor believed that Baptist college programs in religious work should be tailored to simplify a transition to one of the denomination's seminaries, should the student continue their education beyond the baccalaureate level.[40]

Denominational leaders, then, were quite clear about their expectations of Baptist educational institutions. Every student should be prepared through their education to stand by their denomination and to provide pro-denominational lay leadership in their local congregation. Additionally, students bound for some form of professional, full-time religious work should find in Baptist colleges opportunities to identify their career plans and to receive specialized training appropriate to their calling.

What is less than clear from accounts in Baptist newspapers, however, is the extent to which Baptist educational institutions heeded the call and modified their curricula in order to rise to the expectations of denominational leaders. An examination of four Baptist educational institutions, including the Southern Baptist Theological Seminary of Louis-

The Right Arm of Our Power

ville, Kentucky; Carson and Newman College of Jefferson City, Tennessee; Bessie Tift College of Forsyth, Georgia; and the Woman's Missionary Union Training School adjacent to Southern Seminary reveals that these four institutions, at least, made historically significant changes to their educational programs during the Seventy-Five Million Campaign period.

Students at Southern Baptist Theological Seminary had always been trained for work in local churches, but in 1920 E. Y. Mullins announced that the seminary would be making a permanent attempt through its formal curriculum to familiarize future pastors with the organization of the denomination and to train them in denominationally approved methods of local church ministry and organization.[41] Beginning with the seminary's 1920–1921 school year, Gaines Dobbins's course in "Church Efficiency" was required for students in the seminary's full three-year course and was offered as an option for fulfilling course requirements among the school's two-year students. In no case was the course relegated to the level of a free elective.[42]

An examination of the seminary's catalogs printed during the Campaign period offers insight into the intent of the new course. First, the seminary sought to make sure future pastors would move into the pastorate with a thorough knowledge of and confidence in the organizational structures of the denomination. The 1920–1921 seminary catalog indicates that Professor Dobbins's students would, during the course's first quarter, make a "careful study . . . of the Southern Baptist Convention and its Boards, of the State Mission Boards and of the District Associations." Fascinatingly, Dobbins sought to frame this study of the denomination's polity by placing it at the end of a series of lectures dealing with "New Testament ecclesiology" and "the application of New Testament principles to present-day Baptist denominational and church polity."[43] Such an explicit connection between the developing organization of the Southern Baptist Convention and "New Testament ecclesiology" hearkens back to E. Y. Mullins's contention in *The Axioms of Religion* that the methods of administration used by churches to accomplish their ends are "susceptible of infinite development."[44] In other words, Dobbins sought to reinforce Mullins's opinion that the burgeoning organizational structures of the Southern Baptist Convention were fully legitimate, even by biblical, Baptist standards. This aspect of the curriculum remained more or less unchanged throughout the Campaign period.[45]

Students in the new course were thoroughly familiarized with the denomination's various programs and ministry methods. Although this

Southern Baptist Higher Education and the "Scarborough Synthesis" material was dealt with during the course's third quarter during the 1920–1921 school year, in subsequent years this material found its way into the course's second quarter. To the end of studying "efficiency in organization," students learned about the Baptist Young People's Union, the Woman's Missionary Union, the Laymen's Movement, and "the unifying of the auxiliaries for effectiveness in the total life of the church."[46] Each of these organizations focused their efforts on creating bonds between individual Baptists and their denomination, eliciting financial support for the denomination, or both. In other words, students at Southern Seminary during the Seventy-Five Million Campaign were trained to organize their churches in such a way that they would yield adequate financial support for the larger denomination.

Southern Seminary responded to the Convention's call for a more denominational education by adding a formal emphasis on denominational programs and loyalty to its existing programs of professional preparation. Tennessee's Carson and Newman College, on the other hand, began its attempt to respond to the denomination one step behind the Seminary, entering the Campaign period with almost no curricular emphasis on professional training for ministers at all. In fact, the school's 1919–1920 catalog indicates that while the college boasted an active Baptist Young People's Union and a "Mission Band" dedicated to studying "different phases of missionary endeavor" and deepening "the spiritual lives of the young people who expect to go to the foreign fields" on Sunday afternoons, the college's only formal religion courses were lectures in the Old and New Testament.[47] Students could elect to graduate with a Bachelor of Arts in Ministry, but the requirements were minimal, consisting only of two years of Latin or Greek and one additional year each of Philosophy and Bible beyond what was required of other Bachelor of Arts graduates.[48]

By the publication of the following year's catalog, Carson and Newman's administrators had responded to the denomination's new attitude toward its colleges and their curricula by reorganizing its Bible offerings into a new "School of Christianity." Retaining the Bible courses required of all students, the School also offered a number of new courses that were intended to formalize the preparation of pastors and, to a lesser extent, missionaries at Carson and Newman. Future pastors would be able to elect courses in "Homiletics and Missions," "Pastoral Problems and Personal Work," "Evangelism," "New Testament Greek," and "Reading and Public Speaking."[49] Although the designation "School of Christianity" appeared only in the 1920–1921 catalog, most of the courses that made up its curriculum persisted as a part of Carson and Newman's Bible curriculum throughout the Campaign period.[50]

College administrators made sure that the meaning behind this curricular change would not be lost on readers of their school's catalog. "For the last fifty years," administrators explained, "the Denominational Colleges have been called upon for Christian leaders in social and religious service, yet few of these schools have provided courses of study sufficient to inspire this service. Since a large number of preachers attending College never go to a Theological Seminary, it is urgent upon the Denominational Colleges to provide such training as will equip the ministers the better for their chosen work."[51] Carson and Newman's administrators wanted to signal to Southern Baptist leaders that they were sensitive to the denomination's professionalizing mood.

Upon closer inspection, however, Carson and Newman's curricular changes failed to meet all of the criteria laid out by denominational leaders. For one thing, the new "School of Christianity" seems to have placed no formal emphasis on either denominational loyalty or methodology. If Carson and Newman's administrators had any interest in inculcating their students with a loyalty to the denomination, they must have trusted this task to their Baptist Young People's Union or some other extracurricular organization. Secondly, and more interestingly, the paragraph reproduced above reveals clear slippage between the college's affirmation of their mission to provide training for "leaders in social and religious service" and their promise to provide training for "preachers" and "ministers." Carson and Newman's School of Christianity offered little formal training for women aspiring to full-time forms of religious service or for men interested in non-pastoral work. Carson and Newman, then, ultimately offered only a qualified response to denominational leaders' wishes.

When compared to Southern Seminary and Carson and Newman College, Baptist women's institutions made much more trenchant adjustments to their curricula during the Seventy-Five Million Campaign period. Because much new, specialized coursework was oriented towards training people bound for positions in Christian education, denominational work, and other non-pastoral positions, men's institutions such as Southern Seminary that trained students first and foremost for the pastorate made subtler changes to their curriculum than those that attracted students primarily bound for non-ordained full-time positions. Further, because Southern Baptist women of this period did not enter the pastorate, the average student at women's institutions was most likely to be bound for an alternative form of full-time, professional church or denominational service. As a result, the curricula of Baptist women's institutions of higher education were more sensitive to denominational pressures in the direction of professionalization than were coeducational institutions or institutions attended only by men.

J. H. Foster, the president of Bessie Tift College during the first half of the Seventy-Five Million Campaign period, echoed the sentiments of other denominational leaders about the place of a Baptist college within the denomination:

> We are not simply preparing young women for the business
> of the social life, but for the high responsibilities that come to
> those whose citizenship is in heaven. When they go out from
> these college walls, we expect them to be prepared to fall into
> line with their own church work wherever they go and to be
> come efficient leaders in any department of that work. Loyalty
> to the ideals, the doctrines and the organized work of the de
> nomination has given to the Bessie Tift girl the qualifications
> for leadership and to the Bessie Tift College a name of which
> we are not ashamed.[52]

Foster was aware of his denomination's expectations, and he signaled to his colleagues that he intended to live up to them.

During the years leading up to World War I and the Seventy-Five Million Campaign, Bessie Tift College had placed some emphasis on preparing students for religious work. The bulk of this work, however, was done through non-academic courses provided by the college's Young Woman's Auxiliary, "directed by the students," and through a daily "twilight prayer-meeting."[53] Bible courses were consistently required of all students, but a note in the catalog explaining that the Bible course was intended in part to help students "become conversant with our Baptist organized life" was dropped in 1917 when President Foster began teaching the courses on the Bible himself.[54]

Curricular changes that appeared in the Tift College bulletin published during the months preceding the 1919–1920 school year show that President Foster was responding to the educational emphases of the Seventy-Five Million Campaign. To prepare for the opening of the fall semester, the college added an entire "Department of Denominational Ministries" to its curriculum. The description of the department's new coursework noted that its purpose was to "help insure a distinctly denominational product from a distinctly denominational institution. The *aim* of the course, therefore, is that the student may be thoroughly acquainted with, and instructed in, the *origin*, the *object* and the *function* of each *unit* and of each *organization* within the denomination." Not only were students to be instructed in the structure of the denomination; they were also to be inculcated with a loyalty to its institutions. "Denominational loyalty and efficiency will come only from definite knowledge of, and consequent conviction upon, the fundamental tenets of the denomination." These were words that could have been pulled verbatim from a Southern Baptist newspaper of the period. Students began their study of "Baptist Organizations and Operations" by first examining "The Individual Soul" and then moving on to "The Local Church," "The Association," "The State Baptist Convention," and "The Southern Baptist Convention," finally concluding with a discussion of "The Baptist World Alliance." Later, students studied "Sunday School and B.Y.P.U. Methods" in order to organize themselves into a local Baptist Young People's Union and to learn methods of Sunday School instruction. The catalog notes that these courses were required for all Baptist students. Additionally, an explanatory note reminds students that while the first semester of freshman Bible would not be offered in the fall, the courses in denominational ministries would "count for the same as Bible toward [the] bachelor's degree."[55] The catalogs of the following two school years, 1920–1921 and 1921–1922, include the same explanatory notes.[56]

During the spring of 1922, a conflict developed at Tift College that caused J. H. Foster to resign as president.[57] In the catalog for the 1922–1923 term, the still-new Department of Denominational Ministries is conspicuously absent, perhaps because Foster's departure had robbed the college of its most strident advocate of the inclusion of denominational studies in the college's curriculum.[58]

Bessie Tift College found a new leader in Aquila Chamlee, a scholarly Georgia pastor with high ambitions for his new charge. Under Chamlee, Tift's support of denominational efforts became more subtle but was still very much in evidence.[59] During the 1923–1924 school year, Tift's four Bible courses concluded with a course on "Church Efficiency," "Doctrines," and "Church Organization and Missions."[60] Later Tift catalogs consistently included some coverage of denominational or ecclesiastical issues as a segment of its Bible curriculum.[61] Catalogs printed between 1924 and 1926 consistently indicated that it was "probable that a course on Church Efficiency will be offered" instead of the listed course in the Acts of the Apostles.[62]

Bessie Tift's curriculum in denominational studies was aimed mostly at a student body whose members would not advance into full-time

151

religious work, although college leaders hoped that their institution provided appropriate preparation for those students who chose to pursue additional studies at the Woman's Missionary Union Training School. In fact, board of trustees records indicate that the college was actively working toward coordinating their coursework with that of the Training School so that students could complete as many as nineteen hours of the thirty-four hour training school curriculum before arriving in Louisville.[63]

That Tift College trustees wanted to coordinate so closely with the WMU Training School provides further evidence of the school's movement toward offering a "distinctly denominational" education. Ironically, however, the Training School itself was slower in its adaptation to the new expectations of the denomination than was its Georgia cousin, showing no serious formal curricular reaction to the Seventy-Five Million Campaign until 1922. This may be because the training school offered, in the words of T. Laine Scales, a "hidden curriculum" meant to inculcate loyalty to the Woman's Missionary Union and, by extension, to the Southern Baptist Convention whose missionary efforts the WMU supported.[64] By 1922, however, the Training School began to exhibit a more formal curricular commitment both to training women for specific denominational careers beyond narrowly defined mission work and to inculcating a loyalty to the WMU and to the Convention through formal coursework.[65]

In 1922 the Training School added courses in "W. M. U. Methods" to its curriculum, providing a formal channel for the inculcation of loyalty to the WMU. The 1922–1923 Training School catalog's description of this course is sparse, noting that students would have been instructed in the history of the WMU, "program making," "Note Book work," and "Missionary Pageantry," but the catalogs for subsequent years provide more detail.[66] The 1923–1924 catalog specifically notes, for instance, that the second-year WMU course "is planned for the specific purpose of training leaders for each of the organizations of Woman's Missionary Union."[67] The following year, the catalog reveals further development in the course. Students taking the WMU course during their first year of studies during the 1924–1925 school year carried out "a detailed study of the organizations of the Graded Union, how to organize and direct them," while second-year students conducted "an intensive study of the Fundamental Principles on which the Woman's Missionary Union is founded."[68] Although students at the Training School must certainly have been exposed to these subjects from the school's founding in 1907, the formal, academic curriculum of the school did not reflect this until the Seventy-Five Million

152

Campaign. Through these WMU courses, students not only developed close ties to the Woman's Missionary Union; they also prepared for professional service within that organization. Carrie Littlejohn, a member of the Training School's faculty, noted in her 1934 Northwestern University MA thesis that of the 275 students who graduated from the Training School between 1920 and 1930, twelve were employed by the WMU itself in 1934, working as young people's secretaries, field workers, and in one case, a state WMU treasurer.[69] All of these women, except for one, were employed full time. At least some Training School students managed to translate their educations into careers as WMU professionals.

During the Campaign period, the Training School also offered other opportunities to women who sought training for particular full-time, professional careers outside of foreign missions. In 1922, Carrie Littlejohn began offering a course in "Christian Social Service," a subject that had formerly been offered as a part of the course work in "Personal Service."[70] By 1925, the course title had been changed to "Social Work." The course's description, which exhibited only minor changes between 1922 and 1925, noted that the course "offers a study of modern problems of the city, town and rural communities," along with a discussion of methods of ameliorating these problems.[71] The 1925–1926 catalog specifically notes that the course would place "special emphasis on methods for Clubs in Good Will Center[s]."[72] Littlejohn notes that as of 1934, five members of her sample worked in Good Will Centers (WMU-supported settlement houses), five others worked in orphanages, and six more had found secular employment in the field of social work.[73]

Perhaps more significantly, the Training School began offering during the 1924–1925 school year a program specifically intended for "church and educational secretaries," providing another professional outlet for career-minded Southern Baptist women. While secretarial work was considered to be well within the women's sphere, T. Laine Scales notes that the creation of this program represented a crack through which Southern Baptist women eventually found their way into jobs in Christian education and church administration, areas originally reserved for men among Southern Baptists.[74] Even during the first year in which the course was offered, students took course work in these two areas.[75] During the 1925–1926 school year, students in the secretarial program also took Littlejohn's Social Work course, suggesting that Training School faculty may have hoped that their graduates would be engaged in a range of activities not traditionally subsumed under the title of "secretary."[76] Littlejohn notes

153

that fifteen of the students she surveyed were working in congregations, and three of those students split their time between secretarial and educational duties. Another two served as educational directors. Of these fifteen graduates, twelve had found full-time employment.[77] Although these secretaries mostly worked for local congregations and not for a denominational agency, Training School graduates working as secretaries and educational directors were in an ideal position to act as advocates for the WMU and its sponsoring denomination.

Noting the kinds of work that WMU Training School graduates had found, Littlejohn believed that the School should modify its curriculum to better prepare its students for the practical work in which they found themselves engaged. "The writer believes that a careful study should be made of the curriculum to ascertain whether it is overweighted with theoretical and theological courses to the exclusion of courses that are sorely needed in the training of women for professional religious work . . . particular attention should be given the types of work in which graduates have been engaged . . . for guidance in the proportion of background and methods courses."[78] For Littlejohn, professionalizing education by emphasizing practical skills at the expense of the theoretical was a positive development. Already much in evidence at the WMU Training School, Bessie Tift College, and Southern Seminary, the emphasis on providing practical, professional training for emerging, denominationally oriented professions, when combined with a parallel curricular emphasis on denominational loyalty, provides strong evidence of how the Seventy-Five Million Campaign and its attendant movement toward denominational bureaucratization affected Southern Baptist educational institutions.

Southern Baptist Education and the "Scarborough Synthesis"

In their simultaneous scrutiny of and reliance upon their institutions of higher education, Southern Baptist leaders were applying the "Scarborough Synthesis." While Northern Baptists moved to the brink of schism because of conflicts generated in part by Fundamentalist anxieties about the curriculum and control of their schools, Southern Baptist leaders channeled their own fears of Modernism in a more constructive direction, using the tense years of the early 1920s as an opportunity for consolidation. Leaders promised to mold their schools into bastions of orthodoxy, thus guaranteeing the Convention's distinctive doctrinal identity. In the meantime, these same schools increasingly offered practical preparation

154

for the people that would eventually hold paid and volunteer positions in the denomination's bureaucracy, guaranteeing sound, denominationally loyal leadership for the organizations that leaders had entrusted with holding back the rising tide of Modernism. To no small degree, leaders pinned their hopes for the Convention's future on their educational institutions, hoping that they would translate the "Scarborough Synthesis" into meaningful action.

In the meantime, many Southern Baptists began to suggest aloud that the centralizing tendencies apparent everywhere in their denominational life had begun to endanger the traditional Baptist practice of democratic decision-making. Some observers believed that their leaders had illicitly taken the denomination's reins, while at least one editor believed that these same leaders actually used their influence to hide the presence of Modernism in their own ranks. In both cases, evidence abounds that not all Southern Baptists uncritically accepted the changes in polity that Progressivism seemed to be bringing to the Southern Baptist Convention.

6

The Empire's New Clothes: Dissent against Denominational Centralization during the Seventy-Five Million Campaign

In *Yet Saints Their Watch Are Keeping: Fundamentalists, Modernists and the Development of Evangelical Ecclesiology, 1887–1937*, J. Michael Utzinger demonstrates the relationship between the Northern Fundamentalist controversies and the centralization that took place among Northern Baptists, Northern Presbyterians, and the Disciples of Christ during the years surrounding the Great War. Utzinger convincingly shows that Northern Baptist Fundamentalists, in particular, were anxious about the increasing centralization of the Northern Baptist Convention because it tended to place Modernists in positions of institutional influence while leaving more conservative Baptists to pay the bills.[1] When Northern Baptist Fundamentalists expressed frustration at the fact that "certain small groups have constituted themselves steering committees of the Convention and have assumed for themselves responsibilities to determine in secret conferences courses of action for the whole body," they were motivated first and foremost not by polity anxieties, but by doctrinal disagreement. Northern Baptist Fundamentalists attempted, with little success, to play the polity card in order to trump Modernist advances within the structures of the still-new Northern Baptist Convention.[2]

Among Southern Baptists, however, a different pattern of protest emerged. While Northern Baptist Fundamentalists criticized centralization as a method of resisting doctrinal change within their denomination, many Southern Baptists expressed doubts about the centralization of their own Convention—but Southern Baptist doubts were expressed as a primary, freestanding concern, independent of any doctrinal anxieties. In a denomination in which leaders were often revered as living saints, many rank-and-file Southern Baptists felt that the inordinate influence of

a small circle of men was subverting traditional Baptist polity. The annual meeting of the Southern Baptist Convention had degenerated, in
many Southern Baptists' minds, from an opportunity to democratically
discuss the denomination's problems and goals into a loud, uncontrollable
mass meeting. Messengers failed to take it seriously, and leaders used
it as a platform for autocratic grandstanding. Further, many frustrated
Southern Baptists believed that the Seventy-Five Million Campaign had
introduced an intolerable element of coercion into Southern Baptist life.
Laypeople, pastors, and even some editors expressed concern that the
Convention's leaders had developed an antipathy for criticism, even of the
most well-meaning kind. They also noticed that Southern Baptists who
failed to do what their superiors required of them were in danger of being
stigmatized through a variety of methods. In fact, some Southern Baptists denounced the program that Southern Baptist leaders developed in
response to the autocratic Interchurch World Movement, asserting that
this new program was also autocratic.

Among editorial critics of Southern Baptist centralization, the most
ardent was the editor of the Kentucky Baptist newspaper, Victor I.
Masters. The South Carolina native brought to his task as the editor of
the *Western Recorder* an urgent, unparalleled concern for the preservation of democratic polity among Southern Baptists. Masters sought to
warn his fellow Baptists about the decline of democracy in Southern Baptist life, but most other editors found his breathless editorializing obnoxious and accusatory. As Masters found himself increasingly isolated from
the rest of the Southern Baptist press, he began to intimate that the unwillingness of other Southern Baptist leaders and editors to confront the
Modernist threat was due not to a desire to avoid controversy for the sake
of the Campaign, but instead revealed the presence of Modernist sym-
pathizers within the Convention's leadership. Masters did not identify
with Northern Fundamentalism more strongly than any of his editorial
colleagues because he was more conservative than they; rather, his frustrations with the increasingly antidemocratic tendencies of Southern
Baptist Convention leaders pressed him into sympathizing with Northern
conservatives. In the process, Masters laid out the rudiments of an alternative to the Scarborough Synthesis, suggesting that Southern Baptist
identity should not focus on regional distinctiveness or allegiance to a
constellation of denominational organizations, but should instead grow
out of Southern Baptist identification with the Fundamentalist movement.

God's Upper Class: Looking Up to Leaders During the Seventy-Five Million Campaign

While bureaucracies are created to govern or organize large groups of people through a set of rules or laws established for the sake of fairness and equality, the officials administering those rules or laws ironically develop into a new "caste" that controls the machinery of their organization.[3] During the Seventy-Five Million Campaign, Southern Baptist newspapers offered ample evidence that at least some Southern Baptists had begun to see their highest echelon of leaders as a people set apart, possessing superior knowledge and wisdom and worthy of almost infinite trust.

In the August 18, 1921 edition of the Virginia *Religious Herald,* editor R. H. Pitt printed an editorial titled "Our Leaders." In it, Pitt praised the Convention's leadership in a way that became increasingly familiar through the years of the Campaign. Of B. D. Gray, the corresponding secretary of the Home Mission Board, Pitt exclaimed, "What an admirable secretary he has made! Genial, lovable, an eloquent master of assemblies, with a statesmanlike grasp of the problems of the South, he adds to these a long stretch of years full of experience and gathered wisdom." Pitt likewise praised the "fine, thoughtful, statesmanlike qualities" of J. F. Love, the leader of the Foreign Mission Board. The editor also lavished praise on the presidents of the two Southern Baptist seminaries, offering words of approval for the "cultured, sagacious" E. Y. Mullins and the "able and energetic" L. R. Scarborough.[4]

Other Southern Baptists offered similar affirmation of the Convention's leadership. One Baptist, writing to the Kentucky *Western Recorder,* claimed "that of the Baptists of the South, the greatest organizer is E. Y. Mullins, the greatest Greek scholar is A. T. Robertson, the greatest orator J. W. Porter, the most all around man J. B. Gambrell, the greatest single missionary force J. F. Love, the greatest combination of doctrine and evangelism Lee Scarborough, the greatest arousing public collector W. D. Powell, the most consecrated man George W. Truett."[5] Similarly, *The Christian Index* carried a group of "TRIBUTES TO OUR LEADERS" overheard in the halls during the 1920 meeting of the Southern Baptist Convention. J. B. Gambrell was listed as "our greatest Baptist commoner," A. T. Robertson was praised as "the greatest New Testament scholar of the age," and E. Y. Mullins was deemed to be "the premier theologian of the age."[6] Such comments illustrate not only the insularity of Southern Baptist life, but also the unusually high esteem in which these men were held by at least some Southern Baptists.

THE CHRISTIAN INDEX

VOLUME 105   ESTABLISHED 1881   NUMBER 2

THE ORGAN AND PROPERTY OF THE BAPTISTS OF GEORGIA
ATLANTA, GEORGIA, THURSDAY, JANUARY 8, 1925

LIBRARY
SOUTHERN BAPT.ST
APR   1972
THEOLOGICAL SEMINARY
LOUISVILLE, KY.

EDGAR YOUNG MULLINS
President of the Southern Baptist Theological Seminary for Past Quarter of the Century—
Great Teacher, Great Preacher, Peerless Theologian, Glorious World
Leader of our Baptist People.

MULLINS ANNIVERSARY NUMBER

A portrait of E. Y. Mullins on the cover of *The Christian Index*, January 8, 1925. Many Southern Baptists came to view their leaders with extraordinary trust and awe. The caption under Mullins' portrait reads: "President of the Southern Baptist Theological Seminary for Past Quarter of the Century–Great Teacher, Great Preacher, Peerless Theologian, Glorious World Leader of our Baptist People." Permission to reprint graciously provided by *The Christian Index*.

Occasionally, editors would identify the boards and agencies responsible for Southern Baptist work so closely with their respective secretaries that refusing to contribute to the work of the Convention was taken as a personal injury to the leaders themselves. In the Oklahoma *Baptist Messenger*, a series of cartoons appeared in 1925 that show D. B. Gray and J. F. Love, representing the two Southern Baptist mission boards, in two difficult situations. In the first cartoon, Gray is shown pressed between a series of blocks. The blocks below him carry labels that describe the board's various responsibilities, such as "CO-OPERATION WITH STATES," "WORK AMONG THE JEWS," and "CUBA AND PANAMA." The board resting on top of him carries only one word, however: "DEBT." Underneath a caption reading "DR. GRAY CALLING," the secretary himself calls out, "HELP! HELP!"[7]

160

The Empire's New Clothes

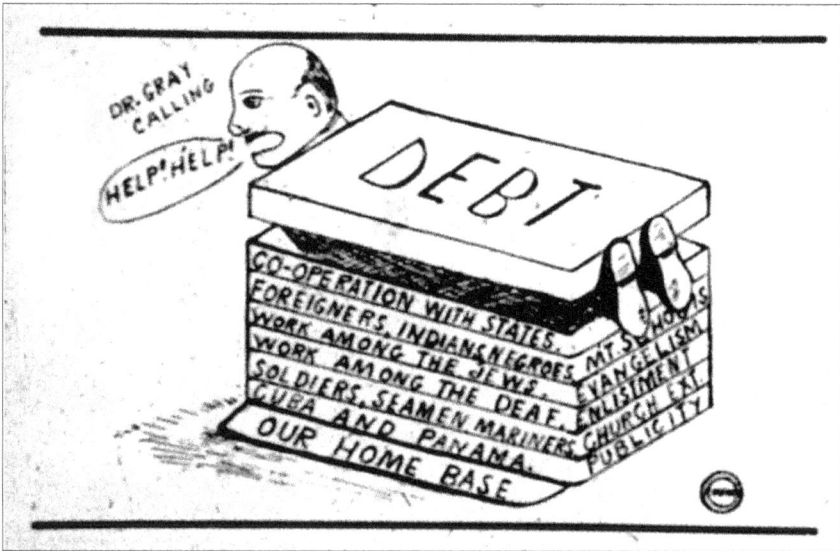

"Dr. Gray Calling," *Baptist Messenger*, February 25, 1925, p. 4. The circle in the bottom right corner of the cartoon is the signature of Mrs. J. B. Rounds, the wife of the man who edited the "Building Our Denomination" page on which the cartoon appeared. Permission to reprint graciously provided by *The Baptist Messenger*.

In another cartoon published the following month, Secretary Love of the Foreign Mission Board appears in a coat and striped pants, sweating profusely, struggling to walk to a door marked "FOREIGN MISSION FIELDS." Unfortunately, Love is burdened by a large sack over his shoulder, marked "FOREIGN MISSION DEBT," and a long-limbed "SATAN" is outrunning him. A caption sums up the appeal: "WHY NOT REMOVE THE HANDICAP AND GIVE HIM A CHANCE TO WIN THE RACE?"[8] In both cartoons, a Southern Baptist leader personifies the organization that he leads, and the financial difficulties of these organizations are identified as personal hardships on the leaders themselves. The boards and agencies of the Southern Baptist Convention were becoming indistinguishable from the personalities that led them.

Further, Southern Baptist colleges participated in the praise of Baptist leaders and seemed to be oriented toward replicating this style of leadership in the future. The last chapter demonstrated the extent to which students at Bessie Tift College and the Woman's Missionary Union Training School received denominational training that was meant to fit them for future denominational leadership. Even while students received this formal training, however, they learned to look up to the leaders of the WMU even

161

Untitled cartoon, *Baptist Messenger*, March 18, 1925, p. 4. Permission to reprint graciously provided by *The Baptist Messenger*.

as the wider Convention looked up to Mullins, Love, and others. Carrie Littlejohn, for instance, noted that Maud Reynolds McLure, the first principal of the WMU Training School, "for the alumnae . . . *was* the School." Many students "were very close to her during student days and loved her devotedly. Some of them stood in awe of her and never paid her a visit unless called in for conference. But without question, they all admired her and had the utmost confidence in her administration of affairs."[9] A blurb in the Tennessee *Baptist and Reflector* offers evidence showing that at least one institution enrolling men sought to make leaders like Mullins, Scarborough, Love, and Gray the models toward which young, aspiring ministers would strive. "Dr. Campbell," the chair of Carson and Newman College's Bible department, "is soliciting funds to place on the walls of the Bible department pictures of the leading Baptist preachers," the newspaper reported. Readers interested in contributing funds to the project were encouraged to contact the department.[10]

When W. J. McGlothlin, Professor of Church History at the Southern Baptist Theological Seminary, said that Christian colleges would train "a religious and moral upper class," he explained that the world needed leaders who "put moral and spiritual considerations above all else and who at the same time are competent and efficient."[11] This is exactly the collection of traits that many, if not most, Southern Baptists saw in their denomina-

The Empire's New Clothes

tional leaders, a group dedicated to expressing the collective faith of the Convention through Progressive-style programs and organization. As a result, during the Seventy-Five Million Campaign Southern Baptist spokespersons encouraged rank-and-file Baptists to reserve their criticisms and support the program because its architects were trustworthy. Georgia editor Louie D. Newton, for example, noted that "Southern Baptists have been blessed through all the years in a leadership which at all times was wholly worthy of the complete confidence of the people. And today," Newton claimed significantly, "we face our enlarging tasks with the growing appreciation of the worthy leadership of all of our secretaries and convention leaders." For Newton, the high quality of the Convention's leadership legitimized a Campaign strategy in which individual Baptists were asked to march in step with the denomination's leaders. "To know that we are thoroughly democratic and yet are reposing great responsibility upon a few men and are absolutely assured of their high fidelity to this trust? [*sic*] Our people are co-operating in a worthy task, we are straightening up the lines, we are moving together, we are keeping step. Our leaders have their faces toward the Dawn. The Captain of the mighty host is leading us on."[12] It is hard to escape the impression that Newton envisioned everyday Southern Baptists following their leaders as their leaders followed "the Captain"; for this editor, leaders especially in tune with the divine will mediated the leadership of Christ.

L. R. Scarborough asked for the same trust in denominational leadership, but was often forced to cast it in negative terms. Instead of describing a church militant marching toward "the Dawn," Scarborough was forced to plead with vacillating Baptists, asking them to withhold their criticism and to give denominational leaders the benefit of the doubt. Faced with suspicions of mismanagement based on discrepancies between the stated amounts that each agency would receive and the amounts that they actually had collected, Scarborough reported that the practice of designated contribution "explains the larger part of the discrepancies widely advertised." Knowing the damage that rumors of malfeasance could inflict on the Campaign, Scarborough appealed to his constituents, asking them to trust their leaders: "I wish to say I have not received or administered one cent of the Campaign money as Chairman of the Conversation [*sic*] Commission and have nothing to do with percentages, but I do know the secretaries and boards, and do not believe that there is a single case of maladministration or misappropriation. I know what our leaders do is in the open, have been approved by their boards and none of them has been arraigned nor discredited by misappropriations." Scarborough had not seen the books, but to do so would be unnecessary because the Campaign's administrators were trustworthy. Scarborough asked his readers to trust the Convention's leadership as implicitly as he did, suggesting that they *"Restrain Criticism* on the *co-operating* forces . . . *Save Now our Over-Taxed Causes*," and "raise *funds*, not suspicions."[13] Many Southern Baptists surely did exactly what Scarborough asked, but a number of others expressed doubts.

Southern Baptist Criticism of Denominational Centralization

At the most superficial level, at least one Baptist thought that constant, effusive praise of Southern Baptist leaders was quite unnecessary. "Without appreciable loss," J. J. Taylor wrote, "we might also dispense with all our agencies of puffery which waste so much valuable space in our religious papers telling of the great men among us."[14] In a more important way, however, the increasing centralization of the Convention and the attending expectation that ordinary pastors and laypeople would participate in the denomination's democratic polity by paying their pledges, loving their leaders, and keeping their thoughts to themselves generated a significant reaction.[15] Although the still-independent and theologically tolerant Baptist newspapers of Virginia and North Carolina were most likely (excepting Kentucky's *Western Recorder*) to carry complaints about the decline of democracy among Southern Baptists, almost every Southern Baptist newspaper published at least a few letters or editorials expressing concern about the Convention's metamorphosis into an "oligarchy."

One cluster of polity concerns centered on the realization that the annual meeting of the Southern Baptist Convention was no longer democratic but had degenerated into a disorderly "mass meeting" dedicated to socializing and long speeches from Southern Baptist leaders. The 1920 meeting of the Convention, held in Washington, DC, served as a wake-up call for many observers of Southern Baptist life. According to R. H. Pitt, the editor of *The Religious Herald*, the registered attendance at the meeting exceeded ten thousand, although the venue in which the meetings were held only seated three thousand five hundred.[16] As a result, the meeting overflowed with attendees, prompting police officers to close the building and refuse entry to thousands of registered messengers.[17] L. L. Gwaltney told stories of spouses separated from each other and of at least one pastor who abandoned the sessions entirely in order to watch a movie.[18]

164

Similar problems plagued other sessions of the Southern Baptist Convention held during the first half of the decade. In 1923, for instance, messengers lingering in the lobby of the Convention's meeting place to talk proved so disruptive that a policeman had to be called; during that same meeting the messengers constantly burst into rowdy applause, behavior forbidden by the SBC's bylaws.[19] The acting editor of the Tennessee *Baptist and Reflector*, O. E. Bryan, commented on the "misery" of the 1925 Convention, saying that he had fielded numerous "complaints of the people regarding the difficulty had in hearing the proceedings. It can truly be said of our convention," Bryan continued, "that it is more of a mass meeting than it is of an orderly convention. From nine o'clock in the morning until nine in the evening, the convention hall was filled with restless humanity. The vast auditorium, built with a view to the comfort of great throngs of people, proved to be a source of torment to multitudes who desired to hear what was being said."[20]

Bryan chalked up part of the messengers' misery to the lack of "horns" in the buildings where they had been meeting, but his remarks point up the polity concerns latent in Southern Baptist anxieties about the deterioration of Southern Baptist Convention meetings. Instead of an opportunity for deliberation, the annual Convention had become a platform for leaders to speak, excluding rank-and-file Baptists from participation and undermining the Convention's democratic purpose. John D. Mell, president of the Georgia Baptist Convention, believed that the unruly conduct of the 1923 Convention was a nadir for that organization. Mell observed:

> We have too many reports, they are generally too long, and
> there are too many appointed speakers. . . . The Convention
> itself, cannot, without breaking its rules, discuss any ques-
> tion it has to decide. We hear only one side, and that side is
> presented by speakers appointed by those interested in the
> matter. . . . We Baptists boast that we are a free people, believ-
> ing in the rights of the individual, and freedom of speech is
> one of our cardinal doctrines. Yet, the greatest Baptist body
> on earth has no freedom of speech for the individual member
> but, on the contrary, operates under a gag rule that permits
> no member to speak on most questions before it unless he has
> been appointed to speak. . . . We have too much harness and
> too little horse.

Dissent against Denominational Centralization

Additionally, Mell was frustrated that messengers moved about during the entire meeting, making it difficult to follow the proceedings.

> We must keep better order so the messengers can hear what
> is going on. Nobody seems for several years to have tried to
> keep order, until we are really not a convention any longer but
> just a religious mob. In Kansas City is [*sic*] was just like a big
> moving picture show, a large crowd coming in and another
> large one going out all the time. Those that were going out had
> become disgusted because they could not hear, and those that
> were coming in were hopeful that they might hear, but a little
> later on they joined the crowd that were going out. Only a few
> comparatively, who were up close to the speaker, could hear.
> I studied this situation carefully and, so far as I can recall, no
> serious effort was made by anybody to stop this disorder.[21]

Not only had the Convention become disorderly; this disorder was apparently immaterial to its presiding officers.

Mell framed his critique as an attempt to promote the best interests of an organization he loved. Other commentators, however, saw something more sinister in the new shape of the SBC annual meetings. Writing in the *Baptist Standard*, M. T. Andrews noted that Baptists would soon lose patience with the Convention's preference to deal with business through committees rather than through open debate: "It is much easier sometimes to get a thing done in a small committee meeting than it is to make the right of it apparent before the larger representative body; but if we pursue such a policy persistently, it will not be long until we will reap the consequences of our folly in the broken confidences of our people. Baptists ought not to boast of more democracy than other people, and practice less."[22] More trenchantly, Allen Hill Autry of Little Rock seemed to indicate that leaders were actively conspiring to limit lay and pastoral participation.

> As for "deliberation," that word might as well be eliminated
> from Southern Baptist vocabulary, first, because very few
> speakers could be heard by more than one-fourth of the dele-
> gates assembled, and, second, it seems to be the convention's
> policy to settle everything in committees. And it seems to
> be understood among many of the "leaders" that is it next to
> high treason for anyone to raise objection to the report of any

The Empire's New Clothes

committee, if there is a unanimous report. In this way many important reports are never settled before the body at all, except as it acquiesces in the committee's report, and that often without discussion, except by those appointed beforehand to speak. To give "one-fourth" of the time allotted to a given report to general discussion, and three-fourths of the time to the chairman of a committee or his appointee, is a farce upon its very face. Five thousand nine hundred and fifty of the delegates have one-fourth of the time, while probably 50 will have three-fourths of the time. That's just an "all-day sucker" to keep the brethren quiet.[23]

Southern Baptist leaders, having taken control of the Convention's programs, worked to keep it that way.

Thus, this first cluster of complaints about the Convention, gathered around the realization that the annual meeting was "really not a convention any longer but just a religious mob," leads directly into the second.[24] A number of observers believed that the Southern Baptist Convention was silently replacing its democracy with a less participatory form of polity. In particular, many of these observers believed that the leaders of the denomination had turned to methods of coercion inappropriate for an organization claiming to be democratic.

Many Southern Baptists, including some newspaper editors, expressed considerable alarm at the coercive tendencies that denominational leaders had exhibited during the Seventy-Five Million Campaign.[25] Criticisms of this tendency among rank-and-file Baptists ranged from subtle to sarcastic. One author, for instance, expressed his concerns about the behavior of SBC leaders in relatively gentle terms, granting that a lack of organization was also undesirable. "It is too lamentably true that democracy has been often discredited by some who were partakers of its choicest benefits. . . . On the other hand, some men have advanced to positions of leadership in the Baptist denomination who have sought diligently to so centralize its democracy that they could issue commands with all the authority of a military officer. Now, with these two parties democracy fares badly, they pierce it through with many sorrows, although both profess to be its loyal friends."[26] Other Baptists complained about leaders who "issued commands" in less irenic terms. A. T. Smith of Haynesville, Louisiana wrote to his state's newspaper to express his frustration with his denomination's leaders:

Dissent against Denominational Centralization

> I know our churches have a right to send messengers . . . to
> Conventions who can have a part in forming the plans of our
> work; but in reality our programs are made before the Con-
> ventions meet, by a few of the "leading brethren." Actually, the
> policies of the Southern Baptist Convention are controlled by
> not more than twenty-five leaders. Of course, I or any other
> "small fry" could get up and object, but what good would it
> do? How many brethren are willing to be classed as "reaction-
> aries," "obstructionists," etc., and besides get nowhere.[27]

Smith's comments underscored the tendency among Convention leaders to apply unsavory labels to their critics, a strategy that seems to
have generated significant resentment. "I do resent being classed as non-
cooperative or a kicker when I cannot follow the hobby of some leader,"
Smith admitted.[28] An author in the Texas *Baptist Standard* made a similar point when he expressed his frustration toward "a disposition on the
part of some to want to brand as 'disloyal' all who do not agree with them
in their thinking. That word has become so distasteful that it nauseates
some of us every time we hear it used. Yet it is all too common. When the
day comes that a Baptist can not think for himself, and even express those
thoughts, we are rapidly heading toward an ecclesiasticism that is worse
than any hierarchy on the face of the earth but Romanism."[29]

Just as some Baptists felt anger toward their leaders because of
their tendency to label their opponents, other Baptists believed that the
Campaign had not been executed as a voluntary fundraising effort but
had been levied as a tax undergirded by denominational coercion. In 1922,
The Alabama Baptist printed a set of resolutions passed by "a certain
association in Alabama" in which the association stated their intention to
"deny and denounce any right the Alabama convention has assumed over
us in taxation and otherwise, we do not expect to conform to its dictation
nor that of the state board."[30] While these unidentified Baptists might have
had a tenuous relationship with the Southern Baptist Convention even before the Campaign was launched, J. B. Salmond, a Baptist writing in the
Mississippi *Baptist Record* in November 1923, pled his own loyalty to the
Convention before offering his critique. "It has always been a pleasure and
not a pain for me to give," he noted. At the same time, however, Salmond
believed that the Campaign represented a "golden calf" that needed to be
destroyed. "It is violative of distinct Baptist doctrine . . . that some Board
or Committee has assumed the authority or right to tax, or assess, or 'ap-
portion' the individual independent Baptist churches and its members

The Empire's New Clothes

thereof, so much per head," Salmond asserted. The author also noted that leaders used undesirable methods to add bite to their demands for money, mentioning their tendency to call uncooperative Baptists "a 'slacker' or some other unkind and un-Christian name" and to intimate that pastors so described "would not be 'acceptable' as a pastor within the bonds of the Southern Baptist Convention."[31]

Underneath periodic flashes of anger about the fundraising methods of Southern Baptist Convention leaders, however, lay the growing realization that these methods were indicative of a shift in organizational form among Southern Baptists. Because of the Seventy-Five Million Campaign, Southern Baptists were adopting a more centralized form of polity. In other words, Southern Baptists were not only behaving in new ways; they were changing into a new thing. Again, some comments were gentler than others. B. F. Fronabarger believed that part of the blame for this trend lay with pastors and laypeople.

> I fear that many of us to whom in the beginning our brethren
> entrusted leadership in Baptist affairs—state, associational
> and community . . . have come to think that the world would
> not go forward without some of us tried and true fellows to
> plan the work and direct the other brethren in doing their part,
> even to the extent . . . of giving instructions as to the whens
> and the wheres and hows of procedure in the doing of the
> thing. . . . On the other hand, many of us, especially pastors,
> had rather take up these plans and directions furnished by
> those who have come to feel that it is theirs to keep the pas-
> tors and missionaries toned up, trained up, and lined up, and
> meekly to carry them out, rather than take the initiative and
> plan their own procedure and put the thing over in their own
> way—the way their own consecrated common sense tells
> them is best suited for their people to do the thing and grow
> in the doing.[32]

J. O. Heath made a similar point in the Oklahoma *Baptist Messenger*, but he was unwilling to divert any of the blame from the leaders who worked to consolidate the denomination's power in their own hands.

> There are indications sufficiently palpable to convince the
> incredulous, that Southern Baptists are drifting from . . . de-
> mocracy. . . . The present tendency is away from the churches
> and it toward the centralizing of power in the hands of a few

Dissent against Denominational Centralization

men. And "a centralized democracy may be as tyrannical as an absolute monarch." The Baptists are professedly democratic, yet many of their conventions are run by committees that are under instructions to carry out the decisions of previous caucuses. In those caucuses zeal, honesty and ability may be represented, but certainly democracy has no voice in those momentous meetings.[33]

Heath seemed to believe that these tendencies might lead to a radically revised polity among Southern Baptists. "Among some Baptists free speech is losing its popularity, and a method that would prevent the exercise of the right of legitimate criticism is gaining in favor with them."[34]

Most Southern Baptist state newspapers carried at least a few letters or editorials during the Seventy-Five Million Campaign that gave vent to frustrations among rank-and-file Baptists about the behavior of their leaders and the denomination's consistent movement toward centralization. Three editors, however, dedicated themselves to expressing concerns with particular vigor about these trends among Southern Baptists. R. H. Pitt, editor of the Virginia *Religious Herald;* Livingston Johnson, editor of the North Carolina *Biblical Recorder;* and Victor I. Masters, editor of the Kentucky *Western Recorder* were each especially concerned with issues of denominational polity. Johnson and Pitt, in particular, had much in common. First, they both served East Coast constituencies whose members seem to have somewhat resisted denominational centralization and, later, the adoption of the *Baptist Faith and Message.*[35] Secondly, and perhaps more importantly, both refused to sell their newspapers to their respective state conventions, meaning that their newspapers were almost the only Southern Baptist state newspapers still unowned by a denominational agency throughout the Campaign period.[36] In each case the editors refused to sell, due at least in part to their belief that only a newspaper financially independent of the denomination could truly foster the kind of dialogue needed to defend Baptist democracy.[37] Given their perspective on the importance of democracy as an aspect of Baptist polity, it is no surprise that these editors used their positions to criticize the SBC's progress towards centralization.

In addition to printing numerous letters and guest editorials criticizing the bureaucratic tendencies of the Southern Baptist Convention, North Carolina's Livingston Johnson expressed constant concern that the denomination's continuing centralization was smothering Southern Baptist democracy. In an editorial titled "Tendencies of the Times," Johnson lamented the fact that while German autocracy had been defeated, "America and the allies had swung far toward the very autocracy which they had condemned." The federal government had been "centralized" and represented a form of "bureaucratic rule," and in matters of religion the Interchurch World Movement had become "the most gigantic effort at centralization in religious affairs that has ever been made on the face of the earth, with the possible exception of the Roman Catholic Church." At the same time, however, Johnson believed that the Southern Baptist Convention offered too little resistance to this worldwide trend toward centralization, instead becoming another example of its irresistible influence. "We claim that it was the principle of Baptist democracy that shook the world and caused the nations of the earth to desire that form of government, and yet there is a tendency toward centralization that, if not guarded with greatest care, will bring about a sacrifice of much of our boasted democracy. As in the war we submitted to many things to which we would not have submitted in times of peace, so in the late campaign we surrendered, temporarily, some of the things that, according to our democratic principles, we could not be willing to surrender permanently." While many Southern Baptist leaders touted the Seventy-Five Million Campaign as the religious analogue to the triumph of American democracy at the conclusion of the Great War, Johnson asserted that it represented a capitulation to the same autocratic spirit that undergirded both German aggression and the Interchurch World Movement. As a result, Johnson believed that denominational success was not worth surrendering the spirit of centralization: "As great as was our victory in securing pledges for the 75 Million Campaign, that victory would be dearly bought if secured at the price of our sacredly cherished democracy."[38]

Johnson focused much of his criticism on the Convention's failure to close the Seventy-Five Million Campaign's headquarters in Nashville, Tennessee following Victory Week. Although pledges remained to be collected, Johnson believed that state conventions were competent to look after this aspect of the Campaign:

> We do not believe that we need to maintain a central office
> at considerable expense to "send out proclamations." The
> writer was in hearty sympathy with the methods used in
> the 75 Million Campaign. It was necessary to have some cen-
> tralized agency to accomplish the special work we had un-
> dertaken. That the central agency did its work admirably is
> abundantly shown by the success of the movement; but since

the work for which it was created has been finished, all the extra machinery, except what is needed in the several States, should be abolished, and as quickly as possible we should come back to the simple methods which Baptists have always used, and which comports with the spirit of democracy which has always characterized our people. . . .

What we need throughout the South, and in all our States, is not something new, but a better use of what which we already have. Once again let us say that one of the most important things before us now is to guard our Baptist democracy.[39]

The following year, Johnson became even more explicit about the possible effects of allowing the Campaign headquarters to stay open despite its having completed its task. If nothing else, supporting organizations that had outlived their usefulness was a waste of time and money. "In a few days there will be a gathering at Nashville that will call together, perhaps, a hundred men and women from all over the South. Of course, their expenses will come, directly or indirectly, out of the denominational treasury. Just what they are to do we do not know, but we suspect that the time will be taken up in discussions that will not amount to a great deal." More ominously, however, Johnson believed that the longevity of the denomination's Campaign "machinery" did not bode well for the future of democratic polity among Southern Baptists. "When the campaign was launched we were told that the machinery was temporary and would automatically go out of business when the work of securing the pledges was completed, but the central office is being maintained certainly at considerable cost. There is danger of having a Baptist oligarchy fastened upon our denomination."[40]

While Livingston Johnson publicly fretted about the growth of the Southern Baptist denominational apparatus in North Carolina, R. H. Pitt, Johnson's editorial colleague in Virginia, wrote several editorials that drew attention to the Convention's changing polity. While Johnson's worries focused on the denomination's bureaucratic growth, Pitt's criticisms dealt more directly with his belief that illegitimate authority and coercion were already sprouting in the Convention's new bureaucratic soil. When leaders of the Campaign realized after Victory Week that they had failed to include the denomination's seminaries' building programs in the publicized apportionment of funds, they unilaterally announced that they would be funneling some Campaign money originally intended for the mission boards into the seminaries instead. R. H. Pitt did not hesitate to offer his opinion on what he considered to be an illegitimate assumption of authority on the part of the Campaign's administrators.

> Under the circumstances it would have been considered an act of disloyalty to intimate that the managers had made a blunder, though it was quite natural for them to do so in the hurry of projecting a $75,000,000 enterprise. The whole policy was to avoid divisive issues during the campaign; to raise money first and ask questions afterwards. In this spirit some of us silently "stood by consenting" when a number of things were said and done which did not at all commend themselves to our judgment and will not stand the test of time. They were part of the program that we must unhesitatingly support or be accounted slackers, and no good Baptist wanted to lie under suspicion of opposing, or being out of sympathy with the great movement. Just as in the world war all loyal Americans submitted without a murmur to autocratic methods because of the tremendous issues involved, so in our $75,000,000 campaign we Baptists surrendered for the time being certain principles inhering fundamentally in our Democratic faith and practice. This matter of redistribution strikingly illustrates the point.

The editor continued by expressing disappointment that Convention leaders had allowed designation of gifts on paper, while offering "pronounced criticism" of those who had availed themselves of this option in practice.[41]

Lacking the sanguine faith in human progress that so many Southern Baptists exhibited during this period, Pitt believed that democracy and its various foils existed in a dialectical relationship. With one eye on the Russian Revolution, Pitt wrote that "hierarchies and oligarchies breed by a sort of reaction the most intense types of democracy and out of democracies run to seed are born all manner of hateful autocracies and oligarchies." Counter to the claims of many other Southern Baptists who observed recent events, Pitt believed that "the race has not moved steadily toward ordered liberty."[42] Importantly, Pitt did not believe that Southern Baptists were excluded from this trend. In fact, he was worried that they might end up providing a strong example of it. In the early months of the Campaign period, for example, Pitt cautioned his readers: "As we work together for more effective organization of our Baptist forces in our States and in our Southern Convention let us be careful lest in our natural reaction from a loose-jointed, free-and-easy democracy we go into

Dissent against Denominational Centralization

something closely akin to autocracy or at any rate to oligarchy or bureaucracy. Bolshevism in its earlier stages represented an extreme reaction from oligarchy and bureaucracy but after a little developed a quite hateful oligarchy of its own."[43]

It seems that the progress of the Seventy-Five Million Campaign did not brighten Pitt's attitude toward the condition of Baptist democracy. In 1922, the editor was still warning against Southern Baptists providing "an analogue to the Russian program."[44] Later, with the Campaign in ruins and with the adoption of a denominational statement of faith looming on the horizon, Pitt offered a sobering analysis of the state of Southern Baptist democracy:

> We Baptists are fast drifting into what is practically the pres-
> byterial order and presently, if we continue to drift, we shall
> no longer be a democracy with all the freedom which that
> word implies. It is true that we are fond of saying that we sub-
> stitute "influence" for "authority" in the management of our
> cooperative work. Yet as we centralize more and more in these
> practical ways we find and shall continue to find that the line
> between influence and authority grows fainter and fainter.
> Now when we go on to do the same sort of thing which we
> are doing in the practical management of our common work,
> in the realm of Christian doctrine, we shall presently find it
> difficult in that realm to trace the line between influence and
> authority. It is true not only of individuals, but of groups, that
> when they have sent out formularies of faith they are not only
> committed to these personally, but, whatever disclaimers
> they may make, they are apt to consider these declaration as
> having some measure of binding force upon others and as fur-
> nishing tests of Christian fellowship. If this sort of thing goes
> on indefinitely all that will be left of the democratic temper
> and spirit of our folk, the temper and spirit that have made
> them so influential and that have challenged the wonder and
> admiration of the Christian world, will be left to the fractious,
> the cross, the sensation mongers, the kickers, the disturbers
> of Christian peace and brotherhood.[45]

Pitt's opposition to the *Baptist Faith and Message* was not a freestanding aversion to creeds or to doctrinal definition but was instead a function of his concern for what he considered to be traditional, democratic Baptist polity.

174

Victor I. Masters: The Scarborough Synthesis Questioned

Even while editors Johnson and Pitt criticized their denomination for its increasing tendency to appropriate illegitimate authority, they never seem to have denied that the Southern Baptist Convention was, for all its flaws, what L. R. Scarborough said that it was: an effective instrument to protect true Baptist doctrine against the encroachment of Modernism, owing to the organization's regional ties. The same cannot be said for Victor I. Masters, the editor of the Kentucky *Western Recorder*. During the Seventy-Five Million Campaign, Masters used the *Western Recorder* to express his own acute anxieties about the future of Southern Baptist democracy, only to be rebuffed publicly by other denominational leaders. As a result, Masters came simultaneously to distrust the Convention and to suggest that, rather than being an effective bulwark against the encroachment of Modernism, the denomination was actually a safe haven for heterodox theology. In the process, Masters provided the rudiments of an identity for Southern Baptists that had the potential to serve as an alternative to the Scarborough Synthesis.

Although he later found himself at cross-purposes with many Southern Baptist leaders, V. I. Masters owed his position at the *Western Recorder* to E. Y. Mullins. After a conflict between Mullins and the Kentucky State Board of Missions that caused J. W. Porter—a personal enemy of Mullins and the Seminary at Louisville—to resign from the editorship of the *Western Recorder*, the Board sought a new editor with whom Mullins was willing to work. When the Board settled on V. I. Masters, the director of publicity at the Home Mission Board, Mullins was pleased enough with the decision to personally encourage Masters to accept.[46] Beginning in February 1921, Masters served as the editor of the newspaper, which he would continue to do until his retirement in 1942.

Upon arriving at the *Western Recorder*, Masters almost immediately used his position as editor to publicize his belief that the centralization inherent in the Seventy-Five Million Campaign was endangering traditional Baptist polity. Writing in the second issue of the newspaper issued under his leadership, Masters sounded a familiar theme:

> Southern Baptists in their own life and work are not entirely free from danger of . . . trying to make the "matured judgment" of their leaders take the place of initiative and independent thought and expressions of thought by all our people. This danger has not risen from among the people themselves. It is an unfortunate byproduct which has come from among our

175

leaders—especially since the 75-Million Campaign gave us a lot of money to manage.

The Recorder stands for our leaders. It heartily believes in them. But it does not stand with its mouth closed and its eyes shut. As God gives it light this paper is responsible to all our Baptist people, as well as to the chosen men who lead them. Since both the leaders and the people are equally emphatic in their declaration for real Baptist democracy, we shall expect as much support from our leaders as from our people in any aid our utterances may give toward the maintenance of full-length democracy. . . .

Our denominational agencies are granted and must freely and unhampered exercise the power to conduct the work committed to them. Within the limits prescribed for them they ought to go forward with initiative and constructive policies. . . .

But their activities should be conscientiously held within the lines laid down by the denomination and should unfailingly conform to the requirements of its known fundamental principles. Nor should they use their great official prestige to foster schemes by which new programs shall be pressed on the general meetings of the denomination for its adoption, without opportunity being given for full and free discussion by our people.[47]

Masters continued by discussing the problems inherent in the "unwieldy" nature of the annual Southern Baptist Convention meeting. In fact, Masters seems to have come to the *Western Recorder* having completely accepted the sort of denominational critique that editors Johnson and Pitt had been making since early 1920.

Masters's analysis of his denomination's tendencies toward centralization was far from unique, but the editor's atypical sense of the denominational newspaper's role gave his criticisms an unusually sharp edge. While most Southern Baptist editors accepted that the function of a state Baptist newspaper was to serve as the means by which the denomination's leadership funneled information to pastors and laypeople while refusing to publish material "which directly antagonized any policy adopted by the Convention," Masters envisioned a more active role for the

Western Recorder.[48] To express his commitment to Baptist democracy, Masters made it a point to seek out specific instances in which the actions of Baptist leaders endangered traditional Baptist polity and to draw attention to them in the *Recorder,* a goal that necessarily put him on a collision course with the denomination's leadership. Only weeks after he assumed his editorial duties, Masters found himself mired in the first of many controversies that developed between himself and denominational leaders: a quarrel over whether the secretaries of the various state boards of missions should be allowed to meet "behind closed doors."

In an editorial that relied upon information published in H. Boyce Taylor's *News and Truths,* an independent Southern Baptist newspaper published in Murray, Kentucky, Masters pointed out that a group of state secretaries had held a "secret meeting." He suggested that these secretaries avoid holding meetings of an "inspirational" character without inviting any Baptist that might care to come, though he conceded that "executive" sessions might be held in private.[49] Masters's editorial was not particularly accusatory and was intended to shield Kentucky's own secretary from criticism, but it seems to have hit a nerve among secretaries already sensitive to criticism of the denomination's ongoing centralization. Arch Cree, the Secretary of the State Secretaries' Association, chided Masters for calling the motives of the secretaries into question. "To insinuate or imply that these men met in an unworthy way with an unworthy purpose would be promptly resented by those who know them and trust them. . . . Yet the editorial clearly implies that there was something 'secret,' something questionable, something unbaptistic and possibly unbrotherly in the State Secretaries holding such a meeting."[50]

In a reply to Cree's article, Masters was clearly stung, remarking that he and Dr. Cree had been personal friends in Atlanta during the editor's time at the Home Mission Board. In focusing on the implied accusations in the original editorial, Masters pleaded that Cree's interpretation was "an entire shift of the argument away from where our editorial placed it" and that he had never proposed to question the secretaries' intentions. As the editor continued, however, his democratic motives became clearer. "If these meetings shall become official or quasi-official in fact, even though not in form, they shall inevitably, to that extent, inure in their influence against the responsible agencies that have been evolved by the wisdom and experience of the denomination itself, through its State Conventions and the Southern Baptist Convention." Masters saw in the meeting in question the seed of a new, anti-democratic form of Baptist polity with the potential to quietly undermine the Convention's official channels of

177

leadership. In fact, Masters believed that in some places, that seed had already begun to germinate.

> A prominent minister, who was for years member of a state board, tells us that his State Secretary often came before his Board and said: "The State Secretaries discussed 'such and such' a proposition, and decided it would be wisest to do 'thus and so.' Now, of course it is up to you brethren. But all the other states will carry on this matter in this way. What will you do?" "After a while," says our friend, "some Board member would rise and say: 'Well, we don't want to be Bolshevists. I move to do what our Secretary suggests.'"
> THIS IS A REACTION CONTRARY TO WHAT THE STATE CONVENTIONS HAD PROVIDED FOR IN APPOINTING THEIR BOARD. THE REACTION . . . TENDS TO DISTURB THE EQUILIBRIUM OF THE CONSTITUTED AND RESPONSIBLE AGENCIES OF THE SOUTHERN BAPTIST CONVENTION, BY THE INJECTION OF AN UNANTICIPATED AND NONOFFICIAL BUT CONFESSEDLY STRONG MORAL FORCE INTO THE SITUATION.[51]

Masters understood, as did R. H. Pitt, that the line between unofficial influence and ecclesiastical authority among Southern Baptists was growing thin indeed. The editor concluded by warning the denomination's leaders that he had no plans to be cowed into silence. **"This State Secretary incident is only one of the little straws. Its importance exists only in the fact that they are in each State the trusted leaders of the people. There are other dangers greater than this. We are going to love everybody and trust every man's judgment, so far as we can. But we are going to clean up centralization from fastening its power-loving fangs in the throats of the liberties of Southern Baptists."[52]** Although many Southern Baptists used their newspapers to suggest that Southern Baptist democracy was in a state of decline, Masters, unlike Johnson and Pitt, cast himself in an antagonistic relationship with other Baptist leaders.

The results of Masters's editorial were predictable. By the end of the month, Masters had endured strong criticism not only from the secretaries themselves, but also from other Southern Baptist editors. J. D. Moore, the editor of the Tennessee *Baptist and Reflector*, for instance, referred to Masters as a "bush-whacking bandit."[53] The entire ordeal, precipitated

The Empire's New Clothes

in part by the editor's own use of unnecessarily strong language, seems to have convinced Masters that a conspiracy existed to keep the denominational press from looking too closely into Convention policies.

> There always seems to be a preponderance of reason why a responsible Baptist paper can never tell the truth about any questionable actions of an official of the denomination. Fortunately—we thank God for it daily!—the paper is entirely free from such restraints locally in Kentucky, or any occasion for them, so far as we know or believe.
>
> The Recorder wants to be truthful without being radical. But a stone wall is what we face when it comes to saying anything about unwise or unworthy administration of official trust by Baptist Boards or officials. We have not yet decided whether the "moral suasion" that scotches talking out about our officials when the use of our people's money is concerned, is actually prohibitive to a denominational paper!
>
> **If it is, shame upon us Baptists! Let us hang our heads, for it is a crying shame!**
>
> "But," says the by-the-card monitor, "this paper has already hurt our work." "It throws suspicion on our organized work." "If it was any good, it would not be a grouch."
>
> Oh, yes; we know all the stock phrases for whipping a "recalcitrant" into line. **All the same, shame!**"[54]

Despite the restraints that bound him as an editor, however, Masters still believed that the denomination would eventually find a way to set itself right.

> Somehow, sometime, our Baptist people are going greatly to help their work by taking time to clean up with every Baptist official or group of officials who discourage liberality by their autocratic lust for power, their abuse of a trusting people's confidence, or their tragic lack of constructive indignation or initiative.
>
> **Somehow, sometime, our papers are going to come to think more of the rights of the rank and file of our people than of the "divine right" of any plausible and soft-worded, but small-souled and lusting-for-power official. . . .**

Dissent against Denominational Centralization

> When they do, we shall have a new impetus for all of
> our work. Faithful leaders will be appreciated and the
> shrewd schemer that has long kept about three jumps
> ahead of the wrath of an informed constituency will be
> separated from his pap, and his place given to a real man
> of God.[55]

While Masters was not the only editor that discussed the problems facing Southern Baptist democracy, he was the only one who regularly framed his opinions in such colorful language. Needless to say, Masters's strategy won him few friends.

Although Masters spent a lot of time sparring with denominational leaders during his first few years at the *Western Recorder*, he reserved enough space in his newspaper to deal with other issues as well. In particular, like other Southern Baptist editors, Masters kept an eye on developments among Northern Baptists, occasionally offering his own opinion. In 1921, when the Northern Baptist Convention's Home Missionary Society was offered and accepted an anonymous gift of $1,750,000 on the condition that the Society use the funds to support only missionaries that affirmed a specific list of Christian beliefs, Masters mistakenly reported to his readers that the Society rejected the gift.[56] Masters identified this non-event as evidence of democracy's decline among Northern Baptists and as a triumph of Modernism, a phenomenon for which Masters had reserved an especially profound hatred even during his tenure at the Home Mission Board. In frustration, Masters drew an important connection between the Northern Convention's polity and their theological decline, identifying Northern Baptist Modernism as a "hidden enemy":

> While a sense of democracy has been growing among
> our Northern brethren, the power of this hidden enemy
> of Christian faith has among them also been growing.
> It has been stealthily doing its work in certain Baptist
> quarters, as among other Christian bodies. This enemy
> hates democracy. It is also astute in its abilities to cheat
> and subvert real democracy. True, it is right now devel-
> oping a campaign under the aegis of "liberty". But it
> wants license, not liberty. It is for spiritual anarchy,
> not freedom in Christ.[57]

Masters did not conclude his analysis there; instead, he went on to suggest that the Southern Baptist Convention was in no way immune to similar in-

The Empire's New Clothes

fluences. "The democracy of the young Northern Convention . . . has been beset throughout its life by a corresponding increase of this subtle power, the purpose of which is to cheat democracy of its fruits. This is not worse with Northern Baptists than with any other Christian body into which the apostasy of rationalism has clandestinely crept. It is not worse than the situation shall yet be among Southern Baptists, if we ever allow this diabolical enemy to gain a similar foot-hold among us. Moreover, there is more danger that it shall do so than most of us seem to realize."[58]

In this editorial, Masters provided ideological material that had the potential to disrupt the new, synthesized Southern Baptist identity that was just beginning to appear among Convention leadership. While Scarborough would eventually tie the denomination's burgeoning bureaucracy to its role as defender of Baptist orthodoxy, Masters instead identified centralization with Modernism, noting that "Modernism claps its hands for the builder."[59] Furthermore, while Scarborough relied heavily on the idea of the South as a special region especially immune to heterodox influences, Masters instead insisted that the Southern Baptist Convention was no less vulnerable to the influence of Modernism than were Northern religious bodies. Masters had himself been responsible for popularizing the idea that the South possessed a special religious vocation, but by 1921 he seems to have concluded that the cultural influences that had made the "New South" possible also exposed it to Northern forms of religious and political thought.[60]

As a result, Masters confronted Modernism head-on in the pages of the *Western Recorder*. While other Southern Baptist editors tended to juxtapose their editorializing on the subject of Modernism with assurances that the problem lay entirely with Northern Baptists, Masters refused to make such a distinction. By March 1922, for instance, Masters had already rejected out of hand the idea that the SBC's regional identity could protect the denomination from Modernism. In response to an article by William Bell Riley about the interregional importance of the Fundamentalist movement, Masters wrote that the Minnesota pastor was "**right in saying that it is essentially a world-movement which we confront, and not a sectional movement. May his words sink deeply into many Southern hearts. They are the words of truth and soberness. The sooner we come to realize it, the better.**"[61] Furthermore, Masters defended J. Frank Norris and other Baptists pastors that chose to join interdenominational fundamentalist organizations, a move that other Baptist leaders saw as an unforgivable breach of solidarity with the denomination. "We see no more guilt in a Baptist preacher identifying himself with this Fundamentalist Movement than with the evangelical group in the Anti-Saloon League Movement. As between open barrooms and the Bible-scrapping Rationalism which the Fundamentalists fight, we regard a thousand barrooms less dangerous that one great educational center of Rationalism."[62]

Needless to say, Masters's refusal to admit that Southern Baptists were immune to the dangers of Modernism and constant editorializing on its dangers earned him a significant amount of criticism, resembling in many ways the lambasting he received after the "secret meeting" controversy. L. L. Gwaltney of Alabama sarcastically referred to Masters as a "watch dog," while Z. T. Cody of South Carolina suggested that "Mastersean" be used as a synonym for "hysterical" among Southern Baptists.[63] The criticism of other editors only served to further isolate Masters, pressing him closer to making an open Fundamentalist-style critique of the Southern Baptist Convention. Masters complained about the treatment he had received at the hands of editors Pitt and Cody as they rebuffed his tirade about the dangers of the evolution theory:

> With all proper respect and consideration for the persons
> of the editors of our venerable contemporaries, we now call
> attention to that their attitude toward those who differ with
> them on this particular subject, is of the same flavor of intol-
> erant disrespect as that shown by the rationalistic professors
> of learning who, in hundreds of educational institutions in
> America, are seeking to ram their half-baked God-limiting the-
> ories down the throats of the young people who shall be the
> intellectual leaders of the next generation. We protest against
> their persistent attitude as unfair to themselves, unjust to
> their brethren and subversive of the truth of Christ. They do
> not belong with the group to which they show far more res-
> pect than their own brethren.[64]

In this instance, Masters stopped short of suggesting that his fellow editors were actually Modernists in disguise, but the seed had been planted.

In fact, after only a few months, Masters began to sense a close connection between the refusal of Southern Baptist leaders to directly confront the problem of Modernism and the centralizing tendencies of Southern Baptist leadership. The Kentucky editor, having endured severe censure for his comments on Southern Baptist polity and on his treatment of Modernism, came to suspect that Baptist leaders were actively

The Empire's New Clothes

seeking to keep the Southern Baptist press from drawing attention to either. In other words, Masters was beginning to sense among Southern Baptists the same connection between Modernism and centralization that he had first detected among Northern Baptists in 1921. As a result, he began to insinuate that some Southern Baptist leaders refused publicly to criticize Northern Modernist spokespersons because they secretly harbored heterodox opinions of their own, raising acutely the question of their fitness for service in a democratic denomination with an overwhelmingly conservative membership. Reacting against Southern Baptist criticism of the Fundamentalist movement, Masters suggested that his readers "**beware of men who in these perilous days refuse to give any clear testimony in exposing the fallacies of rampant infidelity, but who are diligent in their personal relationships and, when they dare, in their writings, are seeking to be-little and discredit those of their own brethren who are honestly using their talents and opportunities to withstand the enemies of Christ.**"[65] The editor questioned whether leaders critical of Fundamentalism could be trusted by rank-and-file Southern Baptists: "Any Southern Baptist who uses his prestige to try to throw this truth in doubt, must in the minds of unprejudiced brethren raise a question as to whether he is willing aforetime to hedge against the growth among Southern Baptists of an organized fight against the encroachments of Rationalism and the 'New Theology.' If he is willing to do so, he . . . suggests the question as to whether he is a trustworthy note-sounder for this great body of the people of God."[66] The editor failed to recognize that many Southern Baptist leaders, while theologically conservative, struggled to forestall a Fundamentalist-style controversy in the South as a way of protecting the fragile Seventy-Five Million Campaign. The editor interpreted leaders' reliance upon college and seminary boards of trustees to identify and dismiss Modernist professors through the same lens. "Why is it so difficult to get at these men? Why is it that even among Baptists, where democratic fearlessness in telling the truth is supposed to reign supreme, there is so often, when it comes to specific cases, a system of checks and restraints that enables you only with the greatest difficulty to get the truth across, and at the risk of being accused of disloyalty to the denomination?"[67] For Masters, a truly democratic denomination would be able to remove professors from their positions at will, and the fact that Southern Baptist leaders discouraged this approach revealed their antidemocratic tendencies and hinted at the presence of heterodoxy among them.

Dissent against Denominational Centralization

By late 1923, Masters was willing to make explicit his belief that at least some of the leaders of the Southern Baptist Convention were Modernists who used their influence to squelch free debate of doctrinal issues: "For the first time in our history this Evolution-bred apostasy of Modernism has found some influential leaders among us who appear to be unwilling to lead God's hosts to a warfare against error and in witness to revealed truth, **and equally unwilling that others than themselves should disturb this placid front of compromise by loyal warnings to the masses of our people that all is not well.**"[68] The leaders of the Convention could not be trusted to foster Baptist democracy as Masters understood it; nor could they be trusted to defend Baptist orthodoxy. Heterodoxy and centralization went hand in hand in the Southern Baptist Convention, exactly as they did among Northern Baptists.

This interpretation of the Southern Baptist Convention struck at the very heart of the Scarborough Synthesis. Scarborough and other leaders who aligned with him had hoped to prevent a full-scale Fundamentalist controversy within the boundaries of the Southern Baptist Convention by suggesting that Southern Baptist institutions, preserved from Modernist influence because of their Southern roots, could themselves be trusted to defend Southern Baptists from creeping Modernism. Masters, on the other hand, rejected this interpretation out of hand as he insisted, much to the chagrin of other leaders, that the South was not immune to Modernist influence. Furthermore, the editor saw the increasing centralization of the Southern Baptist Convention not as the development of an orthodox Baptist empire, but as the creation of a bureaucracy controlled by leaders whose theology was not beyond reproach. As Masters sought to expose the dangers of Modernism and the decline of democracy among Southern Baptists, he provided the rudiments of what might be considered an alternative to the Scarborough Synthesis. For Masters, Southern Baptists could fulfill their vocation not through regional identity or institutional development alone, but through full participation in the Fundamentalist movement.

Alternatives to the "Scarborough Synthesis"

Although Southern Baptist leaders sought to paint a picture of their denomination as united in both doctrine and purpose, the contents of the denominational press reveal a more nuanced picture of the denominational mood during the Seventy-Five Million Campaign. While some Southern Baptists were more than willing to praise denominational leaders in superhuman terms, such rhetoric belied the ambiguous attitude that many other Southern Baptists held toward them. Some rank-and-file Baptists affirmed as a truism the idea that the annual meeting of the Southern Baptist Convention had degenerated into an opportunity for leaders to speak to a disenfranchised constituency and failed to provide an opportunity for communal decision-making. A significant number of Baptists also feared that the leaders of the Southern Baptist Convention were steering the denomination toward a more centralized, bureaucratic form of polity.

Even some editors used their positions to criticize the Southern Baptist tendency toward centralization. Livingston Johnson of North Carolina warned against the waste inherent in maintaining excessive denominational "machinery," while R. H. Pitt of Virginia cautioned that the Southern Baptist Convention was drifting into the "presbyterial order." More than either of these, however, Victor I. Masters of the Kentucky *Western Recorder* articulated a sharp critique of his denomination's centralization that eventually transformed into a criticism of the way denominational leaders had chosen to deal with the theological controversy raging among Northern Baptists. Finding himself at the center of denominational criticism after trying to warn his readers about the dangers inherent in the increasingly bureaucratized nature of the Southern Baptist Convention, Masters soon decided that denominational centralization and theological modernism were two sides of the same coin. Unlike other editorial critics of the Convention's centralization, Masters eventually came to see bureaucratization as a threat not only to Baptist democracy but to Baptist orthodoxy as well. As a result, Masters tacitly rejected the idea that the Southern Baptist Convention could be defended from Modernism through financial investment in its network of seminaries and mission boards and through its identification with a region of the country especially immune to Modernist influence. Instead, Masters hoped that Southern Baptist leaders would engage Northern controversies as direct participants rather than observers. Although Masters did not live to see his dream realized, he helped inject into the bloodstream of the Southern Baptist Convention an alternative to the centralizing goals of many other SBC leaders.

Conclusion

The Legacy of the Seventy-Five Million Campaign and the Impact of Fundamentalism among Southern Baptists

The Seventy-Five Million Campaign has been remembered by denominational insiders and identified by historians as a failure. Although pledges to the campaign far exceeded the seventy-five million dollars that leaders wanted, in the end they collected less than fifty-nine million, miring the board and agencies of the denomination deeply in debt. Although this shortfall could largely be blamed on the economic difficulties that choked the South in the aftermath of the Great War, Southern Baptist leaders must bear a share of the blame as well. Dashing into the largest fundraising program the SBC had ever attempted, leaders realized too late that such a sum could never be raised through a "whoop-em-up" method; only emphasizing systematic budgeting and giving could provide the steady stream of funds that SBC boards and agencies needed.[1] Leaders also assembled the apportionment figures for the campaign so quickly that they accidentally failed to dedicate a portion of the expected receipts to the two seminaries. Embarrassingly, leaders had to publicly rearrange the campaign's expected disbursements after having already gathered pledges.[2] Such public errors could hardly have inspired confidence among the many Southern Baptists whose opinions about their denomination's activities during this period have been lost to history. Perhaps most devastating was the habit among denominational workers of spending campaign monies before they had been collected.[3] Exuberant spending, often based on the hopelessly faulty assumption that every nickel pledged to the campaign would be paid, guaranteed that the SBC would struggle in debt for years to come. Leaders were unable to bridge the gap between their dreams of a professionalized denomination and their own inexperience in large-scale fundraising.

At the same time, however, the program of centralization inherent in the Seventy-Five Million Campaign continued after its conclusion. After having learned some valuable lessons during the previous five years, Southern Baptist leaders chose to continue trying to finance the work of the denomination through annual fundraising drives modeled after the Seventy-Five Million Campaign.[4] The "Co-operative Program," as these drives were called, bore all the marks of the original campaign's centralizing goals. The "First Annual Report of the Future Program Commission to the Southern Baptist Convention," presented to the SBC in 1925, showed that the anxieties associated with the new program differed little if at all from the old. Leaders responsible for framing the new program continued to worry that many Southern Baptists did not take a Southern Baptist state newspaper, ensuring that they continued to be "almost wholly uninformed."[5] They also expressed frustration that Southern Baptists failed to solicit new Christians for financial contributions to the denomination as a part of their evangelistic activities,[6] worrying aloud that "destructive criticism" would be allowed to scuttle the new program.[7]

In response, the framers of the new program sounded a familiar note: Southern Baptists must be enlisted in the work of the denomination, and this work must happen through the involvement of pastors and all other participants in Southern Baptist life. The financial needs of the denomination should be featured in associational meetings, revivals, and every other conceivable setting until all Southern Baptists have been welded into "a great and mighty host of never-failing supporters of Kingdom causes."[8] Leaders sought to emphasize that Southern Baptists should give to the whole program without designating their gifts, thus ensuring that the distribution of funds would remain in the hands of the denomination's leadership. As one writer put it in 1926, "It is generally known that this plan was worked out by about fifty of what are supposed to be the wisest Baptist men and women in the South, after months of careful survey of the whole field; and designations, whether so designated or not, tend to discredit both them and their plan."[9] Centralized management of the funding for the SBC's boards and agencies had come to stay. Although a significant number of churches and individual Southern Baptists were never incorporated into this vision of the Southern Baptist Convention, the Cooperative Program provided the core of the denomination's continuing centralization; by 1982, one respected scholar of Southern Baptist life noted that the businesslike methods of the SBC's Progressive shapers had been taken into the life of ninety percent of the denomination's congregations.[10]

This continuing centralization reached a milestone in 1931, when the denomination voted to establish a method of choosing Boards of Trustees for Southern Baptist boards and agencies that would rotate them regularly. These trustees were, in turn, formally tasked with the direct oversight of the various boards and agencies of the Convention.[11] Although these institutions had already had trustees for years, this development helped to formalize the method of oversight that Scarborough and other leaders had advocated during the Seventy-Five Million Campaign as part of the Scarborough Synthesis. Later, the role that these Boards of Trustees played in the SBC would figure prominently in the controversies that rocked the denomination between 1980 and 2000.

In 1925, as the Seventy-Five Million Campaign wound down, L. L. Gwaltney of the *The Alabama Baptist* reminded his readers, "It is well to remember in the connection that Southern Baptists have become more centralized in polity in the last five years than in a generation."[12] That the polity of the Southern Baptist Convention had been permanently altered by the events of the early 1920s did not escape the notice of attentive Southern Baptists. A later student of these events might rightly identify a number of factors that contributed to this rapid centralization, such as the Progressive Era's emphasis on professional management, Southern Baptists' desire to imitate the centralizing goals of the Interchurch World Movement or the fundraising and institution-building of other denominations, and the seeds of bureaucratization that were already planted in the history of the denomination before the Seventy-Five Million Campaign even began. Each of these factors certainly played a part in transforming the shape of the Southern Baptist Convention, but to these another factor could be added: the Southern Baptist encounter with Fundamentalism. Working under the shadow of Fundamentalist criticisms that threatened to discredit the Seventy-Five Million Campaign, Southern Baptist leaders suggested that the Southern Baptist Convention itself, because of its regional distinctiveness, could be trusted to keep its boards and agencies free from heterodoxy. Rejecting Fundamentalist critics of the SBC such as J. Frank Norris as enemies of the cause of Christ owing to their non-support of denominational agencies, Lee Scarborough and others articulated support for the denomination as a key aspect of Biblical faith. In other words, Southern Baptist leaders sought to turn the centrifugal force of Fundamentalism into the centripetal force of cooperation. Had Southern Baptist leaders not made these arguments in the course of their efforts to shore up the struggling Seventy-Five Million Campaign, the denomination's centralization might not have continued at such a brisk pace.[13]

Southern Baptists, then, participated in the Fundamentalist movement to an extent that has heretofore not been acknowledged by students of Southern religion. Southern Baptist leaders wrote to an audience of laypeople that had been exposed to the doctrinal disagreements disturbing other Christian denominations; that their leaders sought to incorporate that conflict into their own fundraising efforts shows that they, too, were aware of, and influenced by, developments in the Fundamentalist-Modernist controversy. By the time Southern Baptist leaders found themselves having to articulate the idea that the South was a world set apart, the theological boundaries between the South and the rest of the United States were already beginning to crumble. When those walls were finally breached in the 1980s, Southern Baptists would be forced once again to face many of the same questions that had been raised decades before.[14]

Conclusion

Appendix

J. Frank Norris's Relationship to the Southern Baptist Convention

The 1980 publication of George Marsden's *Fundamentalism and American Culture* provided a clear portrait of Fundamentalism to which other scholars have added. Scholars of Southern religion, however, have been rather sluggish in appropriating Marsden's work in their attempts to discern the extent to which Northern-style Fundamentalism has influenced the religious life of the South. The assumptions that historians have brought to their examinations of J. Frank Norris, for instance, illustrate this point. While authors writing about Norris in the 1980s failed to clarify the relationship between Norris's fighting Fundamentalism and the native conservatism of Southern Baptist life, scholars approaching the subject more recently have come to realize that Norris, while a Baptist and a Southerner, took his theological cues not from the Southern Baptist tradition, but from radical, Northern-style Fundamentalism. As a result, Norris's own thought, while an important part of the history of Fundamentalism, is not directly relevant to a study of Southern Baptist reactions to the Fundamentalist movement.

James J. Thompson, Jr.'s *Tried as by Fire: Southern Baptists and the Religious Controversies of the 1920s* helps to illustrate the extent to which scholarship on Southern Baptists in the early 1980s tended to identify Norris as a ringleader among Southern Baptist "Fundamentalists." This work, published in 1982, does not mention Marsden's work or benefit from his analysis of Fundamentalism because Thompson completed his study long before Marsden's work was published; the work originated as a doctoral dissertation at The University of Virginia. Given that the author worked without the benefit of Marsden's *Fundamentalism*, the monograph makes some points about Southern Baptist identity in the 1920s that show it to be a competent work of scholarship still worthy of attention.

Thompson, for instance, brings forward the rural and agrarian identity of Southern Baptists during this time period and shows the extent to which Southern Baptist thinkers married agriculture, Southernness, and chosenness in their thoughts on the Southern Baptist Convention's mission.

Thompson's treatment of J. Frank Norris, however, shows that his analysis glosses over differences that one must observe in order to grasp the nature of doctrinal infighting among Southern Baptists during the early 1920s. The author rightly identifies the Southern Baptist Convention as an organization without any real modernists in its ranks. Alongside this ambient conservatism, the author posits the existence of a strain of "Fundamentalism," in quotations here because of the tension between Thompson's use of the word and the now generally accepted use resting on Marsden's work. *Tried as by Fire* lumps Norris and his followers together with more traditional, Landmarkist conservatives in the convention despite the fact that Norris committed the cardinal Landmarkist sin of offering his pulpit to non-Baptists. Additionally, Thompson offers a serious flaw in his analysis by offering J. R. Graves, the leading figure of nineteenth-century Landmarkism, as a significant source of dispensationalism among Southern Baptists, following that up with the statement, "Dispensationalism's most important feature for Baptist fundamentalists was its conception of the Church. The 'Church' in dispensational language referred not to Baptists, Methodists, Presbyterians, or Episcopalians, but to the faithful few whom God gathered out of these denominations to await the second coming."[1] No statement could be further from Graves's own ecclesiology. By positing Norris as the leader of Southern Baptist "Fundamentalism," Thompson obscures the real differences that existed between genuine Marsden-style Fundamentalists led by Norris and denominational conservatives who found their doctrinal roots elsewhere.

William Ellis's "*A Man of Books and a Man of the People*": *E. Y. Mullins and the Crisis of Moderate Southern Baptist Leadership* remains one of the most helpful monographic looks at conflicts in Southern Baptist life during the early twentieth century. The book's successfully defended thesis is that E. Y. Mullins found himself leading a denomination in which there were two parties: conservatives, often styled "Fundamentalists," and moderates, whom conservatives tended to brand as "modernists." Because the leftward-leaning party in the convention was actually only moderate to begin with, Mullins's attempts to strike a balance between the two warring parties failed.

Ellis's book is a gem, but its treatment of J. Frank Norris betrays some of the same assumptions about Norris's relationship to other conservatives

Appendix

in the denomination that can be found in Thompson's work. Ellis identifies Norris as a "leader of the fundamentalists," which in light of more recent scholarship is a difficult proposition to sustain.[2] Ellis is able to quote Norris as accusing Mullins of "disturb[ing] the peace of our Southern Baptist Zion."[3] This juicy evidence is a red herring, however; the Baptist General Convention of Texas had been refusing to seat messengers from Norris's church since 1923 because he had formed a separatist denomination. The point to be made here is that Ellis does not clearly identify two separate strands of conservatism in the Convention—a genuinely Fundamentalist strand under Norris and a more traditional strand made up of twentieth-century Landmarkists. To be fair, though, Ellis identifies Norris as different from other conservative leaders, portraying him as being especially aggressive. At the very least, Ellis does not artificially conflate Norris's Fundamentalism with Landmarkism. Instead, he leaves the relationship of these two factions in Southern Baptist life unexamined.

Barry Hankins's *God's Rascal: J. Frank Norris & the Beginnings of Southern Fundamentalism* represents a sharp departure from these earlier interpretations of Norris's relationship to conservatism within the Southern Baptist Convention. In fact, Hankins's monograph is driven by the assumption that Norris is best understood not as a leader among Southern Baptists, but as the first Fundamentalist on Southern soil. As such, he managed to shape Southern religion; in the process, however, Norris managed to alienate Southern Baptist leaders of every stripe and even the Northern Fundamentalists with whom he aligned himself. For Hankins, Norris was far from representing Southern Baptists or even Fundamentalism. Instead, he was a figure so exceptional that he must be examined on his own terms.

Hankins does not explicitly analyze the relationship between Norris's brand of Fundamentalism and the denominational conservatives who did not associate with him; his exploration of Norris's relationship with the Convention is largely limited to moderate Convention elites. At the same time, Hankins does provide some clues that illustrate the extent to which his own practice was out of line with the Landmarkism that defined much of the conservatism that had run deep through Southern Baptist life since the nineteenth century. First, by 1948 Norris was willing to reject the Southern Baptist Convention as "soft on communism" and as compromised as its Northern counterpart. Secondly, Norris associated freely with similarly minded ministers in other denominations, including Disciples of Christ firebrand Gerald L. K. Smith. Finally, Norris was even willing to suggest a political alliance with Roman Catholics

193

against Communism late in his career.[4] In short, while he does not describe the Landmarkist conservatives who would not make common-cause with Norris, Hankins provides everything needed to explore their incompatibility.

These ingredients all finally come together in William Glass's *Strangers in Zion: Fundamentalists in the South, 1900–1950*. In this monograph, Glass suggests that Southerners, who generally saw Modernism as a Northern problem, mostly resisted Fundamentalism. Southerners refused to abandon denominations soaked in the rhetoric of the Lost Cause in order to endorse a cause that made little sense outside of the rapidly industrializing and rationalizing North. Additionally, Southerners had built a society that rested on the reality of racial segregation, and theological development that did not threaten this bedrock doctrine of mainstream Southern religion tended to be taken in stride.

Given these aspects of Southern religion, J. Frank Norris appears in *Strangers in Zion* as something of an oddity. While his power and popularity are not obscured, he is classified among "separatist Fundamentalists" who had placed themselves outside of denominational structures. As a result, their fuming hardly affected contemporary Southern religion as a whole (although Glass strongly hints that many aspects of their ideology would seep into the mainstream later in the century). For instance, Glass claims that Southern Baptists were impervious to Norris's carping, calculated to sever churches from the denomination. Furthermore, Glass notes that after the formation of the Baptist Bible Fellowship, a group that splintered off from Norris's orbit of churches in 1950, many Southern Baptists embraced the BBF as a viable alternative to the Southern Baptist Convention because it provided an opportunity to leave the Convention without associating with Norris. By the end of Norris's life, allegiance to his brand of Fundamentalism had become fundamentally incompatible with membership in mainstream Southern religious life.[5]

Glass also offers the story of E. P. Alldredge, a lifelong bureaucratic servant of the Southern Baptist Convention who finally, in 1948, expressed his frustration over the increasing likelihood that Southern Baptists would eventually participate in the Federal Council of Churches. Several things about Alldredge's complaint, which was representative of complaints made by other vocal Southern Baptists of the time, show the difference between Norris and these conservatives. First, Alldredge's concern over Southern Baptist participation in the FCC was classically Landmarkist: he was unwilling to compromise on certain traditional Baptist doctrines. While Fundamentalists had accused the FCC of being rife with Modernism, Alldredge and others were unwilling to cooperate with Christians who did not practice believer's baptism, to offer one example. Secondly, in order to get a hearing, Alldredge was forced to deny any connection with Norris often, even as his opponents constantly made just that accusation in order to discredit him. Finally, Alldredge's long history of service to the Convention placed him far outside the separatist camp in which Norris held court.[6] In short, Alldredge is a prime example of Landmarkist conservatives that had been present in Southern Baptist life since before the Civil War, owing little to the Fundamentalist movement. Glass shows that this strain of critique is fully distinct from that of Norris.

Essentially, in the years since *Fundamentalism and American Culture* was published, there has emerged a new clarity regarding the relationship between J. Frank Norris and the Southern Baptist Convention. While Norris was a Southerner who claimed that identity when it suited his polemic purposes, his identification with the South was little more than geographical. Theologically and ecclesially, Norris identified with radical Northern Fundamentalists, placing him outside the scope of a study of Southern Baptist reactions to the Fundamentalist movement.

195

Notes

Introduction

1. For an account of these controversies, see David T. Morgan, *The New Crusades, The New Holy Land: Conflict in the Southern Baptist Convention, 1969–1991* (Tuscaloosa: Univ. of Alabama Press, 1996) or Bill J. Leonard, *God's Last and Only Hope: The Fragmentation of the Southern Baptist Convention* (Grand Rapids, MI: William B. Eerdmans, 1990), ch. 6. More conservative accounts can be found in James C. Hefley, *The Truth in Crisis: The Controversy in the Southern Baptist Convention* (Dallas: Criterion Publications, 1986) or Jerry Sutton, *The Baptist Reformation: The Conservative Resurgence in the Southern Baptist Convention* (Nashville, TN: Broadman and Holman Publishers, 2000).

2. A selection of these figures will be discussed in the book's sixth chapter.

3. The most influential work on Fundamentalism, George Marsden's *Fundamentalism in American Culture* provided an explanation of Fundamentalism vastly superior to those that had come before but did not discuss the movement's influence in the South. Marsden correctly notes that, despite the assumptions of his 1980 audience, Fundamentalism was more northern and urban than southern and rural. Marsden's work shows clearly that the rise of Fundamentalism was a reaction to the preceding rise of Modernism among Northern Protestants, and therefore that Southern Protestants, who were almost uniformly theologically conservative to begin with, had no immediate need to join the movement in order to stamp out ideas that Southerners identified as Northern and, therefore, alien. At the same time, however, Marsden believes that Fundamentalism eventually moved South, although how this occurred is not clear. George M. Marsden, *Fundamentalism in American Culture* (New York: Oxford University Press, 2006), 103. For a classic example of the tendency to associate Fundamentalism with rural religion, see H. Richard Niebuhr, *The Social Sources of Denominationalism* (New York: Henry Holt and Company, 1929), 184.

4. Although most (if not all) Fundamentalists spent at least some time and energy discussing the dangers of the theory of evolution, antievolutionism had a constituency and logic of its own, mustering support among people and in areas where Fundamentalism made little headway. The South was the most important

of those areas in which antievolutionism flourished despite the residents' disinterest in organized Fundamentalism; Edward Larson paints a lurid picture of the success of antievolutionist efforts to ban the teaching of evolution in public schools in the state of Tennessee in Edward J. Larson, *Summer for the Gods: The Scopes Trial and America's Continuing Debate over Science and Religion* (Cambridge, MA: Harvard Univ. Press, 1997), 48–59.

William E. Ellis's *"A Man of Books and a Man of the People": E. Y. Mullins and the Crisis of Moderate Southern Baptist Leadership* is one example of a scholarly work that conflates Fundamentalism and antievolutionism. *A Man of Books*, the only scholarly biography of Southern Baptist leader E. Y. Mullins, describes Mullins' struggle against antievolution legislation in Kentucky in considerable detail. While preparing to discuss this conflict, Ellis notes that during the 1920s, "premillennialism and fundamentalism had become synonymous, and the teaching of evolution had become the principal adversary of this ultraconservative movement." Later, Ellis notes that by defeating antievolution legislation, Mullins and his allies had "averted a fundamentalist victory." While it is true that Fundamentalist leaders from the North, W. B. Riley in particular, looked on approvingly as a faction among Kentucky Baptists pressed for antievolution legislation, Ellis's framing of the issue this way in *A Man of Books* obscures the fact that Fundamentalism and antievolutionism were separate phenomena. William E. Ellis, *"A Man of Books and a Man of the People": E. Y. Mullins and the Crisis of Moderate Southern Baptist Leadership* (Macon, GA: Mercer Univ. Press, 1985), 151, 158.

While *A Man of Books* and many other works that equate antievolutionism and Fundamentalism were published after Marsden's *Fundamentalism*, Marsden himself cannot be blamed for the conflation of Fundamentalism and antievolutionism in accounts of Southern religion during the 1920s. On the one hand, Marsden indicates that Fundamentalism "flourished on two fronts. In the major denominations fundamentalists battled against those who denied, or would tolerate denials of, the fundamentals of the traditional faith. In American culture as a whole they fought to stop the teaching of evolution in the public schools." On the other hand, Marsden notes, "Darwinism never became a major issue in the church controversies themselves." In fact, Marsden notes that in the South, antievolutionism took on a life of its own, independent of Fundamentalist agitation in the Northern denominations: "Both the premillennial movement and denominational fundamentalism had been confined mostly to Northern states, but anti-evolution swept through the South and found new constituencies in rural areas everywhere. Many people with little or no interest in fundamentalism's doctrinal concerns were drawn into the campaign to keep Darwinism out of America's schools." In other words, Marsden's 1980 text contains a warning against identifying widespread antievolutionism in the South with a triumph of Fundamentalism in that region. Marsden, *Fundamentalism*, 164, 169, 170.

198

5. William R. Glass, *Strangers in Zion: Fundamentalists in the South, 1900–1950* (Macon, GA: Mercer Univ. Press, 2001), xiv.

6. Ibid., 2.

7. While J. Frank Norris was a Baptist in Texas who spent his time criticizing Southern Baptist leaders, he was excluded from the Texas General Conference in 1924. While some historical work on Southern Baptists, such as James J. Thompson, Jr.'s *Tried as By Fire*, has identified Norris as the leader of Fundamentalists among Southern Baptists, historians of Southern religion now seem to realize that Norris was viewed as an outsider by most Southern Baptists and must be excluded from any analysis of Fundamentalism in the SBC. Glass, *Strangers*, 77–78.

8. Paul Harvey, *Redeeming the South: Religious Cultures and Racial Identities Among Southern Baptists, 1865–1925* (Chapel Hill: Univ. of North Carolina Press, 1997), 3.

9. Samuel S. Hill, conclusion to *Churches in Cultural Captivity: A History of the Social Attitudes of Southern Baptists*, by John Lee Eighmy (Knoxville: Univ. of Tennessee Press, 1987), 202.

10. Ibid.; Harvey, *Redeeming the South*, 23–31.

11. Leonard, *God's Last and Only Hope*, 15.

12. Arthur Emery Farnsley II, *Southern Baptist Politics: Authority and Power in the Restructuring of an American Denomination* (University Park: Pennsylvania State Univ. Press, 1994), 6.

13. See, for instance, E. B. Hatcher, "How Can We Raise at Least $35,000,000 For Home and Foreign Missions Within Five Years?" *The Baptist World*, 15 May 1919, p. 8; J. Fred Eden, Jr., "A Big Baptist Publicity Program," *The Christian Index*, 1 May 1919, p. 9.

14. L. R. Scarborough, *Marvels of Divine Leadership* (Nashville, TN: Sunday School Board Southern Baptist Convention, 1920), 22–27.

15. Ibid., 96.

16. L. R. Scarborough, "The Creeds of Dead Hands," *Baptist Standard*, 22 September 1921, p. 6.

17. L. L. Gwaltney, "Ten Thousand Strong," *The Alabama Baptist*, 11 March 1920, p. 3; Gerorge W. McDaniel, "The Approaching Southern Baptist Convention," *The Religious Herald*, 1 April 1920, p. 11.

18. Livingston Johnson, "Cashing In," *Biblical Recorder*, 11 August 1920, p. 6.

19. See, for instance, L. L. Gwaltney, "A Campaign for Tithers," *The Alabama Baptist*, 14 July 1921, p. 4; L. R. Scarborough, "Southern Baptists In for a Great Campaign for Souls," *Baptist Standard*, 22 June 1922, p. 12.

20. Barry Hankins, *God's Rascal: J. Frank Norris and the Beginnings of Southern Fundamentalism* (Lexington: Univ. Press of Kentucky, 1996), 27.

21. "Introduction," in H. H. Gerth and C. Wright Mills, *From Max Weber: Essays in Sociology* (New York: Oxford Univ. Press, 1958), 51.

22. Max Weber, "Bureaucracy," in Gerth and Mills, *Weber*, 198.

23. Ibid., 200.

24. Ibid., 240.

25. Max Weber, *The Theory of Social and Economic Organization*, trans. A. M. Henderson and Talcott Parsons (New York: Oxford Univ. Press, 1947), 339. (This is an English translation of the first part of Weber's *Economy and Society*.)

26. Weber, "Bureaucracy," 208.

27. Ibid., 199.

28. Ibid., 196.

29. Ibid., 231.

30. Ibid., 240.

31. Dewey Grantham, *Southern Progressivism: The Reconciliation of Progress and Tradition* (Knoxville: Univ. of Tennessee Press, 1983), 82–83.

32. Ibid., 103.

33. Robert H. Wiebe, *The Search for Order, 1877–1920* (New York: Hill and Wang, 1967), 166.

1. The Transformation of Baptist Identity

1. Bill Leonard, *Baptist Ways: A History* (Valley Forge: Judson Press, 2003), 391; Ernest A. Payne, *The Baptist Union: A Short History* (London: The Baptist Union of Great Britain and Ireland, 1958), 159–65.

2. Fisher Humphreys, "E. Y. Mullins," in Timothy George and David S. Dockery, eds., *Baptist Theologians* (Nashville, TN: Broadman Press, 1990), 332.

3. Russell Dilday, "The Significance of E. Y. Mullins's *The Axioms of Religion*," *Baptist History and Heritage* XLIII, no. 1 (2008): 86.

4. See, for instance, C. Douglas Weaver, "The Baptist Ecclesiology of E. Y. Mullins: Individualism and the New Testament Church," *Baptist History and Heritage* XLIII, no. 1 (Winter 2008): 18–34 and H. Leon McBeth, "God Gives Soul Competency and Priesthood to All Believers," in Charles W. Deweese, ed., *Defining Baptist Convictions: Guidelines for the Twenty-First Century* (Franklin, TN: Providence House Publishers, 1996). Weaver, in particular, recognizes that Mullins was criticized for his emphasis on individualism, but Weaver defends him on the grounds that many of his critics read in his work an "excessively individualistic" anthropology that Mullins himself would not own and took care to avoid.

5. Harold Bloom, *The American Religion: The Emergence of the Post-Christian Nation* (New York: Simon and Schuster, 1992), 201–2.

6. Winthrop S. Hudson, "Shifting Patterns of Church Order in the Twentieth Century," in Winthrop Still Hudson, ed., *Baptist Concepts of the Church: A Survey of the Historical and Theological Issues which have Produced Changes in Church Order* (Philadelphia: Judson Press, 1959), 215–16.

200

7. R. Albert Mohler, introduction to *The Axioms of Religion: A New Interpretation of the Baptist Faith*, by Edgar Young Mullins (Nashville, TN: Broadman and Holman, 1997), 16.

8. William E. Ellis, *"A Man of Books, A Man of the People": E. Y. Mullins and the Crisis of Moderate Southern Baptist Leadership* (Macon, GA: Mercer Univ. Press, 1985), 80–81. C. Douglas Weaver also provides an excellent account of the widespread acceptance of *The Axioms* in C. Douglas Weaver, introduction to *The Axioms of Religion* by Edgar Young Mullins (Macon, GA: Mercer Univ. Press, 2010), 18.

9. Mohler, introduction to *The Axioms of Religion*, 18.

10. C. Douglas Weaver connects Mullins to Progressivism more strongly than any of his other interpreters, noting that Mullins embraced a moderate Social Gospel. At the same time, Weaver's description of Progressivism as it impinged on Mullins's career begins and ends with social reform and does not extend to Mullins's concerns with centralization and organizational development. See C. Douglas Weaver, "E. Y. Mullins: Soul Competency and Social Ministry," *Perspectives in Religious Studies* 36, no. 4 (Winter 2009): 451. Additionally, see Weaver's introduction to his edition of *The Axioms* in Weaver, ed., *The Axioms of Religion*, 26–29.

11. Paul Harvey, *Redeeming the South: Religious Cultures and Racial Identities Among Southern Baptists, 1865–1925* (Chapel Hill: Univ. of North Carolina Press, 1997), 90.

12. The classic statement of Landmark claims is James Robinson Graves, *Old Landmarkism: What Is It?* (Ashland, KY: Calvary Baptist Church Book Shop, 1880). Graves couples the sole ecclesial legitimacy of Baptist churches with his identification of the Baptist movement with democracy, casting other churches as institutional embodiments of tyranny. For Graves and his followers, Baptist churches were institutional embodiments of political and religious liberty, often oppressed throughout history by tyrannical churches and governments, but never extinguished.

13. Harvey, *Redeeming the South*, 149–50.

14. E. Glenn Hinson, "Oh, Baptists, How Your Corporation Has Grown!," in Marc A. Jolley with John D. Pierce, eds., *Distinctively Baptist: Essays on Baptist History, A Festschrift in Honor of Walter B. Shurden* (Macon, GA: Mercer Univ. Press, 2005), 20.

15. William G. McGlothlin, *Isaac Backus and the American Pietistic Tradition* (Boston: Little, Brown and Company, 1967), 107.

16. Lee Canipe, *A Baptist Democracy: Separating God from Caesar in the Land of the Free* (Macon, GA: Mercer Univ. Press, 2011), 40.

17. Elder John Leland, "The Government of Christ a Christocracy," in L. F. Greene, ed., *The Writings of the Late Elder John Leland, Including Some Events In His Life, Written By Himself, With Additional Sketches, &c.* (New York: G. W. Wood, 1845), 275.

201

18. E. Brooks Holifield, *The Gentlemen Theologians: American Theology in Southern Culture, 1795–1860* (Durham, NC: Duke Univ. Press, 1978), 34. Southern clergy were not attempting to create a professional identity that clergymen had never held, but were actually trying to recover something that had been de-emphasized during settlement of the frontier. See also Burton J. Bledstein, *The Culture of Professionalism: The Middle Class and the Development of Higher Education in America* (New York: W. W. Norton & Company, Inc., 1976), 80ff.

19. Ibid., 11.

20. Ibid., 12.

21. Ibid., 28.

22. Ibid., 4.

23. Charles Reagan Wilson, *Baptized in Blood: The Religion of the Lost Cause, 1865–1920* (Athens: Univ. of Georgia Press, 1980), 58.

24. R. B. C. Howell, for instance, remains Graves's best-remembered opponent, but he clearly adhered to the successionist idea that Baptists are not Protestants. R. B. C. Howell, "Organization of the Church with Respect to its Officers" (Ordination sermon for Peter Lindsley), Microfilm 894, Southern Baptist Historical Library and Archives, Nashville, Tennessee.

25. Marty Bell, "James Robinson Graves and the Rhetoric of Demagogy: Primitivism and Democracy in Old Landmarkism" (Ph.D. diss., Vanderbilt University, 1990), 96–101.

26. Ibid., 98–100.

27. Ibid., 68.

28. Harvey, *Redeeming the South*, 89.

29. Bell, "James Robinson Graves," 182.

30. Ibid., 196. R. B. C. Howell (1801–1868) was a native Virginian who twice served as the pastor of the First Baptist Church of Nashville, Tennessee, once from 1835 until 1850, and again from 1857 until 1867. During his first pastorate, Howell invited Graves to serve as the assistant editor of *The Baptist*, the denominational newspaper that Howell edited. Even before Howell left Nashville in 1850 to pastor a church in Virginia, however, Graves increasingly used the newspaper, now renamed *The Tennessee Baptist*, as a platform to promote Landmarkism, even willing to target his critics by name in its pages. Graves's controversial activities eventually caused such turmoil at First Baptist Church that the congregation voted to recall Howell as pastor, certain that he was the one person who could quell Landmarkist controversy and restore order to the church. Howell, however, was unable to defuse the controversy; instead, the two men found themselves locked in a personal feud that involved differing visions of denominational life, church discipline, and particularly the role of the Southern Baptist Publication Society, with which Howell was associated but which Graves viewed as an impediment to his own publishing interests. The controversy became so heated that it reached the floor of the Southern Baptist Convention, where Graves and his allies were unable to prevent Howell's reelection

202

as the Convention's president; Howell, however, resigned, seeking to keep the controversy from infecting the Southern Baptist Convention. The best treatment of Graves's life, and this controversy in particular, can be found in James Patterson, *James Robinson Graves: Staking the Boundaries of Baptist Identity* (Nashville, TN: Broadman and Holman Academic, 2012), 34–44, 127–53.

31. *The Tennessee Baptist* 15, no. 37 (May 21, 1859): 2, quoted in Bell, "Graves," 200.

32. Paul Gaston, *The New South Creed: A Study in Southern Mythmaking* (Baton Rouge: Louisiana State Univ. Press, 1970), ch. 1 passim.

33. Ibid., 189.

34. Ibid., 41, 221.

35. C. Vann Woodward, *Origins of the New South, 1877–1913* (Baton Rouge: Louisiana State Univ. Press, 1971), 3. The Redeemer Democrats were actually formed by a forced alliance between Southern Democrats and Southern Whigs, both of which sought to end reconstruction and the rule of Radical Republicans. The pro-business slant of the new party, which failed for years in some places even to refer to itself as a "Democratic Party," was drawn from the Whig side of the new alliance. For the relationship between Southern Baptists and this new Democratic Party, see John Lee Eighmy, *Churches in Cultural Captivity: A History of the Social Attitudes of Southern Baptists*, with revised introduction, conclusion, and bibliography by Sam Hill (Knoxville: Univ. of Tennessee Press, 1987), 41.

36. Robert H. Wiebe, *The Search for Order, 1877–1920* (New York: Hill and Wang, 1967), 13–18; 138–45.

37. Bledstein, *The Culture of Professionalism*, 90. Urban Southern ministers, it will be remembered, fit this description well.

38. Wiebe, *The Search for Order*, 11. The Progressive Era (1890–1917) was the period of American history during which bureaucratic solutions were most widely applied to the growing nation's problems.

39. Ibid., 160.

40. For information about the burgeoning cities of the South and their growing pains during the Progressive Era, see Dewey Grantham, *Southern Progressivism: The Reconciliation of Progress and Tradition* (Knoxville; Univ. of Tennessee Press, 1983), 277. For information about the peculiar plight of the Southern farmer during these years, see Lawrence Goodwyn, *The Populist Moment: A Short History of the Agrarian Revolt in America* (New York: Oxford Univ. Press, 1978), 21–23.

41. Grantham, *Southern Progressivism*, 112, 118; C. Vann Woodward, *The Strange Career of Jim Crow*, 2nd rev. ed. (New York: Oxford Univ. Press, 1966), 83. When the ruling classes of the Southern states justified disfranchisement on the grounds that it barred from voting the "ignorant and vicious of *both races*," they were hearkening back to classical republican fears that common people were unable to practice the virtues necessary for democratic self-rule.

42. Ibid., 43.

43. Bell, "Graves," 269.

44. Joseph E. Early, Jr., *A Texas Baptist Power Struggle: The Hayden Controversy* (Denton: Univ. of North Texas Press, 2005), 29, 40.

45. Ibid., 65.

46. Philip Ray Bryan, "An Analysis of the Ecclesiology of Associational Baptists, 1900–1950" (Ph.D. diss., Baylor Univ., 1973), 123–26. Bryan notes that while Hayden identified the new organization upon its creation, he vigorously rejected the idea of a new general body of Baptists until that time. Marty Bell provides a brief account of this conflict in Bell, "Graves," 262.

47. Early, *Hayden Controversy*, 108.

48. Bell, "Graves," 265.

49. Ibid., 269.

50. Although Landmarkism was widespread throughout the Western half of the SBC after the Civil War, many rural Baptists rejected the political implications of antebellum Landmarkism while retaining its unusual ecclesiology. As a result, many Western Baptists enthusiastically supported leaders like E. Y. Mullins despite their committed defense of Landmarkism. See Paul Harvey, "The Ideal of Professionalism in the White Southern Baptist Ministry, 1870–1920," *Religion and American Culture* 5, no. 1 (Winter 1995): 100.

51. Ibid., 269.

52. Harvey, *Redeeming the South*, 90.

53. Early, *Hayden Controversy*, 86. The Gospel Mission movement was a push among some Southern Baptists, led by Tarleton Perry Crawford (1821–1902), to abolish the Foreign Mission Board on the grounds that churches are the only organizations with a biblical mandate to send missionaries and channel funds to them. Although the movement is frequently associated with Landmarkism, Adrian Lamkin notes that the movement actually sprang from Crawford's experiences as a missionary in China, only later to be appropriated by Landmarkers for their own ends. Adrian Lamkin, "The Gospel Mission Movement within the Southern Baptist Convention" (Ph.D. diss., Southern Baptist Theological Seminary, 1980), xi, 209.

54. Early, *Hayden Controversy*, 105.

55. Ibid., 115.

56. Christopher Bart Barber, "The Bogard Schism: An Arkansas Agrarian Revolt" (Ph.D. diss., Southwestern Baptist Theological Seminary, 2006), 214.

57. Ibid., 54.

58. Ibid., 54–57.

59. Ibid., 214.

60. Bell, "Graves," 264–65. See also Hinson, "Oh, Baptists," 23.

61. Ellis, *A Man of Books*, 1, 4, 7, 9–10.

62. Ibid., 14.

63. Isla May Mullins, *Edgar Young Mullins* (Nashville, TN: Sunday School Board of the Southern Baptist Convention, 1929), 99.

64. Ibid., 128–29, 145. Harvey, *Redeeming the South*, 151.

65. Ellis, *A Man of Books*, 25–26.

66. Progressivism sponsored by the clergy was known as the "social gospel." Wiebe, *The Search for Order*, 207–8.

67. E. Y. Mullins, *The Axioms of Religion: A New Interpretation of the Baptist Faith* (Philadelphia: The Griffith and Rowland Press, 1908), 19.

68. Ibid., 53.

69. Ibid.

70. Ibid., 51.

71. Ibid., 127.

72. Ibid., 131.

73. Ibid., 250.

74. Ibid., 35.

75. Ibid., 22.

76. For example, see Friedrich Schleiermacher, *On Religion: Addresses in Response to its Cultured Critics*, trans. Terrence N. Tice (Richmond, VA: John Knox Press, 1969), 73.

77. Mullins, *The Axioms of Religion*, 20.

78. Mullins's conservative critics tend to interpret him as suggesting that religious knowledge is mined primarily from experience, a process in which the Bible plays only a secondary role. This is an overreading of his position, at least as it is laid out in *The Axioms*; Mullins never believed that religious experience could be a source of knowledge independent from the Bible. Mohler, introduction to *The Axioms of Religion*, 9–10.

79. Ibid., 92–93.

80. Ibid., 127.

81. Ibid., 143.

82. Ibid., 32.

83. Ibid., 134.

84. Ibid., 131.

85. Ibid., 213.

86. Ibid., 147.

87. Ibid., 148.

88. Ibid.

89. Furthermore, Mullins restricts the role of the denomination to "missions and education." Baptists can never organize beyond the level of the local church in order "to try heretics or to impose creeds or to pass general laws." Ibid., 262.

90. Ibid.

91. Mullins is certainly not the first to think of Southern Baptist democracy in terms of consensus. Arthur Emery Farnsley II, *Southern Baptist Politics:*

Authority and Power in the Restructuring of an American Denomination (University Park: Pennsylvania State Univ. Press, 1994), ch. 3 passim.

92. Mullins, *The Axioms of Religion*, 56.

93. Ibid., 55.

94. Ibid., 129.

95. As Mullins himself noted to a correspondent in 1919, "You may be familiar with the word 'Landmarkism,' but perhaps you do not know all that is implied in it. The center of gravity has shifted towards the Southwest, and the type of opinion described by the above word is very much in evidence in the present constituency of the Convention, especially when it meets within range of that territory." Mullins, a master politician, was well aware of the influence of Landmarkism in the Southern Baptist Convention; there is no reason to believe that he would have written *The Axioms of Religion* without tending closely to this fact. Letter, E. Y. Mullins to Clarence Barbour, 3 May 1919, cited in Harvey, *Redeeming the South*, 89. For information on Mullins as a consummate politician, see Walter B. Shurden, *Not an Easy Journey: Some Transitions in Baptist Life* (Macon, GA: Mercer Univ. Press, 2005), 176.

96. Ibid., 134.

97. Ibid., 60.

98. Ibid., 63–64.

99. See, for example, J. R. Graves's discussion of Methodist ordination practices in J. R. Graves, *The Great Iron Wheel; or, Christianity Backwards and Republicanism Reversed* (Nashville, TN: Graves and Marks, 1855), 143–52.

100. Farnsley, *Southern Baptist Politics*, 40–42. Farnsley correctly notes the influence of common sense realism on Southern Baptist assumptions about democracy.

101. *Proceedings of the Southern Baptist Convention, 1913*, in Ibid., 6.

102. *Southern Baptist Convention Annual, 1917*, in Ibid, 6.

103. L. L. Gwaltney, "Time and 75 Millions," *The Alabama Baptist*, 7 August 1919, p. 3.

104. F. M. McConnell, "Building a Denomination," *Baptist Messenger*, 25 June 1919, pp. 4–5.

105. L. R. Scarborough, "The Baptist Pot is Boiling," *The Religious Herald*, 4 September 1919, p. 3.

106. L. R. Scarborough, "The Convention and the Campaign," *Baptist Advance*, 28 October 1920, p. 9.

107. J. B. Gambrell, "Right and Wrong Uses of Liberty," *Baptist Standard*, 30 October 1919, p. 12.

108. J. B. Gambrell, "Some Lessons From The Great Campaign," *Baptist Advance*, 1 January 1920, p. 2.

2. The Clock of the World

1. Lester G. McAllister and William E. Tucker, *Journey in Faith: A History of the Christian Church (Disciples of Christ)* (St. Louis: Chalice Press, 1975), 335.

2. "Report to Mr. R. A. Long on the Men and Millions Movement," 1913–1919, p. 8. Disciples of Christ Historical Society, RG 119, A. 260.

3. McAllister and Tucker, *Journey in Faith*, 336.

4. "Report to Mr. R. A. Long," 12.

5. Ibid., 13.

6. Ibid., 27.

7. *The Christian Advocate* (New York), 27 September 1917, cited in John Lankford, "Methodism 'Over the Top': The Joint Centenary Movement, 1917–1925," *Methodist History* 2 (Oct. 1963): 27.

8. Lankford, "Methodism 'Over the Top,'" 28.

9. Alfred E. Cornebise, *War as Advertised: The Four Minute Men and America's Crusade, 1917–1918* (Philadelphia: The American Philosophical Society, 1984), 110, 67.

10. *The Christian Advocate* (Nashville), 6 December 1918, in Lankford, "Methodism 'Over the Top,'" 29.

11. *The New York Times*, 6 October 1918.

12. Robert Wuthnow, *The Restructuring of American Religion: Society and Faith since World War II* (Princeton: Princeton Univ. Press, 1988), 35.

13. Eldon G. Ernst, *Moment of Truth for Protestant America: Interchurch Campaigns Following World War One* (Missoula, MT: Scholars Press, 1972), 38.

14. Ellis W. Hawley, *The Great War and the Search for a Modern Order: A History of the American People and Their Institutions, 1917–1933*, 2nd ed. (Prospect Heights, IL: Waveland Press, 1992), 41.

15. Ibid., 39.

16. Ernst, *Moment of Truth*, 38.

17. This was the southern branch of the Presbyterian Church.

18. Ernst, *Moment of Truth*, 44–45.

19. Quoted in Ibid., 45.

20. Quoted in Ibid.

21. Ibid., 51.

22. William Adams Brown, *The Church in America: A Study of The Present Condition and Future Prospects of American Protestantism* (New York: The MacMillan Company, 1922), 119.

23. Ernst, *Moment of Truth*, 52.

24. Ibid.

25. Ibid.

26. Delavan L. Pierson, "A New Inter-Church Missionary Alliance," *The Missionary Review of the World* XLII (February 1919), 82.

27. Ernst, *Moment of Truth*, 56.

28. Ibid., 98.

29. Ibid., 96.

30. Ibid., 95.

31. Ibid., 96.

32. Ibid., 60.

33. Milton G. Evans, "Why Christian Enlistment Now," *The Standard*, 16 November 1918, p. 262, quoted in Ibid., 59.

34. *World Call* II (May 1920), p. 3, quoted in Ibid., 140.

35. Martin Marty, *Modern American Religion*, vol. 1, *The Irony of It All* (Chicago: Univ. of Chicago Press, 1986), 279.

36. Ernst, *Moment of Truth*, 145. Out of forty million dollars expected from "friendly citizens," only three million were received.

37. Ibid., 150–51.

38. As briefly noted above, Southern Baptists had harbored anti-ecumenical tendencies since at least the 1850s because of Landmarkism's pervasive influence. Although the roots of Landmarkism in Southern Baptist life have much to do with social and political conflict, Landmarkism is, on the surface, a series of ecclesiological claims. For Graves, Landmarkism's most important founder, only Baptist churches were true churches, because only Baptist churches could trace an unbroken line of succession from the present day back to the early church. Graves denied that Baptist churches could be properly called "Protestant," because Protestants had abandoned Roman Catholicism during the Reformation while Baptist churches had always existed separate from that body. Because no historical connection exists between Baptists and all other Christian groups, Graves taught that Baptists should never preach in non-Baptist pulpits, allow non-Baptist ministers into their own pulpits, take communion in non-Baptist churches, or weaken the boundaries between the Baptist and non-Baptist churches in any way. This perspective, which was pervasive among Southern Baptists west of the Appalachians by the end of the Civil War, gave Southern Baptist life an anti-ecumenical flavor that lingers, in many places, until the present day. Southern Baptist opposition to the Interchurch World Movement was galvanized by the way the military had dealt with religion during the war, but Southern Baptists would never have approved of an ecumenical enterprise like the IWM even in a best case scenario. For Graves's anti-ecumenical read of non-Baptist denominations, see James Robinson Graves, *Old Landmarkism: What Is It?* (Ashland, KY: Calvary Baptist Church Book Shop, 1880).

39. Z. T. Cody, "The Convention," *The Baptist Courier*, 29 May 1919, p. 4.

40. Paul Harvey, *Redeeming the South: Religious Cultures and Racial Identities among Southern Baptists, 1865–1925* (Chapel Hill: Univ. of North Carolina Press, 1997), 222.

41. J. B. Gambrell, "The Baptists and Others on War Problems," *Baptist Standard*, 5 June 1919, p. 5.

42. George W. McDaniel, "Let Us Know the Truth About the Y.M.C.A. in France," *Western Recorder*, 1 May 1919, pp. 6–7.

43. J. W. Porter, "The Y. M. C. A. and the Soldiers," *Western Recorder*, 8 May 1919, p. 8.

44. *Southern Baptist Convention Annual, 1919*, p. 110.

45. Ibid.

46. J. W. Porter, "Otherwise Engaged," *Western Recorder*, 8 May 1919, p. 8.

47. V. I. Masters, "*Who Steers (?) And Stokes the Union Boat?*" 15 May 1919, p. 1.

48. J. W. Cammack, "Southern Baptist Convention, Atlanta, Georgia, May 14 to 19, 1919," *Religious Herald*, 22 May 1919, pp. 5–7.

49. *Southern Baptist Convention Annual, 1919*, 111.

50. Harvey, *Redeeming the South*, 224.

51. *Southern Baptist Convention Annual, 1919*, 110.

52. B. C. Hening, "The Times Reset to Baptist Doctrines," *Baptist Standard*, 11 September 1919, p. 3.

53. E. C. Routh, "The Baptist 75 Million Campaign," *Baptist Standard*, 11 September 1919, p. 16.

54. Amos Clary, "The Democratization of Christianity," *The Baptist Courier*, 12 June 1919, p. 2.

55. O. W. Greer, "The Uplifting Power of the Campaign," *Western Recorder*, 4 September 1919, p. 3.

56. Rufus W. Weaver, "The Baptist Problem in this Age of Reconstruction," *Baptist Standard*, 12 June 1919, pp. 6, 21–23.

57. A. C. Campbell, "Christianity and World Construction," *Biblical Recorder*, 23 July 1919, p. 5.

58. E. P. Alldredge, "The Inter-Church World Movement," *Baptist Advance*, 4 March 1920, pp. 2–3.

59. Ibid.

60. Ibid.

61. Livingston Johnson, "Efficiency," *Biblical Recorder*, 17 December 1919, p. 6.

62. Ibid.

63. Interestingly, leaders of the SBC seem to have assumed that the 1919 Convention's decision to reject the IWM was binding to local congregations.

64. J. W. Mitchell, "Take Due Notice, Brethren," *Florida Baptist Witness*, 30 October 1919, p. 2.

65. J. B. Gambrell, "The Inter-Church World Movement in the South," *The Alabama Baptist*, 20 November 1919, p. 6.

66. L. L. Gwaltney, "Living Unto Themselves," *The Alabama Baptist*, 20 December 1919, p. 4.

67. Ibid.

68. Curtis Lee Laws, "The Glorious Victory of Southern Baptists," *The Baptist Courier*, 25 December 1919, p. 2.

69. L. R. Scarborough, "Denominationalizing Baptist Schools," *Western Recorder*, 15 May 1919, p. 2.

70. C. H. Wetherbe, "An Unfavorable Sign," *Western Recorder*, 5 June 1919.

71. E. Y. Mullins, "Keeping Steady," *Baptist Standard*, 8 May 1919, pp. 9, 52.

72. L. R. Scarborough, *Marvels of Divine Leadership* (Nashville, TN: Sunday School Board Southern Baptist Convention, 1920), 13.

73. *Southern Baptist Convention Annual, 1919*, p. 112.

74. J. S. Compere, Editorial, *Baptist Advance*, 26 February 1920, p. 4. Boldface in the original.

75. R. H. Pitt, "Let Virginia Baptists Keep Step," *The Religious Herald*, 3 June 1919, p. 1.

76. B. J. W. Graham, "Baptist Seventy-Five Million Campaign," *The Christian Index*, 10 July 1919, pp. 1–2.

77. J. W. C. (J. W. Cammack), "Who 'Started' It and What For?" *The Religious Herald*, 9 October 1919, p. 10.

78. Scarborough, *Marvels of Divine Leadership*, 16–17. Note the idea here and in the previous quotation that the messengers of the Convention were understood to "represent" other Southern Baptists.

79. Scarborough, *Marvels of Divine Leadership*, 17.

80. J. B. Gambrell, "A Challenging Call to Baptists of America," *Baptist Standard*, 1 May 1919, p. 8.

81. L. R. Scarborough, "Truth Tremendously Imperilled," *The Baptist Courier*, 8 May 1919, p. 3.

82. E. B. (Eldridge) Hatcher, "At The Threshold," *The Baptist World*, 8 May 1919, p. 10.

83. Scarborough, *Marvels of Divine Leadership*, 22.

84. L. R. Scarborough, "Two of the Greatest Baptist Days," *Biblical Recorder*, 9 July 1919, p. 3.

85. B. C. Hening, "We Will Win," *Biblical Recorder*, 6 August 1919, p. 1.

86. Livingston Johnson, "Words Baptists Do Not Like," *Biblical Recorder*, 23 July 1919, p. 6.

87. B. J. W. Graham, "Incidents in the Baptist 75 Million Campaign," *The Christian Index*, 6 November 1919, p. 3.

88. B. C. Hening, "The Baptist Unanimous Elective Draft," *Baptist Messenger*, 23 July 1919, pp. 8–9.

89. L. R. Scarborough, "Important Announcement," *Biblical Recorder*, 19 November 1919, p. 1.

90. L. L. Gwaltney, "Things Needed Now," *The Alabama Baptist*, 30 October 1919, p. 3.

91. Unsigned Editorial, "August and the 75 Million Campaign," *The Religious Herald*, 7 August 1919, p. 7.

92. E. B. (Eldridge) Hatcher, "A Steep Hill," *The Baptist World*, 31 July 1919, p. 6.

93. Scarborough, *Marvels of Divine Providence*, 29; L. R. Scarborough, "Looking to Victory—The Thing Most Needful Now," *The Religious Herald*, 21 August 1919, p. 9.

94. W. A. Hobson, "Tremendously Important," *Florida Baptist Witness*, 4 September 1919, p. 10.

95. J. W. Mitchell, "Pledge Cards," *Florida Baptist Witness*, 13 November 1919, p. 6.

96. E. Y. Mullins, "Reasons Why Southern Baptists Should Raise Seventy-Five Million Dollars," *Baptist Messenger*, 10 September 1919, p. 18.

97. Alex W. Bealer, "A Record Breaking Convention Held in the Georgia Capital," *The Christian Index*, 22 May 1919, 1–20, 22.

98. J. W. Mitchell, "The Final Word," *Florida Baptist Witness*, 5 June 1919, p. 2.

99. Livingston Johnson, "Dangers to Democracy, No. 1," *Biblical Recorder*, 17 September 1919, p. 6.

100. M. B. Humphrey, "Safeguarding Our Baptist Principles," *Biblical Recorder*, 1 October 1919, p. 5.

3. The Fundamentalization of Cooperation

1. I. M. Haldeman, *Why I Am Opposed to the Interchurch World Movement* (n. p., n. d.), 14, 17, 22, in *The Fundamentalist-Modernist Conflict: Opposing Views on Three Major Issues*, edited by Joel A. Carpenter (New York: Garland Publishing, Inc., 1988). Italics in the original.

2. Ibid., 4–5. Italics in the original.

3. Ibid., 26.

4. Premillennial dispensationalism was a variety of conservative Protestant theology that emerged in the early 1800s from the ministry of John Nelson Darby, a clergyman of the Church of Ireland. For Darby, the Bible taught that Jesus was to return soon and that this return would take the form of a "secret rapture" that would remove the church from the earth before Jesus' visible coming. Additionally, Darby taught that the coming of Jesus was imminent because he believed that history was separated by the Bible into a number of discrete periods, or "dispensations." During each dispensation, the nature of God's activity was thought to be distinct. Darby taught that the foundation of the church was a "parenthesis" between the penultimate and final dispensation, and thus believed that the rapture of the church would end this parenthesis and usher in the final judgment. These beliefs would eventually enter the bloodstream of early Fundamentalism. See Ernest R. Sandeen, *The Roots of Fundamentalism: British and American Millenarianism, 1800–1930* (Chicago: Univ. of Chicago Press, 1970), 62–70.

5. The "Five Fundamentals" were a list of non-negotiable doctrines originally set out by the Presbyterian General Assembly in the context of a controversy in that denomination in 1910. The fundamentals, laid out in response to questions

211

about some graduates of Union Theological Seminary in New York, concerned "(1) the inerrancy of Scripture, (2) the Virgin Birth of Christ, (3) his substitutionary atonement, (4) his bodily resurrection, and (5) the authenticity of the miracles." Although this list was not intended to become a definitive statement of Fundamentalist belief, it eventually became a conservative rallying cry during the controversies of the 1920s. George M. Marsden, *Fundamentalism in American Culture* (New York: Oxford Univ. Press, 2006), 117.

6. Ibid., 103.

7. Mary Beth Swetnam Mathews claims that Fundamentalism became associated with the South in the popular American mind through the influence of popular print media whose coverage of antievolutionism in the region and the rise of the Ku Klux Klan cast the South as a region "religiously different." Mary Beth Swetnam Mathews, *Rethinking Zion: How the Print Media Placed Fundamentalism in the South* (Knoxville: Univ. of Tennessee Press, 2006), 68.

8. Kenneth Bailey, *Southern White Protestantism in the Twentieth Century* (New York: Harper & Row, 1964), 45–48.

9. James J. Thompson, Jr. *Tried as By Fire: Southern Baptists and the Religious Controversies of the 1920s* (Macon, GA: Mercer Univ. Press, 1982), 141, 147. Although Thompson's work was published in 1982, two years after the appearance of *Fundamentalism in American Culture*, Thompson notes that it "appeared too late to have much impact on my own interpretation of Southern Baptist fundamentalism." Ibid., 219.

10. Ibid., 81.

11. William R. Glass: *Strangers in Zion: Fundamentalists in the South, 1900–1950* (Macon, GA: Mercer Univ. Press, 2001), xvii.

12. William E. Ellis, *"A Man of Books, A Man of the People": E. Y. Mullins and the Crisis of Moderate Southern Baptist Leadership* (Macon, GA, Mercer Univ. Press, 1985), 201.

13. Marsden, *Fundamentalism*, 170.

14. W. C. Tyree, D. D., "Effects of the Union Movement," *Biblical Recorder*, 31 March 1920, p. 5.

15. Victor I. Masters, "The Value of Christian Doctrine," *Western Recorder*, 13 October 1921, p. 9.

16. J. F. Love, "A Letter to be Pondered by the Thoughtful," *Baptist Messenger*, 28 September 1921, p. 1

17. P. I. Lipsey, "If the Foundation be Destroyed," *The Baptist Record*, 20 January 1921, p. 4. Lipsey alludes to the evolution debate in this editorial as well. A conservative editor, Lipsey had no more patience for evolution than he did for Modernism, but other editors clearly disagreed with him.

18. Vedder became notorious among conservatives during the 1920s for his strident rejection of the substitutionary atonement. Details of Vedder's opinion on the matter can be found in Henry C. Vedder, *The Fundamentals of Christi-*

212

anity: A Study of the Teachings of Jesus and Paul (New York: The MacMillan Company, 1922), 194–95.

19. Unsigned editorial, "Dr. Vedder of Crozer," *The Baptist Message*, 24 March 1921, p. 6.

20. J. F. Love, "Dr. Vedder on the Atonement," *The Religious Herald*, 17 February 1921, p. 5.

21. R. H. Pitt, Untitled Editorial, *The Religious Herald*, 15 April 1920, p. 10.

22. R. H. Pitt, Untitled Editorial, *The Religious Herald*, 30 September 1920, p. 11.

23. Ibid.

24. J. D. Moore, Untitled Editorial, *Baptist and Reflector*, 3 March 1921, p. 6.

25. Norman H. Maring, "Conservative but Progressive," in Gilbert L. Guffin, ed., *What God Hath Wrought: Eastern's First Thirty-Five Years* (Philadelphia: The Judson Press, 1960), 23.

26. Ibid., 26.

27. Livingston Johnson, "The Solid South," *Biblical Recorder*, 20 June 1923, p. 6.

28. Z. T. Cody, "The Virgin Birth," *The Baptist Courier*, 24 August 1922, p. 2.

29. Curtis Lee Laws, "Fundamentalism a Protest," *Florida Baptist Witness*, 29 June 1922, p. 14.

30. Frank E. Burkhalter, "Fundamental Conference of the Northern Convention," *The Baptist Message*, 22 June 1922, p. 9.

31. Z. T. Cody, Untitled Editorial, *The Baptist Courier*, 26 May 1921, p. 4. Note that the *Watchman-Examiner* is described as a paper that "we" read.

32. Finley W. Tinnin, Untitled Editorial, *The Baptist Message*, 9 June 1921, p. 2.

33. Finley W. Tinnin, "The Southwestern Bible Conference," *The Baptist Message*, 13 December 1923, p. 6; P. I. Lipsey, "A Great Bible Conference," *The Baptist Record*, 8 March 1923, p. 3.

34. P. L. Johnston, "Bible Conference at Miami First Church," *Florida Baptist Witness*, 13 March 1924, pp. 6–7.

35. J. Michael Utzinger, *Yet Saints Their Watch are Keeping: Fundamentalists, Modernists, and the Development of Evangelical Ecclesiology, 1887–1937* (Macon, GA: Mercer Univ. Press, 2006), 191.

36. P. I. Lipsey, Untitled Editorial, *The Baptist Record*, 5 May 1921, p. 4.

37. J. S. Compere, Untitled Editorial, *Baptist Advance*, 12 February 1925, p. 2.

38. Frank Goodchild, quoted in Maring, "Conservative but Progressive," 25.

39. J. S. Compere, Untitled Editorial, *Baptist Advance*, 14 February 1924, p. 3. Moderate Fundamentalists in the North did found new seminaries, such as Northern Baptist Theological Seminary and Eastern Baptist Theological Seminary, but moderates tried, with mixed success, to ensure that the Northern Baptist Convention would recognize these new institutions. These institutions were meant to be alternatives within the NBC, supplying pastors to NBC churches, rather than separatist institutions. Joel Carpenter, *Revive Us Again:*

213

The Reawakening of American Fundamentalism (New York: Oxford Univ. Press, 1997), 19.

40. Utzinger, *Yet Saints*, 186.

41. Ibid., 189; R. H. Pitt, "Three 'Movements,'" *The Religious Herald*, 26 April 1923, p. 10.

42. Although the BBU's confession did not commit all members to premillennial dispensationalism, its most important members held this opinion. Utzinger, *Yet Saints*, 199–200.

43. Ibid., 201.

44. Curtis Lee Laws, quoted in Finley W. Tinnin, Untitled Editorial, *The Baptist Message*, 10 May 1923, p. 6.

45. L. L. Gwaltney, "The American Baptist Bible Union: 'A Trojan Horse,'" *The Alabama Baptist*, 1 February 1923, p. 3. The most intense Fundamentalists of the 1920s were typically convinced that premillennial dispensationalism was the only legitimate way to read the Bible. More moderate Fundamentalists, however, believed that conservatives could legitimately claim some interpretive latitude in their doctrine of last things. Southern Baptists, who were rather diverse in their beliefs about the end times, agreed and resented the implication that this diversity represented a lack of conviction. L. L. Gwaltney, for his part, seems to have believed that the Baptist Bible Union did require premillennial beliefs of its members. See Marsden, *Fundamentalism*, 233.

46. Utzinger, *Yet Saints*, 201.

47. R. H. Pitt, "Hurting Instead of Helping," *The Religious Herald*, 31 May 1923, pp. 10–11.

48. J. W. Mitchell, "Baptist Bible Union," *Florida Baptist Witness*, 5 April 1923, p. 2.

49. Ibid.

50. L. R. Scarborough, "Is the Baptist Bible Union Needed in the South?" *The Baptist Message*, 10 May 1923, p. 4.

51. R. H. Pitt, "Uniting by Dividing," *Biblical Recorder*, 18 April 1923, p. 5.

52. W. B. Riley, "Orthodoxy and Organization in the Northern Convention," *The Baptist Message*, 17 March 1921, p. 14.

53. Ibid.

54. Finley W. Tinnin, "Baptist Bible Union," *The Baptist Message*, 19 April 1923, p. 6.

55. L. R. Scarborough, "Kept Sacredly Separate," *The Baptist Record*, 4 September 1924, p. 2.

56. Barry Hankins, *God's Rascal: J. Frank Norris and the Beginnings of Southern Fundamentalism* (Lexington: Univ. Press of Kentucky, 1996), 27.; R. H. Pitt, "A Defamatory Utterance," *The Religious Herald*, 20 April 1922, p. 10.

57. Glenn Thomas Carson, *The Life and Work of Lee Rutland Scarborough: Calling Out the Called* (Austin, TX: Eakin Press, 1996), 46.

58. Carson, *Lee Rutland Scarborough*, 49, 102–3. Over the last fifteen years, historians have come to see J. Frank Norris not as a Southern Baptist, but as a radical Fundamentalist working on Texas soil. As a result, Norris's own theological opinions are not directly relevant to a study of Southern Baptist attitudes towards Fundamentalism. See the Appendix for more information on the evolution of scholarly attitudes toward Norris.

59. L. R. Scarborough, "The Weakness of the Fundamentalists," *The Baptist Message*, 9 March 1922, p. 4.

60. L. R. Scarborough, "Two Kinds of Fundamentalism," *Baptist Standard*, 2 November 1922, p. 27.

61. R. H. Pitt, "Fundamentals and Fundamentals," *Biblical Recorder*, 2 May 1923, p. 1.

62. P. I. Lipsey, Untitled Editorial, *The Baptist Record*, 30 March 1922, p. 1.

63. R. H. Pitt, "Keep the Record Clear," *The Religious Herald*, 17 May 1923, p. 10.; J. D. Moore, "Dr. Laws on Baptist Bible Union," *Baptist and Reflector*, 3 May 1923, p. 1.

64. J. E. Dillard, "Fundamentalists and Modernists," *The Alabama Baptist*, 31 January 1924, p. 7.

65. Len G. Broughton, "'Why Call Him a Fundamentalist?,'" *Baptist Messenger*, 2 April 1924, p. 2.

66. Charles Reagan Wilson, *Baptized in Blood: The Religion of the Lost Cause, 1865–1920* (Athens: Univ. of Georgia Press, 1980), 13, 15.

67. Victor I. Masters, *The Call of the South* (Atlanta: Publicity Department of the Home Mission Board of the Southern Baptist Convention, 1920), 17.

68. Ibid.

69. Ibid., 18.

70. Ibid., 19–20.

71. Ibid., 209.

72. Anonymous, "Five Fundamentals of Evangelism," *Baptist Standard*, 4 March 1920, p. 1.

73. Frank E. Burkhalter, "Do Southern Baptists Believe God's Word," *Baptist and Reflector*, 24 January 1924, pp. 4–5.

74. L. R. Scarborough, "Is The Baptist Bible Union Needed in the South?" *The Religious Herald*, 3 May 1923, p. 8.

75. Ibid., 13. Note that Scarborough qualifies his rejection of evolution in order to include theistic evolutionists like W. L. Poteat; conservatives on the evolution issue, such as C. P. Stealey, would never have made such a qualification.

76. L. R. Scarborough, "The Finest of the Fine Arts," *The Religious Herald*, 7 June 1923, p. 2

77. By 1925 Missouri Baptists had voted to align solely with the Southern Baptist Convention, severing their NBC ties. A few churches in large cities retained their alignment with the Northern organization, but the author of this letter,

hailing from a small town in Western Missouri, probably considered himself a singly aligned Southern Baptist. In referring to himself as an "exile" in his letter, he most likely was referring to his exile from Arkansas, not the SBC.

78. J. B. Rose, "An Exile Discusses the Controversy," *Baptist Advance*, 6 August 1925, p. 8.

79. L. L. Gwaltney, "Some Criticisms," *The Alabama Baptist*, 2 February 1922, p. 3. Though Gwaltney is discussing evolution here, this article serves as evidence that many Southern Baptist leaders and editors were willing to accept evolution even while they rejected tenets of Modernism such as denial of Christ's divinity. The editor continues: "**If it can be shown that there are teachers in Baptist schools in Alabama who by reason of any evolutionary theory they may hold deny God or the Christian religion, the editor of The Alabama Baptist will use what influence he may have with the trustees to get such teachers dismissed. If, on the other hand, it is proposed to drive out those who believe in the growth and development in all material and spiritual things and who acknowledge the work of God in all such processes, which is simply called by many 'evolution,' then the editor of this paper will have no part in it.**" Boldface in the original.

80. J. D. Moore, "Action of William Jewell Trustees," *Baptist and Reflector*, 21 December 1922, p. 7. Italics in the original.

81. J. W. Mitchell, "Trouble at Mercer," *Florida Baptist Witness*, 23 October 1924, p. 3.

82. Ibid.

83. Louie D. Newton, "The Fox Case," *The Christian Index*, 16 October 1924, p. 14.

84. L. R. Scarborough, "How Our Schools Can Hold the Confidence and Support of Our People?" *Baptist Messenger*, 29 April 1925, p. 13. See also L. R. Scarborough, "Paul's Three Great Words," *Baptist Messenger*, 27 July 1921, p. 3. Emphasis in the original.

85. L. R. Scarborough, "The Creeds of Dead Hands," *Baptist Messenger*, 5 October 1921, p. 5, 7.

86. J. W. Mitchell, "The War Is On," *Florida Baptist Witness*, 6 March 1924, p. 3.

87. Anonymous, "Preaching for Preachers to Preach," *Baptist Advance*, 28 February 1924, p. 1. See also L. R. Scarborough, "A Four-Fold Answer to Modernism," *The Baptist Record*, 4 June 1925, p. 2. The cartoon associated with the Moody Bible Institute first appears with attribution in the November 15, 1923 issue of the *Baptist Advance*.

88. L. R. Scarborough, "The Heresy of Non-Co-operation," *The Baptist Message*, 17 November 1921, p. 4. It must be acknowledged that Scarborough did not invent the idea of "cooperation" as the method by which Baptist congregations could work together to accomplish tasks that a single congregation could not. The idea can be traced at least back to 1900, when the SBC appointed a "Committee on Cooperation." E. Glenn Hinson, "Oh, Baptists, How Your Corporation

216

Has Grown!" in Marc A. Jolley with John D. Pierce, eds., *Distinctively Baptist: Essays on Baptist History, A Festschrift in Honor of Walter B. Shurden* (Macon, GA: Mercer Univ. Press, 2005), 24. Additionally, E. Y. Mullins advocates the idea in his little book *Baptist Beliefs*, noting in 1912 that mission work is partly done through the "co-operation with missionary boards" and that Baptist efforts in education were important in part because they created that "intelligence and breadth of view" that inspired people to cooperative effort. E. Y. Mullins, *Baptist Beliefs* (Philadelphia: The Judson Press, 1925), 73–76.

89. L. R. Scarborough, "The Unfinished Task," *Baptist Standard*, 22 December 1921, p. 7.

90. L. R. Scarborough, "Is Cooperation a New Testament Doctrine?" *Baptist Advance*, 11 May 1922, p. 6.

91. The 1922 SBC declined to appoint a committee to frame a joint confession with the Northern Baptists on the grounds that the informal joint committee requesting the appointment had no authority to do so, and also out of fear of framing any "creedal statement" at all. Those favoring the creation of a statement tended to be those most familiar with the conflict among Northern Baptists. Livingston Johnson, "Unwritten History," *Biblical Recorder*, 5 July 1923, p. 6.

92. Scarborough seems to be assuming that the new confession would be based on the New Hampshire Confession, which contains eighteen articles.

93. Finley W. Tinnin, Untitled Editorial, *The Baptist Message*, 4 May 1922, p. 6.

94. Victor I. Masters, "Proposes that 'Co-operation' be Made a Baptist Article of Faith," *Western Recorder*, 18 May 1922, p. 9.

95. H. F. Aulick, "Advantages of the Budget Plan of Church Finances," *Baptist Standard*, 11 January 1923, p. 10.

96. J. S. Compere, Untitled Editorial, *Baptist Advance*, 23 February 1922, p. 4.

97. J. S. Compere, "How's Your Baptisity," *Baptist Advance*, 12 July 1923, p. 4.

98. See, for instance, L. R. Scarborough, "Information and Inspiration," *The Religious Herald*, 28 August 1924, p. 3.

99. E. Y. Mullins, "Our Weakness," *Baptist Advance*, 10 June 1920, p. 3.

100. C. P. Stealey, Untitled Editorial, *Baptist Messenger*, 26 January 1921, p. 8. Stealey notes that after this round of purchases, only the *Biblical Recorder* of North Carolina, *The Word and Way* of Missouri, and *The Religious Herald* of Virginia remained independent. Stealey had anticipated the sale of the *Herald*, but Editor Pitt decided not to sell. By my count, Stealey would have been looking at a field of seventeen newspapers.

101. S. M. Brown, "Denominational Ownership of Our Weekly Denominational Papers," *The Word and Way*, 5 June 1919, p. 4.

102. Southern Baptist editors did not abandon the ideal of editorial independence; they simply modified it. The editor of *The Baptist Courier*, for instance, took great pains to explain to his readership that the purchase of *The Baptist Courier* did not, in fact, hamper his freedom as an editor, but merely removed his right to "recklessly attack" the denomination, something he would not have

217

done anyway. Z. T. Cody, "As to Independence," *The Baptist Courier*, 20 July 1921, p. 4. Even editors who were wary of denominational ownership of state Baptist newspapers argued that they had no moral right to administer their newspapers in any way that might be construed as disapproval of denominational programs. Livingston Johnson, editor of the privately owned North Carolina *Biblical Recorder*, told a gathering of the North Carolina State Baptist Convention that "he would not publish articles which directly antagonized any policy adopted by the Convention, or which, in his judgment, would injure the cause of Christ." Livingston Johnson, "Is This Clear?" *Biblical Recorder*, 17 January 1923, p. 6.

103. Anonymous, "The Baptist Record A Factor in Christian and Denominational Life," *The Baptist Record*, 1 February 1923, p. 6. The "right kind of pastoral leadership" may be a reference to radical Fundamentalists like Norris, but Mississippi Baptist leaders seem to have been especially concerned by the inroads made by Pentecostalism and other new religious movements among Mississippi Baptists.

104. E. Y. Mullins, "Discussing Convention Problems," *The Baptist Courier*, 5 July 1923, p. 1.

105. Mullins's willingness to discuss this strategy publicly in the state Baptist newspapers shows that it was not an underhanded attempt at manipulation, but an honest appraisal of the kind of leadership he believed Southern Baptists needed.

106. E. Y. Mullins, "Discussing Convention Problems," 1.

107. L. R. Scarborough, "Southern Baptists in for a Great Campaign for Souls," *The Religious Herald*, 22 June 1922, p. 6. Abundant evidence exists to show that during this period Southern Baptist leaders used the traditional Southern Baptist concern for evangelism as a means of recruiting new participants for the Seventy-Five Million Campaign. Mullins himself noted, "Nothing is more logical than that the young convert should be asked to pledge himself to give liberally to the cause of Christ. Every candidate for baptism should be appealed to in behalf of the kingdom interests upon admission into the church." Even more importantly, in that same month, the Home Mission Board "coordinated" its departments of Evangelism and Enlistment. By placing these two departments under the same superintendent, the members of the board hoped to become more efficient in recruiting new converts to the goals of the denomination. E. Y. Mullins, "The Soul-Winning Campaign," *The Religious Herald*, 6 July 1922, p. 9; O. E. Bryan, "Coordination of Evangelism and Enlistment," *Florida Baptist Witness*, 13 July 1922, p. 5.

108. J. W. Porter, "Associational Meetings," *Western Recorder*, 5 August 1920, p. 8.

109. J. W. Mitchell, editor of the Florida newspaper, said. "We believe it is just as much the duty of a Baptist to seek subscriptions for a Baptist paper as it is to seek subscriptions for missions. Every Kingdom interest is in a large measure

dependent upon the religious paper." J. W. Mitchell, *Florida Baptist Witness*, 5 August 1920, p. 2.

110. John R. Sampey, "Finish the Doing of It," *Florida Baptist Witness*, 28 October 1920, p. 11.

111. R. H. Pitt, "Keep in the Middle of the Road," *The Religious Herald*, 5 January 1922, p. 10; L. L. Gwaltney, "Truth and the Ardor of Its Advocates," *The Alabama Baptist*, 12 January 1922, p. 3; Livingston Johnson, "Is Dr. Poteat's Teaching Dangerous?" *Biblical Recorder*, 3 May 1922, p. 6; V. I. Masters, "The Value of Christian Doctrine," *Western Recorder*, 13 October 1921, p. 9; C. P. Stealey, "Southern Baptists Will Stay with the Book," *Baptist Messenger*, 2 May 1923, pp. 1–2.

112. William E. Ellis, *"A Man of Books, A Man of the People": E. Y. Mullins and the Crisis of Moderate Southern Baptist Leadership* (Macon, GA: Mercer Univ. Press, 1985), 189.

113. Ibid., 190–91.

114. L. R. Scarborough, "Southern Baptists Lift Up A Great Doctrinal Standard," *The Baptist Courier*, 11 June 1925, p. 7.

115. L. R. Scarborough, "A Four-Fold Answer to Modernism," 2.

116. Scarborough, "Southern Baptists Lift Up A Great Doctrinal Standard," 7.

117. Southern Baptist Convention, "Comparison of 1925, 1963 and 2000 Baptist Faith and Message," http://www.sbc.net/bfm/bfmcomparison.asp; Scarborough, "Is Cooperation a New Testament Doctrine?" p. 6.

118. Scarborough, "Southern Baptists Lift Up A Great Doctrinal Standard," 7.

119. J. B. Gambrell, "A Much Desired Union," *Baptist Standard*, 26 June 1919, p. 5.

120. J. B. Gambrell, "The Missouri Situation," *Baptist Standard*, 1 January 1920, p. 3.

121. "Giving is one of the largest means of grace. It is the very heart of the atonement–'For God so loved the world that He gave–,'" "A Pastor," "Advantages of the Budget Plan of Church Finances," *Baptist Advance*, 18 January 1923, p. 16.

122. Martin Marty, "The Protestant Experience and Perspective," in Rodger Van Allen, ed., *American Religious Values and the Future of America* (Philadelphia: Fortress Press, 1978), 40.

4. Carrots and Sticks

1. J. W. Porter, "We Will Pay," *Western Recorder*, 2 December 1920, p. 8.

2. Livingston Johnson, "Points to Guard Against," *Biblical Recorder*, February 9, 1921, p. 6.

3. Ibid.

4. F. M. McConnell, "Some Plain Denominational Business," *Baptist Messenger*, 22 June 1921, p. 4.

5. Ibid.

6. Max Weber, *The Theory of Social and Economic Organization*, trans. A. M. Henderson and Talcott Parsons (New York: Oxford Univ. Press), 340. (This is an English translation of the first part of Weber's *Economy and Society*.)

7. Max Weber, "Bureaucracy," in H. H. Gerth and C. Wright Mills, *From Max Weber: Essays in Sociology* (New York: Oxford Univ. Press), 208; Max Weber, "Class, Status, Party," in Gerth and Mills, *Weber*, 180.

8. Weber, "Bureaucracy," 196.

9. Ibid., 208.

10. J. W. Mitchell, "War in the Churches," *Florida Baptist Witness*, 11 October 1923, pp. 2–3.

11. J. W. Mitchell, "Insurance on Churches," *Florida Baptist Witness*, 8 February 1923, p. 3.

12. Z. T. Cody, "A Point of Confusion," *The Baptist Courier*, 22 January 1920, p. 5. The rejection of the idea that contributions to the work of the church were a form of "benevolence" had roots that stretched back at least into the 1870s. See James Hudnut-Beumler, *In Pursuit of the Almighty's Dollar: A History of Money and American Protestantism* (Chapel Hill: Univ. of North Carolina Press, 2007), 54.

13. Z. T. Cody, "The Spirit of Sacrifice," *The Baptist Courier*, 2 November 1922, p. 2.

14. Z. T. Cody, "Pledges to God and Debts to Men," *The Baptist Courier*, 11 October 1923, p. 2.

15. Livingston Johnson, "The Last Appeal," *Biblical Recorder*, 21 November 1923, p. 6.

16. Livingston Johnson, "Did We Pledge Too Much?" *Biblical Recorder*, 31 October 1923, p. 6.

17. This tendency will be more fully explained in chapter six.

18. See, for instance, Richard T. Hughes, *Reviving the Ancient Faith: The Story of Churches of Christ in America* (Grand Rapids, MI: William B. Eerdmans, 1996), 217–18; and J. Michael Utzinger, *Yet Saints Their Watch are Keeping: Fundamentalists, Modernists, and the Development of Evangelical Ecclesiology, 1887–1937* (Macon, GA: Mercer Univ. Press, 2006), 156.

19. Utzinger, *Yet Saints*, 157.

20. Ibid., 170–71.

21. Ibid., 185, 213, 239.

22. Ibid., 187.

23. Ibid., 188.

24. Ibid., 190.

25. Ibid., 206–7.

26. Paul M. Harrison, *Authority and Power in the Free Church Tradition* (Princeton: Princeton Univ. Press, 1959), 148–49.

27. Utzinger, *Yet Saints*, 157.

28. Lester G. McAllister and William E. Tucker, *Journey in Faith: A History of the Christian Church (Disciples of Christ)* (St. Louis: Chalice Press, 1975), 374.

29. Utzinger, *Yet Saints*, 216.

30. Ibid., 219.

31. Ibid., 231.

32. Edwin R. Errett, "A Convention of Bad Faith," *Christian Standard* 61, no. 48 (27 November 1926): 631, quoted in Ibid., 234.

33. McAllister and Tucker, *Journey in Faith*, 383.

34. Ibid., Utzinger, *Yet Saints*, 236.

35. This theme was repeated endlessly during this period, but for one good example, see L. E. Barton, "Dr. Brown's Open Letter," *Baptist Advance*, 18 August 1921, p. 16.

36. D. T. Andrews, "Building the Denomination," *Baptist Standard*, 22 January 1925, p. 1.

37. L. R. Scarborough, "Two Baptist Pockets," *The Baptist Courier*, 11 September 1924, p. 12. See also L. R. Scarborough, "Kept Sacredly Separate," *The Baptist Record*, 4 September 1924, p. 2.

38. Southern Baptists had emphasized stewardship and tithing during the late nineteenth century; this was, therefore, not a new development but a recovery of an idea that already had significant roots in Southern Baptist soil.

39. L. L. Gwaltney, "Baptists and Democratic Movements," *The Alabama Baptist*, 22 March 1923, p. 3.

40. L. L. Gwaltney, "The Anniston Convention," *The Alabama Baptist*, 27 November 1924, p. 3.

41. J. R. Hobbs, "Convention Notes," *The Alabama Baptist*, 31 May 1923, p. 6.

42. W. Earl Robinson, "Looking Back at the Convention," *Baptist and Reflector*, 9 June 1921, p. 3.; W. S. Farmer, "Kentucky's Program," *Western Recorder*, 13 September 1923, p. 5.

43. J. D. Moore, "Stewardship Undergirding the Campaign," *Baptist and Reflector*, 6 December 1923, p. 1.

44. E. D. Morgan, "A Confession and An Experience," *Baptist Standard*, 8 February 1923, p. 12.

45. H. Boyce Taylor, "Blood River Baptists a Peculiar People," *News and Truths*, 9 June 1920, p. 1.

46. J. J. Taylor, "Piling Up Millions For Preachers," *Baptist and Reflector*, 19 July 1923, pp. 4–5.

47. Selsus E. Tull, "The Question of Designated Gifts," *Baptist Advance*, 19 June 1924, p. 1.

48. Frank E. Burkhalter, "New Year Holds Bright Outlook For 75 Million Campaign," *Baptist and Reflector*, 18 January 1923, p. 7.

49. Forrest Smith, "Foreign Missions and the New Campaign," *Baptist Standard*, 3 July 1924, p. 1.

221

50. J. S. Rogers, "The Story of Two Cows," *Baptist Advance*, 12 April 1923, p. 16.

51. J. S. Rogers, "The One Key To Great Days Ahead," *Baptist Advance*, 12 April 1923, p. 16. Editors and others urged pastors to bypass the subscription process entirely by placing in their church budgets funds for the newspaper to go to every family in their church.

52. R. H. Pitt, "Pastors," *The Religious Herald*, 10 March 1921, p. 10.

53. R. B. Gunter, "Convention Board Department," *The Baptist Record*, 5 March 1925, p. 5.

54. Southern Baptist leaders used the word "enlistment" to describe the process of actively recruiting churches to participate in the denominational program.

55. William A. Moffitt, "How Enlistment Put A Moribund Church On Its Feet," *Baptist and Reflector*, 11 November 1920, p. 25.

56. J. R. Nutt, "The Pastor and His Salary," *Florida Baptist Witness*, 23 March 1922, p. 6.

57. Paul Harvey, "The Ideal of Professionalism in the White Southern Baptist Ministry, 1870–1920," *Religion and American Culture* 5, no. 1 (Winter 1995): 115.

58. F. S. Groner, "Primal Importance of Baptist Standard," *Baptist Standard*, 3 August 1922, p. 3. Boldface in the original.

59. Anonymous, "92-Year-Old Mississippian Picks Cotton Two Days to Pay Her Campaign Pledge," *Baptist and Reflector*, 4 November 1920, p. 8.

60. Frank E. Burkhalter, "Widow Sells Furniture to Pay Her Campaign Pledge," *The Baptist Courier*, 8 May 1924, p. 12.

61. L. R. Scarboro [Scarborough], "How Orphan Children Pay Their Campaign Pledges," *Florida Baptist Witness*, 7 April 1921, p. 11.

62. R. H. Pitt, "Campaign Items," *The Religious Herald*, 12 January 1922, p. 3.

63. J. S. Compere, "Girl Refuses to Die With Pledge Unpaid," *Baptist Advance*, 13 December 1923, p. 14.

64. Z. T. Cody, "Honor Roll Churches," *The Baptist Courier*, 18 January 1923, p. 1; R. H. Pitt, "Baptist Seventy Five Million Campaign: Onward Movement," *The Religious Herald*, 8 April 1920, p. 2.

65. Lloyd T. Wilson, "Churches on the Honor Roll," *Baptist and Reflector*, 13 July 1922, p. 2.

66. For an example of an individual portrait, see *Florida Baptist Witness*, 28 December 1922, p. 1; For a group of portraits, see Anonymous, "Some More of Our Good Preachers and Faithful Workers," *Baptist Advance*, 13 December 1923, p. 16.

67. Livingston Johnson, "Are We In Danger?" *Biblical Recorder*, 25 January 1922, p. 6.

68. J. F. Love, "The Tithing Campaign," *The Religious Herald*, 22 September 1921, p. 7.

69. Z. T. Cody, "The Work of the General Board and the Present Status of the 75 Million Campaign," *The Baptist Courier*, 4 August 1921, p. 1.

70. R. B. Gunter, "Convention Board Department," *The Baptist Record*, 21 February 1924, p. 3; Frank. E. Burkhalter, "Business Man Who Tithed Has Money to Meet Every Legitimate Call," *Baptist and Reflector*, 29 November 1923, p. 10.

71. P. I. Lipsey, Untitled Editorial, *The Baptist Record*, 22 May 1924, p. 4.

72. Charles Reagan Wilson, *Baptized in Blood: The Religion of the Lost Cause, 1865–1920* (Athens: Univ. of Georgia Press, 1980), 68–69.

73. Presbyterian Church in the United States, General Assembly, *Minutes, 1905* (Richmond, VA: 1905), 98, quoted in Kenneth Bailey, *Southern White Protestantism in the Twentieth* Century (New York: Harper & Row, 1964), 3.

74. L. E. Barton, "One More Opportunity to Win," *Baptist Advance*, 1 December 1921, p. 16.

75. A. T. Robertson, "The Preacher Who is a Slacker," *Biblical Recorder*, 4 February 1920, p. 4.

76. J. S. Compere, "Loyalty—To Whom," *Baptist Advance*, 19 July 1923, pp. 4–5.

77. J. F. Tull, "Sell it To the Pastor," *Baptist Advance*, 30 October 1924, p. 13.

78. Finley W. Tinnin, "What Happened to a Minister Who Refused to Tithe," *The Baptist Message*, 10 January 1924, p. 1.

79. L. R. Scarborough, Untitled Editorial, *The Baptist Record*, 24 May 1923, p. 5.

80. G. W. Owens, "Kickerism," *Baptist Advance*, 17 December 1925, p. 3.

81. Anonymous, "Graphic Lesson on Cooperation," *Baptist Messenger*, 22 October 1919, p. 7.

82. W. M. Vines, "The Challenge and the Crisis," *The Baptist Courier*, 27 November 1924, p. 5.

83. W. P. Throgmorton, "The Great Campaign," *The Illinois Baptist*, 19 July 1919, p. 2.

84. B. C. Hening, "We Will Win," *Biblical Recorder*, 6 August 1919, p. 1.

85. R. H. Pitt, "Facing the Facts," *The Religious Herald*, 6 November 1919, p. 10.

86. W. E. Gwatkins, "We Can Carry the Five-year Program Through If We 'Tote,'" *The Baptist Message*, 27 September 1923, p. 16.

87. David M. Kennedy, *Over Here: The First World War and American Society*, 25th Anniversary Ed., (New York: Oxford Univ. Press, 2004), 164–65.

88. Ibid., 166.

89. Paul L. Murphy, *World War I and the Origin of Civil Liberties in the United States* (New York: W. W. Norton & Company, 1979), 222.

90. Kennedy, *Over Here*, 136.

91. In 1916, Congress created the Council of National Defense as a means to coordinate "industries and resources for the national welfare." An umbrella organization embracing state and local chapters of varying effectiveness, these organizations became a chief means by which the federal government encouraged civilians to support the war effort during World War I. Murphy, *World War I*, 88.

223

92. Ibid., 177–78.

93. Gregory A. Wills, *Democratic Religion: Freedom, Authority, and Church Discipline in the Baptist South, 1785–1900* (New York: Oxford Univ. Press, 1997), 8–9.

94. Ed. S. Phillips, "A Needed Drive," *Biblical Recorder*, 15 February 1922, p. 9.

95. A. T. Robertson, "Covetousness and Church Discipline," *Biblical Recorder*, 7 January 1920, p. 1.

96. Finley W. Tinnin, "The Lord's Acres," *The Baptist Message*, 23 October 1924, p. 6.

97. Livingston Johnson, "Most Serious Situation," *Biblical Recorder*, 8 October 1924, p. 6.

98. Finley W. Tinnin, Untitled Editorial, *The Baptist Message*, 27 January 1921, p. 3.

99. Frank E. Burkhalter, "How a Stingy Baptist, Who Refused to Tithe, Was Buncoed Out of a Fortune," *The Alabama Baptist*, 20 December 1923, p. 5.

100. W. E. Farr, "Is It Nothing To You?" *The Baptist Record*, 25 October 1923, p. 7.

101. I. H. Hunt, "The Loyalty of a Layman: Who Will Keep Faith?" *The Baptist Courier*, 14 April 1921, p. 13.

102. Frank H. Leavell, "God's Sacred Tenth: Tithing Promoted," *Baptist Advance*, 12 January 1920, p. 8.

103. J. F. Love, "What Shall the Answer Be?" *The Baptist Record*, 20 December 1923, p. 6. The Foreign Mission Board had borrowed money to support missionaries in anticipation of Campaign funds, much of which never materialized.

104. J. W. Mitchell, "Starving in Sight of Plenty," *Florida Baptist Witness*, 13 March 1924, p. 2.

105. L. R. Scarborough, "An Unfinished Task," *The Baptist New Mexican*, 30 November 1922, p. 5.

106. George W. Truett, "Dr. Truett Says," *Maryland Baptist Church Life*, December 1919, p. 3.

5. The Right Arm of Our Power

1. A portion of this chapter was previously published under the title "Not Only for the Preachers: Comparing Women's and Men's Theological Education among Southern Baptists during the Seventy-Five Million Campaign," in *Baptist History and Heritage* XLVI, no. 2 (Summer 2011). Grateful acknowledgement is offered to *Baptist History and Heritage* for granting permission to reprint this material. Those searching for a more general history of Baptist involvement in higher education in North America may consult William H. Brackney, *Congregation and Campus: North American Baptists in Higher Education* (Macon, GA: Mercer Univ. Press, 2008).

2. Charles A. Israel, *Before Scopes: Evangelicalism, Education, and Evolution in Tennessee, 1870–1925* (Athens: Univ. of Georgia Press, 2004), 56–57,

224

65; William E. Ellis, *"A Man of Books, A Man of the People": E. Y. Mullins and the Crisis of Moderate Southern Baptist Leadership* (Macon, GA: Mercer Univ. Press, 1985), 47–48, 176–77, 199–200. Israel notes that the Tennessee Baptist Convention did not move to provide any kind of systematic funding for their colleges until 1917, leaving their colleges until that time to continually solicit the denomination, associations, churches, and individual Tennessee Baptists for funds. William Ellis notes the similar conditions under which Southern Seminary operated during this time period.

3. Gregory A. Wills, *Southern Baptist Theological Seminary, 1859–2009* (New York: Oxford Univ. Press, 2009), ch. 3 passim; William A. Mueller, *A History of Southern Baptist Theological Seminary* (Nashville, TN: Broadman Press, 1959), 137–39.

4. Mueller, *Southern Seminary*, 160–74.; See also Wills, *Southern Seminary*, ch. 5 and James H. Slatton, *W. H. Whitsitt: The Man and the Controversy* (Macon, GA: Mercer Univ. Press, 2009), chs. 12–18.

5. For a classic example of one Baptist's fear of "false doctrine" in the theological seminary, see James P. Boyce, "Inaugural Address, 1856: Proposed Changes in Theological Education" in *A Sourcebook for Baptist Heritage*, ed. H. Leon McBeth (Nashville, TN: Broadman Press, 1990), 305–312. A discussion of this document can be found in Wills, *Southern Seminary*, 18–19.

6. Z. T. Cody, "A Description, and a Sample?" *The Baptist Courier*, 12 May 1921, p. 4.

7. J. F. Love, "Dr. Vedder on the Atonement," *The Religious Herald*, 17 February 1921, p. 5.

8. Ibid.

9. S. A. Campbell, "A Commentary on Crozer Seminary," *The Religious Herald*, 11 May 1922, p. 6.

10. Livingston Johnson, "Smoke or Poisoned Gas," *Biblical Recorder*, 23 March 1921, p. 6.

11. Livingston Johnson, "Statement as to Agents Accepted," *Biblical Recorder*, 4 May 1921, p. 6.

12. J. F. Love, "Dr. Vedder on the Atonement," *The Religious Herald*, 17 February 1921, p. 5.

13. Livingston Johnson, "Smoke or Poisoned Gas," *Biblical Recorder*, 23 March 1921, p. 6.

14. Conrad Cherry, *Hurrying Toward Zion: Universities, Divinity Schools, and American Protestantism* (Bloomington: Indiana Univ. Press, 1995), 4–5, 169.

15. P. I. Lipsey, Untitled Editorial, *The Baptist Record*, 24 November 1921, p. 4; J. W. Porter, "Not For Sale," *Western Recorder*, 31 July 1919, p. 8; C. W. Stumph, Untitled Editorial, *The Baptist New Mexican*, 31 May 1923, p. 2.

16. Anonymous, "Three Dimensions of Liberty," *Baptist Advance*, 20 June 1921, p. 14.

225

17. W. J. Epting, "Shall Southern Baptists Direct the Policy of Their Institutions or Shall Their Institutions Direct the Policy of Southern Baptists?" *The Baptist Record*, 27 March 1924, p. 6.

18. As in chapter three, this discussion brackets out the controversy over evolution.

19. P. I. Lipsey, "The Denomination and Its Schools," *The Baptist Record*, 19 September 1921, p. 2.

20. L. R. Scarborough, "A Four-Fold Answer to Modernism," *The Baptist Record*, 4 June 1925, p. 2.

21. L. R. Scarborough, "A Visit to the Northern Baptist Convention," *The Baptist Message*, 14 July 1921, p. 4.

22. Livingston Johnson, "Standard of Loyalty," *Biblical Recorder*, 4 January 1922, p. 5.

23. On the exercise of denominational oversight through boards of trustees, see chapter three.

24. R. H. Pitt, "Bad Leaders of a Good Cause," *The Religious Herald*, 22 December 1921, pp. 10–11.

25. See chapter three, p. 107; Louie D. Newton, "The Fox Case," *The Christian Index*, 16 October 1924, p. 14.

26. In fact, some editors did print a good deal of criticism of Baptist colleges, but they mostly printed criticism of colleges in other states, carefully guarding their words in regards to their own state's institutions. R. H. Pitt made this explicit when he wrote, "As far as we can recall, the attacks have been made on colleges in States other than those in whose territory they were printed. Thus we have had Oklahoma attacking Texas, Kentucky and several other States printing attacks on Wake Forest, etc." R. H. Pitt, Untitled Editorial, *The Religious Herald*, 6 April 1922, p. 11. In other words, editors refrained from criticizing schools in which they had a financial stake.

27. G. C. Truitt, "Anent [sic] Denominational Schools and Papers," *Baptist and Reflector*, 1 December 1921, p. 7.

28. W. C. Meadows, "A Final Statement," *Biblical Recorder*, 10 January 1923, p. 12.

29. E. Y. Mullins, "The Seventy-Five Million Dollar Campaign: An Epoch in Baptist History," *The Alabama Baptist*, 11 March 1920, p. 5.

30. Charles A. Israel, *Before Scopes: Evangelicalism, Education, and Evolution in Tennessee, 1870–1925* (Athens: Univ. of Georgia Press, 2004), 59, 64.

31. L. R. Scarborough, "Christian Education," *Florida Baptist Witness*, 25 August 1921, p. 11.

32. Max Weber, "Bureaucracy," in H. H. Gerth and C. Wright Mills, *From Max Weber: Essays in Sociology* (New York: Oxford Univ. Press), 208; Max Weber, "Class, Status, Party," in Gerth and Mills, *Weber*, 240.

33. Ibid., 242–43.

34. L. R. Scarborough, "Denominationalizing Baptist Schools," *Western Recorder*, 15 May 1919, p. 2.

35. Thos. J. Watts, "Denominational Training in Denominational Institutions," *Baptist Courier*, 8 August 1919, pp. 2–3.

36. See chapter four.

37. J. E. Dillard, "A New Day for Baptist Schools," *The Alabama Baptist*, 11 March 1920, p. 8.

38. L. R. Scarborough, *Marvels of Divine Leadership* (Nashville, TN: Sunday School Board Southern Baptist Convention, 1920), 45.

39. Even the idea that Baptist colleges and seminaries could be sites of training in church music bore the marks of the Progressive reform. Paul Harvey notes that Progressive Southern Baptists found the primitive musical practices of small, rural Baptist churches offensive and embarrassing, criticizing the "slow, seemingly discordant style of singing . . . as well as the more upbeat modern gospel hymns." In other words, Progressive Southern Baptist leaders were disturbed not only by the poor quality of congregational singing, but also by the music chosen for performance. Although reformers made some progress in reforming the musical practices of some congregations, many folk worship traditions persisted. Paul Harvey, *Redeeming the South: Religious Cultures and Racial Identities Among Southern Baptists, 1865–1925* (Chapel Hill: Univ. of North Carolina Press, 1997), 97–102.

40. W. T. Connor, "Need of Enlarged Baptist Program of Theological Education," *Western Recorder*, 1 February 1923, p. 6.

41. E. Y. Mullins, "The New Chair of Church Efficiency in the Seminary," *Biblical Recorder*, 7 July 1920, p. 15. Paul Harvey highlights the professionalizing nature of Southern Seminary's curriculum during the Mullins presidency. Harvey, *Redeeming the South*, 150.

42. Southern Baptist Theological Seminary, *Catalogue* (1920–1921), 59.

43. Ibid., 41.

44. E. Y. Mullins, *The Axioms of Religion: A New Interpretation of the Baptist Faith* (Philadelphia: The Griffith and Rowland Press, 1908), 143.

45. In the 1925–26 *Catalog*, the explicit references to "the Southern Baptist Convention and its Boards . . . State Mission Boards and . . . District Associations" is deleted in favor of a study of "application of the principles derived" from the New Testament "to our own denominational life . . . and the programs required to meet the situations." Southern Baptist Theological Seminary *Catalogue* (1925–1926), 47–48.

46. Southern Baptist Theological Seminary *Catalogue* (1921–1922), 45.

47. Carson and Newman College *Catalogue* (1919–1920), 26–27, 43.

48. Ibid., 34.

49. Carson and Newman College *Catalogue* (1920–1921), 29–31.

50. See, for instance, Carson and Newman College *Catalogue* (1925–1926), 66–68. The course on evangelism disappeared from the curriculum with the printing of the 1924–1925 catalog.

51. Carson and Newman College *Catalogue* (1920–1921), 29.

52. J. H. Foster, "Denominational Loyalty in Denominational Institutions," *The Christian Index*, 8 December 1921, p. 12.

53. Bessie Tift College, *Bulletin* 19, no. 2 (1916–1917): 68.

54. Bessie Tift College, *Bulletin* 16, no. 1. (1913–1914): 50; Bessie Tift College, *Bulletin* 19, no. 2 (1916–1917): 44.

55. Bessie Tift College, *Bulletin* (1919–1920), 58–59.

56. Bessie Tift College, *Bulletin* (1920–1921), 54.; Bessie Tift College, *Bulletin* (1921–1922), 54.

57. The reasons for his departure are unclear, but the students calling for his removal claimed that Foster, among other things, "allows personal matters to interfere in moral issues." When some students threatened to meet with the trustees and testify about the president's behavior one by one, the president agreed to leave the college, settling the mysterious controversy but leaving the school leaderless as it approached the new school year. "Resolutions Presented to the Board of Trustees by the Junior and Senior Classes of Bessie Tift College, March 27, 1922," "Classes, 1922," Tift College Archives, Special Collections and Archives, Mercer Univ. Tarver Library, Macon, Georgia.

58. Bessie Tift College, *Bulletin* (1922–1923), 67–69.

59. Chamlee cared about providing academic instruction in denominational doctrine and polity, but he sought to balance this with his own concern for conforming Bessie Tift College to the academic standards of the forerunner of the Southern Association of Colleges and Schools and of the larger institutions in which Tift students might eventually enroll. Chamlee modified the Bible curriculum to include only three-hour courses because he discovered that many colleges and universities would not recognize the one credit hour Bible courses that Tift had been offering. [Aquila Chamlee], "Bessie Tift College December 1923," "Tift Board of Trustees, 1923–24," Tift College Archives, Special Collections and Archives, Mercer Univ. Tarver Library, Macon, Georgia.

60. Bessie Tift College, *Bulletin* (1923–1924), 34.

61. Bessie Tift College, *Bulletin* (1924–1925), 29–30; Bessie Tift College, *Bulletin* (1925–1926), 27–28.

62. Ibid.; Bessie Tift College, *Bulletin* (1926–1927), 29. This may have been an effort on Chamlee's part to retain denominational studies as part of the curriculum while simultaneously retaining his commitment to offer courses that other institutions would recognize.

63. Anonymous, Untitled Typescript, "Tift Board of Trustees, 1920–21," Tift College Archives, Special Collections and Archives, Mercer Univ. Tarver Library, Macon, Georgia.

64. T. Laine Scales, *All That Fits a Woman: Training Southern Baptist Women for Charity and Mission, 1907–1926* (Macon, GA: Mercer Univ. Press, 200), 123. See also Catherine B. Allen, *A Century to Celebrate: History of Woman's Missionary Union* (Birmingham, AL: Woman's Missionary Union, Auxiliary to Southern Baptist Convention, 1987), 273. Paul Harvey notes that the very

existence of the WMU Training School owed much to SBC missionary Charlotte "Lottie" Moon's petition that women be trained for religious work in a Southern institution rather than having to travel North. Although Moon, who was by no means unique in this regard, argued that Southern women should receive Southern training as a way of avoiding unacceptable Northern ideas about womanhood, Harvey claims (probably rightly) that Moon's rhetoric was "disingenuous," intended to lull conservative Southern Baptist men into supporting the foundation of a school providing theological education to women. Harvey, *Redeeming the South*, 212–13.

65. The method of mission promoted by the turn-of-the-century WMU and the curriculum of the early Training School focused on "Personal Service," an idea of mission that excluded preaching before large groups and instead emphasized person-to-person interaction, especially with women and children. Although the most popular career choice for Training School graduates was service with the Foreign Mission Board, this study focuses on careers available to women in the United States. Scales, *All That Fits*, 114; Carrie A. Littlejohn, "A survey of the graduates of Woman's Missionary Union Training School from 1920 to 1930," (Master's thesis, Northwestern Univ., 1934), 35.

66. Woman's Missionary Union Training School, *Catalogue* (1922–1923), 23.

67. Woman's Missionary Union Training School, *Catalogue* (1923–1924), 24.

68. Woman's Missionary Union Training School, *Catalogue* (1924–1925), 24.

69. Littlejohn, "Survey," 35–36. Littlejohn notes that only 144 of these students were unmarried and therefore "employable."

70. Woman's Missionary Union Training School, *Catalogue* (1922–1923), 24. Scales, *All That Fits*, 124.

71. Woman's Missionary Union Training School, *Catalogue* (1925–1926), 25.

72. Ibid., 25.

73. Littlejohn, "Survey," 35, 37.

74. Scales, *All That Fits*, 136.

75. Woman's Missionary Union Training School, *Catalogue* (1924–1925), 17.

76. Woman's Missionary Union Training School, *Catalogue* (1925–1926), 17.

77. Littlejohn, "Survey," 35–36.

78. Ibid., 93.

6. The Empire's New Clothes

1. J. Michael Utzinger, *Yet Saints Their Watch are Keeping: Fundamentalists, Modernists, and the Development of Evangelical Ecclesiology, 1887–1937* (Macon, GA: Mercer Univ. Press, 2006), 157.

2. J. C. Massee, "Opening Address," in *Baptist Fundamentals Being Addresses Delivered at the Pre-Convention Conference at Buffalo, June 21 and 22, 1920* (Philadelphia: Judson Press, 1920), 4, quoted in Utzinger, *Yet Saints*, 189.

3. Max Weber, "Bureaucracy," in H. H. Gerth and C. Wright Mills, *From Max Weber: Essays in Sociology* (New York: Oxford Univ. Press), 240.

4. R. H. Pitt, "Our Leaders," *The Religious Herald*, 18 August 1921, p. 10.

5. W. J. Puckett, Untitled Letter, *The Religious Herald*, 22 July 1920, p. 10. This letter was originally printed in the *Western Recorder* but was reprinted in the *Religious Herald*.

6. Anonymous, "Tributes To Our Leaders," *The Christian Index*, 20 May 1920, p. 13.

7. J. B. Rounds, "Dr. Gray Calling," *Baptist Messenger*, 25 February 1925, p. 4.

8. J. B. Rounds, Untitled Cartoon, *Baptist Messenger*, 18 March 1925, p. 4.

9. Carrie Littlejohn, *History of Carver School of Missions and Social Work* (Nashville, TN: Broadman Press, 1958), 87–88.

10. Harry Clark, "News from Carson and Newman," *Baptist and Reflector*, 25 October 1923, p. 8.

11. W. J. McGlothlin, quoted in H. Boyce Taylor, "God's Upper Class," *News and Truths*, 26 January 1921, p. 5.

12. Louie D. Newton, "Our Southern Baptist Convention Leaders," *The Christian Index*, 26 May 1921, p. 11.

13. L. R. Scarborough, "A Campaign Correction—An Explanation and an Appeal," *The Baptist Courier*, 6 April 1922, p. 1, 4.

14. J. J. Taylor, "The Coming Memphis Meeting," *The Alabama Baptist*, 30 April 1925, p. 8.

15. Bureaucracy's creation of a new "caste" of specialists, who then assume unofficial but real power over those under the bureaucracy's administration, always ensures that the democratically minded will develop an aversion to it. Max Weber, "Bureaucracy," in Gerth and Mills, *Weber*, 240.

16. R. H. Pitt, "The Convention," *The Religious Herald*, 20 May 1920, p. 10.

17. Anonymous, "The 'Blue-Coats': A Necessary Evil," *The Baptist Message*, June 3, 1920, p. 6.

18. L. L. Gwaltney, "After Thoughts of the Convention," *The Alabama Baptist*, May 27, 1920, p. 3.

19. Anonymous, "Convention Notes," *The Word and Way*, 24 May 1923, p. 3; Louis D. Newton, "The Convention," *The Christian Index*, 24 May 1923, p. 12.

20. O. E. Bryan, "The Misery of the Convention," *Baptist and Reflector*, 28 May 1925, p. 2.

21. John D. Mell, "Disorder in the Southern Baptist Convention," *The Christian Index*, 7 June 1923, p. 3.

22. M. T. Andrews, "Denominational Unrest and Its Cure," *Baptist Standard*, 27 September 1923, p. 15.

23. Allen Hill Autry, "Autry's Annotations," *Baptist Advance*, 12 June 1921, p. 8.

24. Mell, "Disorder," 3.

25. See Chapter four.

26. J. O. Heath, "Democracy and the Baptists," *Baptist Standard*, 17 January 1924, p. 10.

27. A. T. Smith, "Another Question of Church Autonomy," *The Baptist Message*, 13 March 1924, p. 7.

28. Ibid.

29. E. F. Adams, "Some Suggestions," *Baptist Standard*, 13 September 1923, p. 11.

30. L. L. Gwaltney, "Non-Cooperative Bodies," *The Alabama Baptist*, 30 November 1922, p. 4.

31. J. B. Salmond, "Some Paints in the Campaign," *The Baptist Record*, 8 November 1923, pp. 4–5.

32. B. F. Fronabarger, "Two Dangers," *Baptist Standard*, 3 February 1921, p. 10.

33. J. O. Heath, "The Baptist Drift," *Baptist Messenger*, 17 October 1923, p. 3.

34. Ibid.

35. See, for instance, R. H. Pitt, Untitled Editorial, *The Religious Herald*, 15 April 1920, p. 10. "We have no men or groups of men in Virginia who claim or seek to exercise the right to go up and down the lines, after the fashion of doctrinal martinets, commanding this one to elevate his chin, and that one to pull down his vest."

36. The only other Southern Baptist newspaper that resisted the movement toward Convention ownership of newspapers during this period was the Missouri *Word and Way*. J. B. Cranfill, "Impressions of the Kansas City Convention," *The Religious Herald*, 28 June 1923, p. 5.

37. R. H. Pitt, Untitled Editorial, *The Religious Herald*, 25 March 1920, p. 3; Livingston Johnson, "Dangers to Democracy No. 3," *Biblical Recorder*, 18 September 1919, p. 6.

38. Livingston Johnson, "Tendencies of the Times," *Biblical Recorder*, 11 February 1920, pp. 6–7.

39. Livingston Johnson, "Stabilizing Things," *Biblical Recorder*, 22 September 1920, p. 6.

40. Livingston Johnson, "Rigid Economy," *Biblical Recorder*, 19 January 1921, p. 6.

41. R. H. Pitt, "Redistribution," *The Religious Herald*, 22 January 1920, p. 4.

42. R. H. Pitt, Untitled Editorial, *The Religious Herald*, 1 April 1920, p. 3.

43. R. H. Pitt, Untitled Editorial, *The Religious Herald*, 25 March 1920, p. 3.

44. R. H. Pitt, Untitled Editorial, *The Religious Herald*, 16 February 1922, p. 11.

45. R. H. Pitt, "Dr. Mullins," *The Religious Herald*, 24 October 1924, p. 10.

46. William E. Ellis, *"A Man of Books, A Man of the People": E. Y. Mullins and the Crisis of Moderate Southern Baptist Leadership* (Macon, GA: Mercer Univ. Press, 1985), 151.

47. Victor I. Masters, "Democracy Versus 'Matured Judgment,'" *Western Recorder*, 10 February 1921, p. 8. Boldface type in the original.

48. Livingston Johnson, "Is This Clear?" *Biblical Recorder*, 17 January 1923, p. 6. See also chapter three. Although Livingston Johnson was open about his suggestion that the Southern Baptist Convention needed to shed much of its bureaucratic apparatus, he made his suggestions in the context of his own implicit and then later explicit refusal to "antagonize" the Convention's leadership.

49. Victor I. Masters, "'Secret' Meetings of Baptists?" *Western Recorder*, 17 March 1921, p. 9.

50. Arch C. Cree, "A Grave Injustice Done the State Secretaries," *Western Recorder*, 5 May 1921, p. 2.

51. Victor I. Masters, "Reply by the Editor of the Western Recorder," *Western Recorder*, 5 May 1921, p. 3. Boldface type and capitals in original.

52. Ibid.; boldface type in the original.

53. Victor I. Masters, "The State Secretaries' Meetings Discussed," *Western Recorder*, 26 May 1921, p. 5.

54. Victor I. Masters, "Did this Article 'Hurt our Work?'" *Western Recorder*, 21 July 1921, p. 4. Boldface type in the original.

55. Ibid.; boldface type in the original.

56. J. Michael Utzinger, *Yet Saints Their Watch are Keeping: Fundamentalists, Modernists, and the Development of Evangelical Ecclesiology, 1887–1937* (Macon, GA: Mercer Univ. Press, 2006), 195. In fact, the Society accepted the gift.

57. Victor I. Masters, "An Interpretation of the Northern Convention Conditions," *Western Recorder*, 7 July 1921, p. 4. Boldface type in the original.

58. Ibid.

59. Victor I. Masters, "Challenging a Bit of Cheap Optimism," *Western Recorder*, 14 July 1921, p. 8.

60. For an example of how Masters popularized the idea that the South is a religiously special place, see Victor I. Masters, *The Call of the South* (Atlanta: Publicity Department of the Home Mission Board of the Southern Baptist Convention, 1920), 17–18.

61. Victor I. Masters, "What Shall We Think of Northern Baptist Fundamentalists?" *Western Recorder*, 23 March 1922, p. 8. Boldface type in the original.

62. Victor I. Masters, "Criticises Baptist Pastor for Joining the Fundamentalist Movement," *Western Recorder*, 10 August 1922, p. 9.

63. L. L. Gwaltney, "The Western Recorder, Our Watch Dog," *The Alabama Baptist*, 23 November 1922, p. 3; Z. T. Cody, "'Mastersean,' Not Hysterical," *The Baptist Courier*, 20 April 1922, p. 2. Especially during the first half of the Campaign, Masters saw evolution and Modernism as two closely linked phenomena. Cody's words here refer to Masters's frustrations that many Southern Baptist newspapers were unwilling to position themselves uncritically against the theory of evolution. Later, Masters would focus more closely on the issue of Modernism, independent of the controversy over evolution. Ellis, *A Man of Books*, 161.

64. Victor I. Masters, "Baptist Papers Derided by their Contemporaries," *Western Recorder*, 13 April 1922, p. 8.

65. Victor I. Masters, "It Is Right to Withstand and Refute Error?" *Western Recorder*, 16 November 1922, p. 11. Boldface type in the original.

66. Victor I. Masters, "About Northern Baptist Fundamentalists?" *Western Recorder*, 4 January 1923, p. 12.

67. Victor I. Masters, "Confusion in the Field of Education," *Western Recorder*, 4 January 1923, p. 11.

68. Victor I. Masters, "For Christ Are We On The Offensive or Defensive– Which?" *Western Recorder*, 18 October 1923, p. 11. Boldface type in the original.

Conclusion

1. J. R. Hobbs, "Convention Notes," *The Alabama Baptist*, 31 May, 1923, p. 6; J. D. Moore, "Stewardship Undergirding the Campaign," *Baptist and Reflector*, 6 December 1923, p. 1.

2. R. H. Pitt, "Redistribution," *The Religious Herald*, 22 January 1920, p. 4.

3. Livingston Johnson, "Points to Guard Against," *Biblical Recorder*, 9 February 1921, p. 6.

4. Specifically, Southern Baptist leaders learned much from the Woman's Missionary Union, the only segment of the Southern Baptist Convention that successfully raised its assigned quota of funds during the Seventy-Five Million Campaign. L. R. Scarborough noted that Southern Baptist women were able to raise their appointed sum of fifteen million dollars through constant study of Southern Baptist mission work and systematic effort rather than through reliance on emotional appeals. This lesson was not lost on the leaders of the SBC. L. R. Scarborough, "A Marvelous Achievement and an Inspiring Example," *Baptist Standard*, 24 July 1924, p. 7.

5. *Southern Baptist Convention Annual, 1925*, p. 28.

6. Ibid., 29.

7. Ibid., 30.

8. Ibid., 31.

9. R. T. Vann, "To Designate or Not to Designate: That's the Question," *Biblical Recorder*, 20 January 1926, p. 1.

10. E. Glenn Hinson, "The Baptist Experience in the United States," *Review and Expositor* 79, no. 2 (Spring 1982): 227.

11. Nancy Tatom Ammerman, *Baptist Battles: Social Change and Religious Conflict in the Southern Baptist Convention* (New Brunswick, NJ: Rutgers Univ. Press, 1990), 47.

12. L. L. Gwaltney, "The Southern Baptist Convention and a Statement of Faith," *The Alabama Baptist*, 15 January 1925, p. 3.

13. Paul Harvey claims, "In the 1920s, denominational conservatives perceived that they had lost the culture war to preserve an America dominated by

233

a conservative Protestant morality. But they in fact had won the struggle to define their own denomination. In future years, voices for progressive change often went unheard." Harvey is right if he means that conservatives won significant influence over the SBC's stances on social matters, but when the idea of Progressive influence is broadened beyond Christian social policy to include development in polity, Progressivism emerges as a much more robust influence over Southern Baptist life. Paul Harvey, *Redeeming the South: Religious Cultures and Racial Identities Among Southern Baptists, 1865–1925* (Chapel Hill: Univ. of North Carolina Press, 1997), 226.

14. Barry Hankins, *Uneasy in Babylon: Southern Baptist Conservatives and American Culture* (Tuscaloosa: Univ. of Alabama Press, 2002), 40.

Appendix

1. James J. Thompson, Jr., *Tried as By Fire: Southern Baptists and the Religious Controversies of the 1920s* (Macon, GA: Mercer Univ. Press, 1982), 151.

2. William E. Ellis, *"A Man of Books, A Man of the People": E. Y. Mullins and the Crisis of Moderate Southern Baptist Leadership* (Macon, GA: Mercer Univ. Press, 1985), 189.

3. Ibid., 193.

4. Barry Hankins, *God's Rascal: J. Frank Norris and the Beginnings of Southern Fundamentalism* (Lexington: Univ. Press of Kentucky, 1996), 149, 134, 72.

5. William R. Glass, *Strangers in Zion: Fundamentalists in the South, 1900–1950* (Macon, GA: Mercer Univ. Press, 2001), 259.

6. Ibid., 185–90.

Bibliography

I. Primary Sources

Newspapers

The Alabama Baptist (Birmingham, AL). May 1919–June 1925.

Baptist Advance (Little Rock, AR). May 1919–June 1925.

The Baptist Courier (Greenville, SC). May 1919–June 1925.

The Baptist Message (Shreveport, LA). May 1919–June 1925.

Baptist Messenger (Oklahoma City, OK). May 1919–June 1925.

The Baptist New Mexican (Albuquerque, NM). May 1920–June 1925.

The Baptist Record (Jackson, MS). May 1919–June 1925.

Baptist and Reflector (Nashville, TN). May 1919–June 1925.

Baptist Standard (Dallas, TX). May 1919–June 1925.

The Baptist World (Louisville, KY). May 1919–August 1919.

Biblical Recorder (Raleigh, NC). May 1919–June 1925; January 20, 1926.

The Christian Index (Atlanta, GA). May 1919–June 1925.

Florida Baptist Witness (Jacksonville, FL). May 1919–June 1925.

The Illinois Baptist (Springfield, IL). May 1919–June 1925.

Maryland Baptist Church Life (Baltimore, MA). May 1919–June 1925.

The Missionary Review of the World. February 1919.

News and Truths (Murray, KY). May 1919–June 1925.

The Religious Herald (Richmond, VA). May 1919–June 1925.

The West Texas Baptist (Abilene, TX). May 1925–July 1925.

Western Recorder (Louisville, KY). May 1919–June 1925.

The Word and Way (Kansas City, MO). May 1919–June 1925.

Archival Materials

Bessie Tift College Bulletins, 1916–1927.

Carson and Newman College Catalogues, 1919–1926.

"Report to Mr. R. A. Long on the Men and Millions Movement," 1913–1919. Disciples of Christ Historical Society, RG 119, A. 260.

Southern Baptist Convention Annual, 1919, 1925.

Southern Baptist Theological Seminary Catalogues, 1919–1926.

Tift College Archives, Special Collections and Archives, Mercer Univ. Tarver Library, Macon, Georgia. Uncataloged.

Woman's Missionary Union Training School Catalogues, 1922–1926.

Monographs

Brown, William Adams. *The Church in America: A Study of the Present Condition and Future Prospects of American Protestantism.* New York: The MacMillan Company, 1922.

Graves, J. R. *The Great Iron Wheel; or, Christianity Backwards and Republicanism Reversed.* Nashville, TN: Graves and Marks, 1855.

———. *Old Landmarkism: What Is It?* Ashland, KY: Calvary Baptist Church Book Shop, 1880.

Masters, Victor I. *The Call of the South.* Atlanta: Publicity Department of the Home Mission Board of the Southern Baptist Convention, 1920.

Mullins, Edgar Young. *The Axioms of Religion.* Philadelphia: The Griffith and Rowland Press, 1908.

———. *The Axioms of Religion.* Edited, and with an introduction by C. Douglas Weaver. Macon, GA: Mercer Univ. Press, 2010.

———, *Baptist Beliefs.* Philadelphia: The Judson Press, 1925.

Mullins, Isla May. *Edgar Young Mullins.* Nashville, TN: Sunday School Board of the Southern Baptist Convention, 1929.

Scarborough, Lee Rutland. *Marvels of Divine Leadership, or The Story of the Southern Baptist 75 Million Campaign.* Nashville, TN: Sunday School Board of the Southern Baptist Convention, 1920.

Schleiermacher, Friedrich. *On Religion: Addresses in Response to its Cultured Critics.* Trans. Terrence N. Tice. Richmond, VA: John Knox Press, 1969.

Vedder, Henry C. *The Fundamentals of Christianity: A Study of the Teachings of Jesus and Paul.* New York: The MacMillan Company, 1922.

Other Primary Materials

Boyce, James P. "Inaugural Address, 1856: Proposed Changes in Theological Education." In *A Sourcebook for Baptist Heritage*, edited by H. Leon McBeth, 305–312. Nashville, TN: Broadman Press, 1990.

Haldeman, I. M. *Why I Am Opposed to the Interchurch World Movement*. In *The Fundamentalist-Modernist Conflict: Opposing Views on Three Major Issues*, edited by Joel A. Carpenter. New York: Garland Publishing, Inc., 1988.

Leland, Elder John. "The Government of Christ a Christocracy." In *The Writings of the Late Elder John Leland, Including Some Events In His Life, Written By Himself, With Additional Sketches, &c.*, edited by L. F. Greene, pp. 273–281. New York: G. W. Wood, 1845.

II. Secondary Sources

Allen, Catherine B. *A Century to Celebrate: History of Woman's Missionary Union*. Birmingham, AL: Woman's Missionary Union, Auxiliary to Southern Baptist Convention, 1987.

Ammerman, Nancy Tatom. *Baptist Battles: Social Change and Religious Conflict in the Southern Baptist Convention*. New Brunswick, NJ: Rutgers Univ. Press, 1990.

Bailey, Kenneth. *Southern White Protestantism in the Twentieth Century*. New York: Harper & Row, 1964.

Barber, Christopher Bart. "The Bogard Schism: An Arkansas Agrarian Revolt." Ph.D. diss., Southwestern Baptist Theological Seminary, 2006.

Bell, Marty G. "James Robinson Graves and the Rhetoric of Demagogy: Primitivism and Democracy in Old Landmarkism." Ph.D. diss., Vanderbilt University, 1990.

Bledstein, Burton J. *The Culture of Professionalization: The Middle Class and the Development of Higher Education in America*. New York: W. W. Norton and Company, Inc., 1976.

Bloom, Harold. *The American Religion: The Emergence of the Post-Christian Nation*. New York: Simon and Schuster, 1992.

Bryan, Philip Ray. "An Analysis of the Ecclesiology of Associational Baptists, 1900–1950." Ph.D. diss., Baylor Univ., 1973.

Canipe, Lee. *A Baptist Democracy: Separating God from Caesar in the Land of the Free*. Macon, GA: Mercer Univ. Press, 2011.

Carpenter, Joel A. *Revive Us Again: The Reawakening of American Evangelicalism*. New York: Oxford Univ. Press, 1997.

237

Carson, Glenn Thomas. *The Life and Work of Lee Rutland Scarborough: Calling Out the Called.* Austin, TX: Eakin Press, 1996.

Cherry, Conrad. *Hurrying Toward Zion: Universities, Divinity Schools, and American Protestantism.* Bloomington: Indiana Univ. Press, 1995.

Cornebise, Alfred E. *War as Advertised: The Four Minute Men and America's Crusade, 1917–1918.* Philadelphia: The American Philosophical Society, 1984.

Dilday, Russell. "The Significance of E. Y. Mullins's *The Axioms of Religion.*" *Baptist History and Heritage* XLIII, no. 1 (2008): 83–93.

Early, Joseph E, Jr. *A Texas Baptist Power Struggle: The Hayden Controversy.* Denton: Univ. of North Texas Press, 2005.

Eighmy, John Lee. *Churches in Cultural Captivity: A History of the Social Attitudes of Southern Baptists.* With revised introduction, conclusion, and bibliography by Sam Hill. Knoxville: Univ. of Tennessee Press, 1987.

Ellis, William E. *"A Man of Books and a Man of the People": E. Y. Mullins and the Crisis of Moderate Southern Baptist Leadership.* Macon, GA: Mercer Univ. Press, 1985.

Ernst, Eldon G. *Moment of Truth for Protestant America: Interchurch Campaigns Following World War One.* Missoula, MT: Scholars Press, 1972.

Farnsley, Arthur Emery II. *Southern Baptist Politics: Authority and Power in the Restructuring of an American Denomination.* University Park: Pennsylvania State Univ. Press, 1994.

Gaston, Paul. *The New South Creed: A Study in Southern Mythmaking.* Baton Rouge: Louisiana State Univ. Press, 1970.

Gerth, H. H. and C. Wright Mills, eds. *From Max Weber: Essays in Sociology.* New York: Oxford Univ. Press, 1958.

Glass, William. *Strangers in Zion: Fundamentalists in the South, 1900–1950.* Macon, GA: Mercer Univ. Press, 2001.

Goodwyn, Lawrence. *The Populist Moment: A Short History of the Agrarian Revolt in America.* New York: Oxford Univ. Press, 1978.

Grantham, Dewey. *Southern Progressivism: The Reconciliation of Progress and Tradition.* Knoxville: Univ. of Tennessee Press, 1983.

Hankins, Barry. *God's Rascal: J. Frank Norris and the Beginnings of Southern Fundamentalism.* Lexington: Univ. Press of Kentucky, 1996.

———. *Uneasy in Babylon: Southern Baptist Conservatives and American Culture.* Tuscaloosa: Univ. of Alabama Press, 2002.

Harrison, Paul M. *Authority and Power in the Free Church Tradition.* Princeton: Princeton Univ. Press, 1959.

Harvey, Paul. "The Ideal of Professionalism and the White Southern Baptist Ministry, 1870–1920." *Religion and American Culture* 10, no. 4 (Winter 1995): 99–123.

———. *Redeeming the South: Religious Cultures and Racial Identities Among Southern Baptists: 1865–1925.* Chapel Hill: Univ. of North Carolina Press, 1997.

Hawley, Ellis W. *The Great War and the Search for a Modern Order: A History of the American People and Their Institutions, 1917–1933.* 2nd ed. Prospect Heights, IL: Waveland Press, 1992.

Hefley, James C. *The Truth in Crisis: The Controversy in the Southern Baptist Convention.* Dallas: Criterion Publications, 1986.

Hinson, E. Glenn. "Oh, Baptists, How Your Corporation Has Grown!" In *Distinctively Baptist: Essays on Baptist History, A Festschrift in Honor of Walter B. Shurden,* edited by Marc A. Jolley with John D. Pierce, pp. 17–33. Macon, GA: Mercer Univ. Press, 2005.

———. "The Baptist Experience in the United States." *Review and Expositor* 79, no. 2 (Spring 1982): 217–30.

Holifield, E. Brooks. *The Gentlemen Theologians: American Theology in Southern Culture, 1795–1860.* Durham, NC: Duke Univ. Press, 1978.

Hudson, Winthrop S. "Shifting Patterns of Church Order in the Twentieth Century." In *Baptist Concepts of the Church: A Survey of the Historical and Theological Issues which have Produced Changes in Church Order,* edited by Winthrop S. Hudson, pp. 196–218. Philadelphia: Judson Press, 1959.

Hughes, Richard T. *Reviving the Ancient Faith: The Story of Churches of Christ in America.* Grand Rapids, MI: William B. Eerdmans Publishing Co., 1996.

Humphreys, Fisher. "E. Y. Mullins." In *Baptist Theologians,* edited by Timothy George and David S. Dockery, pp. 330–50. Nashville, TN: Broadman Press, 1990.

Israel, Charles A. *Before Scopes: Evangelicalism, Education, and Evolution in Tennessee, 1870–1925.* Athens: Univ. of Georgia Press, 2004.

Kennedy, David M. *Over Here: The First World War and American Society.* 25th Anniversary Ed. New York: Oxford Univ. Press, 2004.

Lamkin, Adrian. "The Gospel Mission Movement within the Southern Baptist Convention." Ph.D. diss., Southern Baptist Theological Seminary, 1980.

Lankford, John. "Methodism 'Over the Top': The Joint Centenary Movement, 1917–1925." *Methodist History* 2 (Oct. 1963): 27–37.

Larson, Edward J. *Summer for the Gods: The Scopes Trial and America's Continuing Debate over Science and Religion.* Cambridge, MA: Harvard Univ. Press, 1997.

Leonard, Bill. *Baptist Ways: A History.* Valley Forge, PA: Judson Press, 2003.

———. *God's Last and Only Hope: The Fragmentation of the Southern Baptist Convention.* Grand Rapids, MI: William B. Eerdmans Publishing Co., 1990.

Littlejohn, Carrie. *History of Carver School of Missions and Social Work.* Nashville, TN: Broadman Press, 1958.

———. "A Survey of the Graduates of Woman's Missionary Union Training School from 1920 to 1930." Master's thesis, Northwestern Univ., 1934.

Maring, Norman H. "Conservative but Progressive." In *What God Hath Wrought: Eastern's First Thirty-Five Years,* edited by Gilbert L. Guffin, pp. 15–49. Philadelphia: The Judson Press, 1960.

Marsden, George M. *Fundamentalism in American Culture.* New Ed. New York: Oxford Univ. Press, 2006.

Marty, Martin. *The Irony of It All.* Vol. 1 of *Modern American Religion.* Chicago: Univ. of Chicago Press, 1986.

———. "The Protestant Experience and Perspective." In *American Religious Values and the Future of America,* edited by Rodger Van Allen, pp. 30–51. Philadelphia: Fortress Press, 1978.

Mathews, Mary Beth Swetnam. *Rethinking Zion: How the Print Media Placed Fundamentalism in the South.* Knoxville: Univ. of Tennessee Press, 2006.

McAllister, Lester G. and William E. Tucker. *Journey in Faith: A History of the Christian Church (Disciples of Christ).* St. Louis: Chalice Press, 1975.

McGlothlin, William G. *Isaac Backus and the American Pietistic Tradition.* Boston: Little, Brown and Company, 1967.

Mohler, Albert R. Introduction to *The Axioms of Religion* by Edgar Young Mullins, pp. 1–32. Nashville, TN: Broadman and Holman Press, 1997.

Morgan, David T. *The New Crusades, The New Holy Land: Conflict in the Southern Baptist Convention, 1969–1991.* Tuscaloosa: Univ. of Alabama Press, 1996.

Mueller, William A. *A History of Southern Baptist Theological Seminary.* Nashville, TN: Broadman Press, 1959.

Murphy, Paul L. *World War I and the Origin of Civil Liberties in the United States.* New York: W. W. Norton and Company, Inc., 1979.

Niebuhr, H. Richard. *The Social Sources of Denominationalism.* New York: Henry Holt and Company, 1929.

Patterson, James. *James Robinson Graves: Staking the Boundaries of Baptist Identity.* Nashville, TN: Broadman and Holman Academic, 2012.

Payne, Ernest A. *The Baptist Union: A Short History.* London: The Baptist Union of Great Britain and Ireland, 1958.

Queen, Edward L., II. *In the South the Baptists are the Center of Gravity: Southern Baptists and Social Change, 1930–1980.* Brooklyn: Carlson, 1991.

Sandeen, Ernest R. *The Roots of Fundamentalism: British and American Millenarianism, 1800–1930.* Chicago: Univ. of Chicago Press, 1970

Scales, T. Laine. *All That Fits a Woman: Training Southern Baptist Women for Charity and Mission, 1907–1926.* Macon, GA: Mercer Univ. Press, 2000.

Shurden, Walter B. *Not an Easy Journey: Some Transitions in Baptist Life.* Macon, GA: Mercer Univ. Press, 2005.

Slatton, James H. *W. H. Whitsitt: The Man and the Controversy.* Macon, GA: Mercer Univ. Press, 2009.

Sutton, Jerry. *The Baptist Reformation: The Conservative Resurgence in the Southern Baptist Convention.* Nashville, TN: Broadman and Holman Publishers, 2000.

Thompson, James J., Jr. *Tried as By Fire: Southern Baptists and the Religious Controversies of the 1920s.* Macon, GA: Mercer Univ. Press, 1982.

Utzinger, J. Michael. *Yet Saints Their Watch are Keeping: Fundamentalists, Modernists, and the Development of Evangelical Ecclesiology, 1887–1937.* Macon, GA: Mercer Univ. Press, 2006.

Weaver, C. Douglas. "The Baptist Ecclesiology of E. Y. Mullins: Individualism and the New Testament Church." *Baptist History and Heritage* XLIII, no. 1 (Winter 2008): 18–34.

———. "E. Y. Mullins: Soul Competency and Social Ministry." *Perspectives in Religious Studies* 36, no. 4 (Winter 2009): 445–60.

Weber, Max. *The Theory of Social and Economic Organization.* Translated by A. M. Henderson and Talcott Parsons. New York: Oxford Univ. Press, 1947.

Wiebe, Robert H. *The Search for Order, 1877–1920.* New York: Hill and Wang, 1967.

Wills, Gregory A. *Democratic Religion: Freedom, Authority and Church Discipline in the Baptist South, 1785–1900.* New York: Oxford Univ. Press, 1997.

———. *Southern Baptist Theological Seminary: 1859–2009.* New York: Oxford Univ. Press, 2009.

Wilson, Charles Reagan. *Baptized in Blood: The Religion of the Lost Cause, 1865–1920.* Athens: Univ. of Georgia Press, 1980.

Woodward, C. Vann. *Origins of the New South, 1877–1913.* Baton Rouge: Louisiana State Univ. Press, 1971.

Woodward, C. Vann. *The Strange Career of Jim Crow.* 2nd rev. ed. New York: Oxford Univ. Press, 1966.

Wuthnow, Robert. *The Restructuring of American Religion: Society and Faith since World War II.* Princeton: Princeton Univ. Press, 1988.

Index

Entries in **boldface** refer to illustrations.

Cody, Z. T., 78, 106, 121, 217n102; and atonement, 77, 138; criticism of V. I. Masters,
182, 232n63
coercion, 55, 158, 167–69, 172; and bureaucracy, 8, 9, 103–5; during the Seventy-
Five Million Campaign, 111, 123–33
colleges, Southern Baptist, 1, 9, 89, 133,
135–37, 138, 161–62; denominational
loyalty of, 144–46, 148, 149, 150; funding
of, 143, 224n2; and orthodoxy, 137, 140,
141, 183, 226n26; and Progressivism,
227n39
communism: and J. Frank Norris, 193–94.
See also Bolshevism
Compere, J. S., 11, 95
Connor, W. T., 146
consensus, 32–35, 85, 141, 205n91; "consensus of the competent," 32, 38, 94, 97
cooperation, 9, 24, 128, 216n88; in *The
Axioms of Religion*, 29, 31, 32; and the
Baptist Faith and Message, 100–101; as
a fundamental doctrine, 71, 85, 91, 92,
94–96, 98, 135, 160, 189; interdenominational, 51, 52, 53, 58; between Northern
and Southern Methodists, 43
Cooperative Program, 188
Cranfill, J. B., 24
Crozer Theological Seminary, 76, 108,
137–39

Damnation. *See* judgment, final
Darwinism. *See* antievolutionism
debt, 7, 103; congregational, 113, 117; denominational, 132, 133, 160, **161**, **162**,
187; Seventy-Five Million Campaign
pledges as, 106
democracy, 5, 38; and *The Axioms of Religion*, 16–18, 28, 32, 33, 34, 97, 205n91;
as a Baptist concern, 18–19, 49, 53, 54,
56, 58, 155, 170–74, 206n100; and bureaucracy, 8–9, 24–26, 230n15; and Classical
Republicanism, 19, 203n14; and denominational criticism, 142, Jacksonian, 21,
27; and Landmarkism, 22, 201n12; and
Progressivism, 12, 13, 23, 28; and the
Seventy-Five Million Campaign, 34, 41,
65–66, 164; and the Southern Baptist
Convention (annual meeting), 158, 164–
65, 166, and Southern Baptist leaders,
163, 167, 169–70; and Southern Baptist

Newspapers, 170; and the University of
Chicago, 139; V. I. Masters's warnings
about, 175–84, 185; and World War I, 43,
45, 53
Dennett, Tyler, 47
depression, economic, 7, 104, 119, 187
Dillard, J. E., 84, 145
Disciples of Christ (denomination), 48,
66, 107, 157, 193; "Men and Millions
Movement," 42; Theological conflicts,
108–10
discipline, church, 104, 129, 202n30
dispensationalism, premillennial, 3, 69, 70,
71, 78, 79, 198n4; and the Baptist Bible
Union Confession of Faith, 214n42,
214n45; and Darby, John Nelson, 211n4;
Southern Baptist suspicion of, 80, 82
dissent, 4, 10, 127, 132, 157; in *The Axioms
of Religion*, 28, 32–34, 65
Dobbins, Gaines, 147
Donatists, 31

Eagle, James P., 26
Eastern Baptist Theological Seminary, 100,
213n39
ecumenism. *See* unionism
education. *See* colleges; enlistment;
seminaries
efficiency, 38–39, 133, 147, 148, 151; and bureaucracy, 8; and Progressivism, 24; and
the Seventy-Five Million Campaign, 60,
66, 114; and Southern Baptist criticism
of the Interchurch World Movement, 54,
59; and Southern Baptist polity, 35
enlistment, 6, 35, 37, 218n107, 222n54; and
the Cooperative Program, 188; and local church organization, 117, 125; and
Southern Baptist newspapers, 96–97
evangelism, 3, 71, 87, 148, 159, 227n50; as
an aspect of the Seventy-Five Million
Campaign, 7, 61, 85, 96, as a method
for promoting the Seventy-Five Million
Campaign, 97, 98, 218n107
evolution. *See* antievolutionism
exceptionalism, Southern, 85–87, 88, 189;
rejected as a basis for Southern Baptist
identity, 158, 175, 181, 184
Executive Board (Southern Baptist Convention), 6, 35

244

Faunce, W. H. P., 80
Foreign Mission Board (SBC), 26, 76, 138, 159, 204n53, 229n65; debt, 161, **162**, 224n103; "Statement of Belief," 75
Foster, J. H., 150–51, 228n57
Four Minute Speakers, 63, 112. *See also* minute men
fundamentalism, 2, 70, 87–88; and J. Frank Norris, 191–95; and Southern Baptists, 4–7, 67, 73–85, 88, 99, 101–2, 183, 187, 189; and Southern Protestantism, 2–3, 71–72; Southern Baptist newspaper editors' opinions of, 11, 158,
fundamentals, 75, 76, 87, 88, 198n4, 211n5; Baptist principles as, 56, 61; Northern Baptist Conference, 77, 78

Gambrell, J. B., 25–26, 36, 37, 38, 119, 159; criticism of the IWM, 55, 61, 65; criticism of the YMCA, 49–51,
Goodchild, Frank, 72, 79
Gospel Mission movement, 26, 204n53
Graham, B. J. W., 58
Graves, J. R., 26, 192, 201n12, 202n24, 202n30, 208n38; and Jacksonian democracy, 20–22, 25
Gwaltney, L. L., 11, 36, 55, 112, 164, 182, 214n45; and denominational centralization, 189; and evolution, 89, 99, 216n79

Haldeman, Isaac M., 69–70, 73
Harper, William Rainey, 139
Hatcher, Eldridge, 62, 64
Hayden, Samuel A., 24–26, 27, 32, 33, 37, 82, 204n46
heterodoxy. *See* modernism
Home Mission Board (SBC), 85, 159, 175, 177, 180, 218n107
Home Missionary Society (Northern Baptist Convention), 180
Howell, R. B. C., 21–22, 202n24, 202n30

immigrants, 86
Interchurch World Movement (IWM), 82; collapse, 48–49, 74, 79, 107; framing, 45–48; fundamentalist criticism of, 69, 70, 73; influences upon, 42–45; influence

on the Seventy-Five Million Campaign, 5, 41, 42, 57–67, 158, 171, 189; Southern Baptist opposition to, 39, 41, 49, 51–57, 74, 75, 144, 208n38, 209n63

James, William, 15, 27, 28
Johnson, Livingston, 54, 103, 106, 120, 130, 178, 217n102; as a critic of denominational centralization, 11, 170–72, 175, 176, 185, 232n48; and evolution, 99; and orthodoxy in Baptist colleges and schools, 138, 141
Joint Centenary Movement (Methodist), 43, 47
judgment, final, 49, 211n4; and failure to pay campaign pledges, 104, 124, 131–33

Landmarkism, 11, 20–22, 25–26, 65, 201n12, 202n30; and *The Axioms of Religion*, 33–34, 206n95; and the Gospel Mission movement, 204n53; and the Interchurch World Movement, 74, 208n38; and Jacksonian Democracy, 17, 18, 24; and J. Frank Norris, 192–94; reconciled to the Southern Baptist Convention, 24, 204n50
Laws, Curtis Lee, 56; influence over Southern Baptists, 73, 77–78; as a moderate fundamentalist, 3, 69, 70, 72, 79, 83
Laymen's Movement, 148
Leland, John, 19
Lipsey, P. I., 11, 75–76, 123, 140, 212n17
Littlejohn, Carrie, 153–54, 162
"Lost Cause", 25, 85, 194
Love, J. F., 121, 132, 159, 160–62, **162**; and the "Statement of Belief," 75; on substitutionary atonement, 76, 138

Marty, Martin, 102
Masters, Victor I., 11, 51, 95; criticism of denominational centralization, 158, 170, 175–85; and modernism, 74–75, 99, 175, 180–85; and Southern exceptionalism, 85–7
McDaniel, George W., 7, 50
McGlothlin, W. J., 65, 162
McLure, Maud Reynolds, 162
Mell, John D., 165–66

245

Men and Millions Movement. *See* Disciples of Christ (denomination)
Mercer University, 25, 53, 89–90, 142
Methodists, 3, 21, 55, 66, 192, 206n99; and postwar fundraising, 42–43, 47
Minute Men, 43, 48. *See also* Four Minute Speakers
Mitchell, J. W., 80–81, 89, 91, 105–6, 218n109
modernism, 11, 69, 192, 194, 195; and the *Baptist Faith and Message*, 99–101; and bureaucratization, 107–10, 157; and Crozer Theological Seminary, 137–39; relationship to evolution, 2–3, 99; impetus for the rise of Fundamentalism; 69, 73; and radical fundamentalists, 79, 80; and Southern Baptist educational institutions, 135–6, 140–42, 154–55; Southern Baptist reactions to, 75, 77, 84, 88–91, **92**, **93**, 98, 190; as related to unionism, 56; and the University of Chicago, 139–40; V. I. Masters's critique of, 158, 175, 180–85
Moody Bible Institute, 91, **92, 93**
Moore, J. D., 178
Mullins, Edgar Young, 10, 36, 175, 205n78, 205n89, 217n88; as the author of *The Axioms of Religion*, 17, 133, 206n95; and the *Baptist Faith and Message*, 99; as a defender of Baptist freedom, 16, 200n4; and consensus, 32–34, 38, 94, 97, 205n91; and conflict over evolution, 73, 198n4; and denominational fundraising, 65, 218n107; and the Interchurch World Movement, 57; as a beloved leader, 159, **160**, 162, 204n50; and denominational newspapers, 96–97, 218n105; as a Progressive, 13, 17–18, 27–34, 35, 38, 201n10, 227n41; and Southern Baptist education, 143; as President of the Southern Baptist Convention, 192–93; as the President of Southern Baptist Theological Seminary, 147; as a theologian, 15
music, church, 146; and Progressivism, 227n39

nationalism, 48. *See also* patriotism
New Era Movement (Presbyterian), 43
New World Movement (Northern Baptist), 81, 108

New Hampshire Confession, 99; as the basis for the *Baptist Faith and Message*, 100, 217n92
"New South", 17, 22–27, 181
Newspapers, denominational: criticism of denominational centralization, 170, 178; criticism of the Interchurch World Movement, 52; as a means of denominational coercion and reward, 118, 119–20, **121**, **122**, 124–26, 129, 130, 131, 167; as a means of denominational influence, 6, 96–97, 98, 111, 114, 115, **116**, 133, 176, 188, 218n105, 218n109, 222n51; and doctrinal controversy, 70, 75, 78, 82–83, 87, 88, 94, 110, 137, 142, 179, 232n63; and education, 146; and J. B. Gambrell, 37; as a primary source, 10–12; and the Seventy-Five Million Campaign, 63; state convention ownership, 64, 96, 164, 170, 217n100, 217n102, 231n36; and Southern Baptist leadership, 159, 164
newspapers, secular, 47, 72, 87
Newton, Louie D., 89, 142, 163
Norris, J. Frank, 3, 5, 71, 105, 181; and antievolutionism, 99; conflict with L. R. Scarborough, 81–3, 88, 90, 91, 94, 99, 101–2, 189; relationship with the Southern Baptist Convention, 191–95
North American Christian Convention, 110
Northern Baptist Convention, 11, 15, 110, 180, 215n77; and *The Baptist*, 75, 77; centralization, 157; doctrinal controversy, 69–70, 75, 81, 108; educational institutions of, 139, 141, 213n39; Fundamentalist movement within, 78, 79, 80, 83; Fundamentals Conference, 77
Northern Baptist Theological Seminary, 78, 213n39

oligarchy, 164, 172, 174
open membership, 109–10

Parker, Daniel, 20, 26
pastors, Southern Baptist, 24, 35, 55, 137, 176; bivocational, 10; and denominational centralization, 158, 164, 166, 169; coerced by the denomination, 123–29, 169; and the Cooperative Program, 188; education of, 147–49; free from modern-

246

ism, 84; concerned with fundamentalism and modernism, 87, 90, 110; as denominational newspaper agents, 114–15, 222n51; as obligated to the denomination, 105, 133; as obstacles to the Seventy-Five Million Campaign, 96, 104, 113; participants in fundamentalist organizations, 181; rewarded by the denomination, 102, 104, 115–18, **116**, 120–23, **121**, **122**; role in eliciting support for the Seventy-Five Million Campaign, 35–36, 61, 64, 96, 98, 111–13; socially stratified, 19–20

patriotism, 48, 60, 63, 127. *See also* nationalism

Pitt, R. H., 11, 58, 127, 164, 226n26; concerns about denominational centralzation, 170, 172–75, 176, 178, 185; tolerant of evolution, 99, 182; concerns about Fundamentalist behavior, 80, 81; concerns about Modernism, 76, 141; and denominational ownership of newspapers, 217n100; and pastoral leadership, 115, 117; praise of denominational leaders, 159; and Virginia Baptist tolerance, 231n35

Porter, J. W., 51, 78, 103, 159, 175

Poteat, William Louis, 73, 142, 215n75

Presbyterians, 19, 45, 73, 192; and denominational centralization, 107, 157; doctrinal conflict, 211n5; and postwar fundraising, 43, 66; southern branch, 3, 4, 123, 207n17

premillennialism. *See* dispensationalism, premillennial

Primitive Baptists, 26

professionalism, 9, 23–25, 139, 189; and Southern Baptist education, 145, 148, 149, 150, 153–54, 227n41; and E. Y. Mullins, 18, 27–34; and Southern Baptist polity, 35, 67, 115, 123, 187; southern ministers as, 19, 202n18;

Progressivism, 5, 12–13, 23–24, 189, 203n38, 203n40; and church music, 227n39; and the Disciples of Christ, 109; and E. Y. Mullins, 17–18, 27–28, 32, 34, 201n10; opposed to Jacksonian democracy, 25–26; and the social gospel, 205n66; and Southern Baptist polity, 35, 38, 58, 96, 102, 163, 188, 233n13

Protestantism, Southern, 11, 123; relationship to fundamentalism, 1, 2, 3, 72, 197n3

rationalism (theology), 77–78, 86, 91, 194; and education 138, 139, 140; and V. I. Masters, 181–83. *See also* modernism

rationalization (sociology), 7–8, 135

Reconstruction, 22, 85, 203n35

"Redeemers" (Democrats), 22, 24, 203n35

Republicanism, classical, 19, 21, 203n41

revivals, 27, 78, 117; as opportunities for denominational promotion, 96–98, 188

reward: as an element of bureaucracy, 8–9, 104–5; during the Seventy-Five Million Campaign, 102, 103, 104, 111, 113, 115–23, **121**, **122**, 123, 128, 133

Riley, William Bell, 81, 99, 181, 197n4; as a radical Fundamentalist, 3, 79, 83

Robertson, A. T., 78, 124–25, 126, 129, 159

Russian Revolution. *See* Bolshevism

salary: as an aspect of bureaucracy, 8–9, 105; pastoral, 113, 115, **116**, 117–18, 124, 125; Samuel Hayden's criticism of, 24

Sampey, John, 78, 98

Scarborough, Lee Rutland, 6, 10, 112, 119, 126; and the *Baptist Faith and Message*, 99–101, 217n92; as a beloved leader, 159, 162; critic of unionism, 56; and designation of campaign pledges, 111; and evolution, 215n75; conflict with J. Frank Norris, 82–83; and Northern Fundamentalism, 78; "Scarborough Synthesis," 85, 88, 90–95, 97–98, 110, 154–55, 158, 175, 181, 184, 189; and the Seventy-Five Million Campaign, 60, 61, 63, 64, 102, 145; soteriology, 132; and Southern Baptist education, 135–37, 140, 141, 143, 144; and Southern Baptist polity, 35–37, 216n88; and trust for Southern Baptist leaders, 163–64; and the Woman's Missionary Union, 233n4

"Scarborough Synthesis." *See* Scarborough, Lee Rutland

Schleiermacher, Friedrich, 15, 27, 28, 30, 34

Scofield Reference Bible, 109

Seminaries, Northern Baptist Fundamentalist, 78, 213n39

Seminaries, Southern Baptist, 1, 136, 159, 227n39; as educating denominational professionals, 9, 62, 133, 144–48, 149, 154; originally excluded from the

Taylor, H. Boyce, 113–14, 177
Taylor, J. J., 114, 164
Taylor, John (primitive Baptist), 20, 102
tithing, 111, 117, 125, 221n38; and final judgment, 131–32; and material blessings,
120–21; as a method of buttressing the
Seventy-Five Million Campaign, 7, 97,
112–13. *See also* stewardship
Torrey, R. A., 100
Toy, Crawford, 137
Triennial Convention, 20
Truett, George W., 95, 132, 159
trustees, boards of, 1, 137, 189; entrusted
with their institutions' orthodoxy, 70,
89–90, 135–36, 141–42, 183, 216n79,
226n23

unionism, 49, 51, 56, 58, 61; and heterodoxy,
74, 75
United Christian Missionary Society, 109
University of Chicago, 108, 109; Southern
Baptist criticism, 137, 139–40

Vance, James, 45–46
Vedder, Henry C., 76, 137–38, 212n18
voluntarism, 32

Wake Forest University, 73, 78, 138, 226n26
Watchman-Examiner, 69, 79; influence
upon Southern Baptists, 73, 77, 78,
213n31

Weber, Max, 7–10
White, J. Campbell, 49, 51
Whitsitt, William, 137
William Jewell College, 89, 142
Woman's Missionary Union (WMU), 136,
148, 152–54, 161, 223n4, 229n65;
involvement in fundraising, 125, 233n4
Woman's Missionary Union Training School,
136, 147, 152–54, 161–62, 228n64–5
World Christian Fundamentals Association,
109
World War I, 4, 5, 77, 85, 150, 223n91; abusive language borrowed from, 124, 126–
28; as preparing the world for Baptist
democracy, 52; as a triumph of democracy, 38–39; and denominational
centralization, 157, 171, 173; ensuing
economic depression, 104, 119, 187;
emphasis on loyalty, 63; as an impetus for denominational fundraising
drives, 42–43; as an impetus for the
Interchurch World Movement, 43–45;
as an impetus for the Seventy-Five
Million Campaign, 6, 41, 57, 62, 66–67,
208n38; YMCA work among soldiers
during, 49–51, 65, 67

Young Men's Christian Association (YMCA),
active in Southern Baptist colleges,
144; ecumenical wartime work among
soldiers, 49–51, 58, 65, 67
Young Women's Christian Association
(YWCA), 144

249